Clearwater Fla.
June - 1976

To Mr. John Dalley
Jerrie Cadek Luchtenberg has
requested me to send you a copy
of this book. I hope you will
enjoy it as she thinks you will.

Best wishes from
Jaroslav Siskovsky

Jaroslav Siskovsky

fiddler ON THE hoof

the odyssey of a concert violinist

jaroslav siskovsky

dorrance & company • philadelphia

It gives us great pleasure to dedicate this opus, in sweet remembrance and appreciation, to Frederica (Vanderbilt Webb) and Cyril Jones (Freddie and Cy), the dearest, most loyal and congenial friends we ever had.

Eunice and Jaroslav Siskovsky

CONTENTS

PREFACE

For years people have been urging me to write my memoirs. Most of them didn't know that writing letters was something always abhorred by me; so the thought of venturing into memoirs seemed preposterous—until the summer of 1966 when my wife and I were spending three weeks with our very dear friend Cyril Jones at his estate at Cotuit on Cape Cod.

Was it the beauty and peace of the place, or was it that it felt so good to be near Cy again? I don't know, but out of the blue the idea struck me—why not live dangerously and give the memoirs a try?

That night, and many thereafter, I sat writing until 3:00 a.m., so that by the time we departed for Clearwater twenty pages of my youth had been completed.

Alas, when we got home, there were so many interesting antique clocks waiting to be repaired for one of the clock shops in town that I tied into those and laid the memoirs aside. Thus they lay neglected for about two years, when one day Irene Albert, a columnist for the Clearwater *Sun*, came for an interview on my life, which appeared in her newspaper a short time thereafter.

In order to save time, I dug up the memoirs and told her to take them home in the event that she might find something which would be appropriate for her article. When she returned them, she surprised me with the query, "Jaro, did you consider finishing these memoirs for book publication? I think they have good possibilities."

That got me started again. But before going any further, let me express my heartfelt thanks to Irene for that push, which got me to a point a little less than the halfway mark, when my gumption ran out and the work was again laid aside.

Thus it lay for another two years, almost forgotten, when some correspondence with a dear friend of long standing, Mrs. Vanderbilt Webb, lit the fuse that lit the fires of inspiration, which resulted in my concentrating on the memoirs exclusively and finishing them within six months. If it hadn't been for her, I doubt that they would ever have been completed. There aren't enough words to express my deep gratitude and appreciation to Aileen Webb.

Except for the chapters describing the trips my wife and I took together, the whole opus was written from memory, excluding dates, which were gleaned from passports, passenger lists, etc. At no time did I resort to hyperbole, feeling secure that in this case the truth was more unique than poetic license.

I did make good use of my wife's diaries on all the trips we made to refresh my memory; but, by and large, I wrote my own versions and impressions.

Finally, let me add many thanks to my wife, Eunice, who was very helpful in checking copy and improving syntax, as well as in other ways; to our friend Sharon Hixon, my appreciation and gratitude for a superb job of typing; and to our dear friends Janet and Hamilton Warren, our gratitude for helpful hints, especially for dreaming up the title.

1

CLEVELAND

I was born in Cleveland, Ohio, on August 8, 1888, of Czech parents who had immigrated to the United States a few years earlier. My birth was attended by a midwife, as was customary among poor people in those days. I was kept swaddled in a blanket, presumably to keep my spinal column growing straight. So primitive was this country then that there was no record of my birth.

My parents had arrived at Ellis Island with just enough cash to pay their railroad fare to Cleveland, where my father's two sisters were living. Some gyp, offering to help them buy their railroad tickets, took their money and disappeared. How they managed to get to Cleveland is still a mystery to me.

In any case, since my father was an expert tailor, he soon found work at his trade. Because of back trouble, however, he could not continue this for long, and in a few years he and my mother opened a small grocery store in an immigrant section of South Cleveland. The neighborhood consisted of newly arrived Czechs, Germans, and Irish.

Since neither of my parents spoke English, I learned to speak two languages at the same time, Czech at home and English when I played with the children in the street. Little did I realize what a great help this would be when, later, I had to learn to speak German and Russian.

I remember the wooden frame house in which we lived on unpaved Martin Street, in the very heart of Cleveland. There were five rooms: in front was a grocery store about eighteen by twenty-one feet; in back of this were two rooms—a kitchen and a living room—each about twelve feet square. Alongside these were two small bedrooms, each one large enough to accommodate a single bed, with about two feet to spare at the foot and on one side. In back of the house was an assortment of three barns, a lean-to, and an outhouse. One barn, adjacent to the house, was used for storing what can best be described as flotsam and jetsam. In the rear was a two-story affair, the lower floor of which was divided in half. One side was used as a horse stall, and the other as storage space for feed for the horse—and as a banquet hall for all the rats in the neighborhood. The second floor was the hayloft, with a door opening just above the manure pile. Into this my sister Sylvia and I, and all the other kids in the neighborhood, found it great fun to jump. Of course, it didn't take many jumps before we were a mess. To put it mildly, our parents weren't too happy about this harmless game.

The lean-to was used to house the wagon, empty barrels, and more flotsam and jetsam. Now we come to the outhouse, which was placed as far away from the house as possible, for obvious reasons. I still shudder when I think how far that distance seemed on a cold winter day, with the thermometer hovering around zero. Worse yet, when I got there, it took me the longest time to unbutton my pants and place my bare backside over that freezing hole.

Although we lived in the center of Cleveland, in the 1890s there were still no sewers in our part of town; so outhouses were common, and no one had a better answer under the circumstances. Of course, over a period of months, deposits accumulated. This problem was solved by crews commonly called "honey dumpers," who made the rounds at night at about four-month intervals with long-handled buckets. With these they scooped up the stuff into barrels, dumped it onto wagons built for the purpose, and hauled it away.

When I was about three, I remember, a major event revolutionized our household. A three-quarter-inch pipe was run into our kitchen from the street. This was connected with the city water supply. Where we got our water before that, I don't know. But since there was no sewer in the street, there was no use for a sink; so a bucket stood under the faucet at all times and was emptied into the back yard when it overflowed. It wasn't until about seven years later that a sewer, constructed of brick, was built some fifteen feet below the center of the street and we could install a sink. A few years later a toilet bowl was added, plus a square water tank anchored close to the ceiling for flushing purposes. And now we thought we had all the modern improvements. The outhouse was chopped up and the hole filled with sand. This got rid of the worst of the barnyard aroma, but the manure pile still remained. Many years later, after I had left home, the health department ordered my father not to keep more than a week's accumulation of manure on the premises.

* * *

Being high-strung, I was continually up to some prank that irked my father. He was a harsh disciplinarian, beating me unmercifully (and all too frequently) with a leather strap or anything that was handy. "Why did you do this?" he would ask. "Why?" To this day I don't know why except that some little imp within me made me do things impulsively. This being the case, I grew up always in some mischief or other. There was plenty of hard work to be done around the grocery store, however, and I developed a hardy physique.

I entered public school at five, a year earlier than was permissible at that time. This may account for the fact that my grades were consistently poor, although there were spurts, especially when they set me back a grade. Then I would show signs of wisdom which warranted their moving me up again.

My dear mother tended the store from 4:00 a.m., when the early shift of steelworkers went to work, till 9:00 p.m. My sister Sylvia and I lived in constant fear of lickings from my father. But those never hurt nearly as much as when, on occasion, he beat our mother. Later in life we saw that he had many good qualities and that it was his ungovernable temper that made him act that way.

* * *

When I was about five, a craving to play the violin possessed me. With very little coaxing, I got my father to buy me a violin in a pawnshop for three dollars. He started me taking lessons at twenty-five cents a lesson. The teacher knew very little about the violin but was a fairly good choral conductor. In spite of this, and the fact that I hated to practice—especially when out of the corner of my eye I saw the boys playing baseball in the street—there was evidence at occasional recitals that this little boy was unusually talented.

When I entered high school at twelve and applied for a place in the school orchestra, it was discovered I was the best among the violinists. This encouraged me no end. Until then, my horizon was limited to some ten blocks around my home and the grammar school. Now it included almost a quarter of the city.

Milk in those days was delivered by a milkman, who drove from house to house with horse and wagon, ladling out milk with a dipper from large cans into any receptacle his customers brought out to him. At this time our milkman offered me my first job. It meant getting up at 3:00 a.m., driving his horse and wagon out to a farm eight miles away, picking up four large cans of milk, and getting back in time for the milkman to start his deliveries at 7:00. For this I would be paid twenty-five cents a day, seven days a week. I accepted with gusto, since twenty-five cents looked very big to me.

Now my daily routine was as follows. Mother awakened me at three. Oh, how I hated to get up, especially in the wintertime, when the little cubbyhole of a bedroom where I slept was unheated and the temperature outside was below zero! But, like the mail, the milk had to be delivered in all kinds of weather, no matter what. After much prodding by mother, I finally would go on the run and soon have the horse hitched up, be on my way, and be back by 7:00. A hurried breakfast, a glass of hot milk and buns or other baked tidbits my mother was so good at, and I was off to high school, oddly enough retracing the first three of the eight miles I had just finished with horse and wagon. But this time I was on foot, because we were too poor to afford the luxury of paying three cents for carfare.

Our store averaged about a dollar a day in profits for seventeen hours' work. The steel mills paid their laborers close to a dollar a day for twelve hours' work. But, all too often, a hearse or ambulance would arrive at the home of a neighbor with the remains of a man who had been killed or maimed at the mills,

4

accompanied by an official expressing regrets and presenting the man's up-to-date paycheck. It was just as simple as that for the company. Why bother with funeral expenses? That was the family's business.

I usually got home from school at three o'clock. Twice a week I walked another mile for my violin lesson and on the other days I would have to practice an hour. Then there were chores about the store which needed attending to. If luck was with me, I was free to go out and play with the other children by 5:00. Supper was at almost any time between 6:00 and 7:00, when mother was free of customers. Then homework, and so to bed by 8:00. This, then, was the routine for two years in high school. Making out my own report card for those days, I should say: Studies, fair; Deportment, ants in his pants; Music, very good.

During the past few years, I had formed a little orchestra, which played for dances, Polish weddings, and such. This earned me an occasional dollar or two. Anybody familiar with Polish weddings knows that the dancing begins as soon as the bride and groom return from the church ceremony, at about nine in the morning, and continues until daybreak the next morning, with much eating and even more drinking, principally beer.

In mid-European countries it was customary to start children drinking beer from the time they learned to walk; so what was more natural than to treat the musicians, every so often, with beer? Not having been brought up on it, I soon had a bun on. Eventually the beer made me sick. But then I threw up and felt somewhat better.

As the party progressed, it got gayer, noisier, and more inebriated, so that we had to keep playing almost continuously. That we were able to go through three or four jags and still continue playing for some twenty hours seems incredible to me now.

Arriving home on very unsteady feet, from both beer and weariness, I would fall into bed and sleep like a log for another twenty hours. Since these weddings were usually planned for Saturdays, I could sleep all the next day. I would not have been allowed to skip school on a weekday.

* * *

5

At the end of the second school year, my parents gave me permission to go out and find a job. I was now fourteen. Finding an ad in the newspaper that read, "Restaurant will hire porter," I applied and got the job at fifteen dollars for a seven-day week, without having the slightest idea what a porter was supposed to do. It didn't take long to find out when they put me to mopping the floor and washing the dishes. After three days I left and soon found another job as usher in a burlesque theater. When my parents got wind of this, they made me quit. Next came a week as a soda jerk in a drugstore. This ended because of my dislike for cleaning those frothy glasses.

Soon I found another job as bookkeeper in a wholesale fruit business, but got fired at the end of a week because my books wouldn't balance. Addressing envelopes at the Winton Motor Company didn't last long either. Finally I did locate a job as office boy at the Standard Oil Company, which lasted about six months. It had to, because the schools were reopening, and if I had quit, my parents would have made me go back to school, something I was determined not to do.

One of my duties at the Standard Oil Company was to climb those high tanks every morning, push a long measuring stick down through a hole in the top, and measure the amount of oil in the tank. Since there were some twenty-five tanks to measure, it follows that my leg muscles became very strong. Standard Oil was notoriously stingy. After six months, when I applied for a raise and it was not forthcoming, I quit.

My inquisitive nature demanded to know what it was like to work in a factory; so I found a job winding coils for armatures in electric motors. This was all piecework, so much per coil. The rate was established by averaging out what a given number of men could produce in a day. After several months I was so handy with the tools and working so hard that my production rose much higher than that of the others. The company proceeded to cut my pay, so I immediately cut my connection with the company.

Now followed a stint of several months as clerk in the office of the New York Central Railroad. The work consisted of posting figures in a ledger about a foot long—for a whole month. At the end of the month these figures had to be added up and balanced with an account kept elsewhere. The first month my books were

My father and mother, Cleveland, Ohio, 1915.

only slightly out of balance; it took me about two days to find two errors. Thereafter I balanced every month for the duration of my stay. To this day I still possess the ability which I acquired then of adding up long columns of figures with accuracy and speed.

At the time I went to work in the factory I was about sixteen. I left home then and went to board with the foreman of the shop, who had befriended me. I was sick of being dictated to at home. I also longed for better living conditions. One day I gathered up enough courage to tell my father that I was leaving. To my joy and admiration, he gave his consent, saying, "My boy, if that is your wish, go. Should you wish to return, you will always be welcome if you return like a gentleman." His attitude took a great load off my mind. At last I was a free man. Of course, he well knew, and I knew, that if he hadn't given his permission, I should have run away anyhow.

Shortly after leaving high school, I stopped taking violin lessons. My teacher's knowledge and proficiency were only those of a dance orchestra player, and I got the feeling that he couldn't teach me much more. I did, however, continue to do some wedding and dance playing with a local orchestra, as well as office or shop work in the daytime.

2

GO WEST, YOUNG MAN

It was my notion to keep expanding my horizon and get as far away from Cleveland as possible. Besides, as an employee of the New York Central, it was easy to get a pass as far as St. Louis. So what was I waiting for? With about fifty dollars in my pocket, a fellow office worker, who had the same notion, and I left Cleveland on February 8, 1907.

At this time I assumed the name of Henry Miller instead of Jaroslav Siskovsky, because it was easier to pronounce. My, how big the world seemed and how exciting it was! The name Texas sounded so romantic that we headed for Fort Worth. Since we had to pay the fare from St. Louis and I landed there with about twenty dollars in my pocket, we found lodgings in a cheap rooming house and immediately set out to look for work.

Since we had had railroad office experience, it seemed logical to apply at the railroad offices first. For three days we tramped the streets, from one office to another, without success. Then turning to newspaper ads, we found one which appealed to us. It went something like this: "Salesmen wanted to sell a book, house-to-house canvassing, called *The House Doctor*. A book every family in America has been waiting for. It tells how to cure every disease known to man. Huge profits are being made by our salesmen. Only honest, diligent, hard-working men need apply from nine to twelve tomorrow morning." We arrived at the designated spot at 8:00 the next day. Already there were several in line, and by nine o'clock there were about fifty applicants. They hired us all.

Then came a sales talk telling some of the tricks of the

trade—sticking your foot in the door so they couldn't close it in your face and, most important, calling yourself a student working your way through college. All the other tricks I could stomach, but this last deception was repugnant to me. I resolved not to use it. Next they passed around a spiel for us to memorize and ordered us to report in the morning. The price of the book we were selling was five dollars, out of which we were to receive one dollar as commission.

The next morning we were divided into groups under captains and assigned certain sections of the city to canvass. At the first house I came to, it took me a half-hour to screw up enough courage to ring the doorbell. Finally I did ring; and when the lady appeared, I forgot my lines. After I had mumbled and stuttered a bit, the lady closed the door in my face. I had even forgotten to put my foot in the door. Persevering the next few days, I made the walk from house to house, without pause, and gave the memorized spiel correctly, but without conviction.

Reports turned in after work showed that the other boys were making sales; but I, at the end of two days, had made none. Maybe it was because they called themselves students working their way through college, I thought. Next morning I decided to cast aside my resolution and try it out. Answering the first doorbell next morning, a straggle-haired woman in her fifties, I suppose, appeared, wearing a shabby dressing gown. Unlike the usual sour faces that greeted me at the door, this woman was all smiles. When I pulled the student gag, she asked me in and gave me a seat on the divan.

She seated herself at the other end of it. Sensing that my chances of making my first sale were almost 100 percent, I recited my spiel, this time with conviction. While I was talking, the distance between us seemed to be getting narrower. When I had finished, she closed the last gap between us in one leap. Patting me on the cheek, she said, "Of course I'll buy a book, dearie." As we talked, she kept patting my leg.

What the woman was up to finally dawned on me. Since I could only take orders, it was up to me to get her to sign a contract to buy the book. One look at the old girl revolted me, but I needed my first sale—and dollar—badly; so now it became a race. Would I get her signature and get out of there as quickly as possible, or would she achieve her desire to seduce me before signing the contract?

I won. Just how I extricated myself from this lecher's grasp remains a blank in my memory. No more sales that day. I lived in a state of apprehension lest she renege on her contract; but she apparently was a good sport, because she paid the five dollars and I got my dollar.

The next day we took the train to a small town named Dublin, where one of the gang conceived the idea that this book should be a necessity for every farmer. Living far away from doctors as they did, having this information close at hand could often mean the difference between life and death. Autombiles were just beginning to appear on the roads, and the popular mode of travel was still the horse and buggy. Another fellow and I were the only ones in the gang venturesome enough or—let's be honest about it—stupid enough to be willing to try out a brilliant new idea. I don't know how much money the other fellow had, but I think it was no more than I had, and that was the dollar earned the day before. To save money, we agreed to ride in one buggy and share the cost.

With great joy we marched to the livery stable. There the owner told us that all his single horses were rented out, but he had a pair of young colts that he would rent us, with buggy, for five dollars a day. The team was hitched up—and two beauties they were—and we drove off. Having been brought up with a horse at the grocery store, I did the driving. The other fellow had had no experience with horses. As we drove past the gang, we felt pretty important and imagined how envious they must feel.

Our manager hailed us to ask if we would do him a favor before starting out, that is, drive to the railroad station to pick up a batch of books that had just arrived. "With pleasure," we said. At the station, we were loading the books into the buggy when along came a locomotive. It blew its whistle just as it got within twenty feet of us. Off like a cannonball dashed the team, with me after them, like a fool, hollering "Whoa," to which they paid not the slightest attention.

Of course, they had me outdistanced in no time. All I could do was stand there and watch that cloud of dust disappearing down the road with our brilliant idea. Now what to do! After much talking, and two hours later, we decided to go to the owner and tell him what had happened and say we had no money at the moment but would make every effort to pay the damages. By this time the owner had already retrieved his badly mauled horses and buggy. (This was a small town.) It was easy enough, because about two miles away from where the horses started they decided to leave the road and head for the woods. Each one picked the opposite side of a tree; so there, with the tree between them, they came to a sudden halt, all tangled up with the smashed buggy behind them.

Now, as the day had progressed, the owner had figured that the damages would amount to sixty dollars. Hour by hour he became more demanding for the money or some evidence that we would be able to pay. I had only one dollar and my partner had even less. Here we were, strangers in a strange land, far from home and with no possible means of raising any money, let alone what was a huge sum to us. Little did he know that we had already cooked up a scheme to stall him off until darkness, when we would head for the railroad tracks and hike back to Fort Worth—a distance of some twenty-five miles.

When darkness fell, we were off, glad to wash our hands of the whole mess. The stillness of the semidesert was eerie. I don't remember hearing even a cricket chirp. Along the way we met two different groups of hoboes sitting around campfires. We chatted briefly with them, and by daybreak we had reached the environs of Fort Worth. Even though we had had the toughening experience of tramping all day from house to house, this hiking on railroad ties and loose rock had made us very footsore and weary.

Arriving in the city, my companion went his own way and I headed for the rooming house my friend from Cleveland and I had left only two days before. By now I owed a debt of almost ten dollars to my landlady. (I had left behind my suitcase and violin as security.) This buddy from Cleveland, Grover Brown, was a nice guy from a well-to-do family, with an easygoing disposition. We were inseparable roommates. On the bookselling hegira we would tramp all day, coming home so weary that after our usual supper of a can of sardines or a can of pork and beans, we would soon hit the hay and sleep like logs.

He had sold only two books up to the time of the runaway and was ready to call it quits. So just before my hasty departure, we arranged to meet at our old boardinghouse the next day. When the landlady heard my tale, her heart softened. After taking a good look at me, she said, "You need a bath badly. Go upstairs, take room number four, have a bath, and then come down for breakfast." Bless her! I had never heard sweeter words. After breakfast, which consisted of five layers of pancakes with syrup, I went to my room and immediately fell sound alseep. At five o'clock I was awakened by my pal Grover. He told about how the sheriff had looked all over town for us until a late hour and then, for fear our manager would leave town, too, woke him at 2:00 a.m. and threatened to arrest him unless he paid the damages. The manager paid and that was that.

We sat up until a late hour discussing what we should do next and decided to try, at least for another couple of days, to find work at the railroad offices. At this we were unsuccessful.

Tramping the streets, we met another fellow employee from the New York Central Railroad office where we had worked. He was in the same fix, looking for a job and unable to find one; but hearing that employment was easier to find further west, he suggested we three hobo it to El Paso. Immediately we were fired with enthusiasm—especially I, who was the most combustible. So we arranged to meet at the freight yards of the Texas and Pacific Railroad the next evening at six.

Back home we went, and neither of us had the nerve to tell our kind landlady the bad news. After hours of indecision, I finally did. Of course, our debt had grown for the three days we had stayed on, but the poor dear couldn't do much about it except hold my violin and our measly baggage as security. Actually, she was doing me a great favor by keeping it. How could a hobo jump a moving freight with a violin and suitcase in his hands?

The sun was just setting when the three of us met. As luck would have it, a freight train was being made up for a journey to the west on the Texas and Pacific Railroad. We had to survey the proceedings from quite a distance, knowing full well that at such a big yard the train would be watched closely by both railroad detectives and trainmen for the likes of us. This meant that we would have to hop the car while the train was moving.

We walked down the tracks and picked out a place where the footing looked good and where the train would not have gathered enough speed to make the hopping difficult. Since there was only one handle and one step at each end of each car, it was decided that I would pick a car, hop on, and our new friend Bick would hop the next one, while my old pal Grover hopped the succeeding one. It was a clear, starry night; there was no moon, but there was enough light to see the handles on the cars.

Along about nine o'clock she came along. To our dismay, she had already gained so much speed that hopping would be a risky business. There was no time for discussion. I grabbed the first handhold that came along and made one jump for the step, but missed. There I dangled for some ten seconds before I could pull my feet up to the step. Now to walk back to the car behind my gondola. (A *Gondola*, in railroad language, is a flatcar with sides three to four feet high.) To my surprise, there was Bick, sitting with about ten other hoboes. They all greeted me like a long-lost friend as I joined the group.

The car behind us was a boxcar. Of course, we kept looking up, expecting Grover to appear. At least a half hour passed. Suddenly a figure appeared above us, and then another. As they approached in the darkness, we saw that they were brakemen, each with a club. "All right, you bums, fork up some money or we'll put you off the train at the next stop." "How much?" queried one of the gang. "Oh, we'll let you off easy at two dollars apiece," he replied. About half paid the two dollars and the rest of us said we were flat broke. "All right, you nonpayers will be put off at the first stop, in about two hours." Since they came from the rear of the train, I asked if they had seen our friend Grover along the way, and they replied, "No one." It looked as though the train had been going too fast for Grover to make it. We didn't give up hope, however, until we reached the first division point, Baird, where the train would be reassembled and all, including the crew, would be changed.

In the meantime, we reached our first stopping point out in the Texas wilderness, with no sign of habitation in sight. True to their threat, the two brakemen appeared with their clubs and put all of us nonpayers off. Bick and I were the last to get off. As we were doing so, Bick told them that we were railroad employees looking for work, that we had tried very hard in Fort Worth without success, that we were hoping for better luck in El Paso, that we were flat broke, and would they please let us stay on. This melted their hearts. One of them replied, "You look like decent kids, too young to know what it's all about. Get on, and good luck." So we rejoined the five others who had paid and with whom we became good friends.

They were professional hoboes who pursued this life all year round. They regaled us with tales of their experiences, especially their encounters with the law, and warned us to stay well hidden when we passed through certain towns where the railroad detectives and local police made a habit of searching for such as we. If we were caught, the punishment could be a month's sojourn in jail, with work on the rock pile.

Up north, we tenderfoot Yankees were brought up with the misconception that it is always warm down south. I had come in my summer clothes. Here we were in an open gondola, traveling between forty and fifty miles an hour, sooty clinkers falling like hail from the coal-burning engine, with ourselves sitting in a circle of seven, telling stories by the yard. Through the night it got colder and colder, so that by early morn it was almost unbearable. Our teeth chattered constantly and if it hadn't been for the kindness of one of the hoboes, exchanging his heavier coat for my light one every so often, I would have suffered even more.

It seemed as though the sun would never rise; but at last it did, and we gradually became more comfortable. Yes and no. Since there was no dining car on this freight train, we suffered from hunger. In this condition we arrived at Baird, the freight division point, at noon. We looked around for a while to see if our friend Grover would hop off the train, but to no avail. We concluded he had simply lost his nerve for making the necessary jump at that speed. I never saw him or heard from him again.

Thus assured that he would not be with us, we hurried into the small town about a half mile away for something to eat. I had forty cents in my pocket, and Bick had about seventy-five cents. Knowing that forty cents would have to last me for at least four days, I figured that ten cents a day was all I could spend for meals. I ordered one cup of coffee at five cents and two doughnuts at five cents.

After this sumptuous meal, and not having slept all night, we were very tired, sleepy, and dirty. Heading for the outskirts of the town, we found a pond and some shade trees, where we washed up and slept. The sun was going down when we awoke, and we hastened down to the freight yards.

As luck would have it, we were just in time to watch a train being made up. This was a small town, and there wasn't the same strict surveillance of hoboes. Also, it was dark; so we decided to choose a place to hide while the train was standing still—a place where we would be protected from the cold as well as from brakemen. Finally we found just what we wanted. It was a flatcar hauling an iron tank about eight feet high and ten feet in diameter, with a manhole in its top.

Looking around to be sure no one was watching, we climbed aboard. Then I hoisted Bick up to the manhole for a smell to see if it was habitable. Ascertaining that it was, he climbed up and then pulled me up; and we both dropped into it. Fortunately it was quite clean. There we were, set for the trip to the next freight division, Big Spring, some 130 miles west. It seemed a very long time before the freight began moving; but long before that we discovered that sitting on the iron bottom was much too cold for our own tender bottoms. There was nothing to do but keep moving around, occasionally punching each other hard to stir up circulation. Even then our feet were numb from the cold, and the appearance of morning light in the manhole overhead was a most welcome sight.

Now to the other extreme. Toward midmorning, with the sun pouring down on the iron tank car, the inside became unbearably hot and we began suffering from the heat. Well, at least we got thawed out and arrived in Big Spring about noon, none the worse for wear, but frightfully hungry. Off to the first small restaurant we could find where again I had a cup of coffee and two doughnuts, assuaging my hunger somewhat.

No sooner had we left this restaurant than we spotted a freight a short distance away slowly pulling out for the west. Quickly we made up our minds to board it, so we ran alongside and chose the first boxcar with an opening in the rear. To our horror, we found it loaded almost to the top with lumps of soft coal. To move to another car would have meant walking along the tops of the cars in plain view of the brakemen, who usually sat in the cupola of the caboose.

The train had by this time gathered so much speed it would have been very risky business to jump off. We decided to crawl in on top of the coal and get out of sight as quickly as possible. It soon became evident that we had crawled into an instrument of torture, the likes of which had never been thought of. Sharp points of coal were sticking up everywhere. We couldn't stand up because we were too close to the roof of the car. There was nothing to do but keep changing position. In a couple of hours we were sore all over. "And this is what they call soft coal?" we kept joking.

After enduring this for about six hours we struck some unexpected luck. It was about nine o'clock in the evening (I still had my watch) when we slowed down and the whole train was shunted off onto a siding. We heard them uncouple the engine and caboose and depart. Our bodies were so sore that we could hardly move, but we got out of our torture chamber as quickly as possible and surveyed the situation. We realized that we were standing on a siding in the middle of the desert, with no habitation in sight.

Since we hadn't had any sleep in thirty-six hours, it didn't take us long to decide to sleep. Staying close to the sidetrack, in case the crew came back to pick up the train, we lay down in the sand and went sound asleep. Oh, how nice and soft that sand felt after what we had just gone through!

We weren't given much time to sleep, however, because about 1:00 a.m. we were awakened by much activity on the sidetrack. At first we thought it was the crew coming back for the train we had just been on; but on further investigation, we saw that it was another freight, sidetracked to let a passenger train pass. As this was out in the wilderness and the crew was not on the alert for us, we had ample time to choose a car suitable for our purpose. After looking over quite a few, mindful of comfort and a place to hide from the brakemen, we chose an oversized boxcar loaded with knocked down Studebaker wagons. Climbing in through a small opening near the top of the rear end, we squirmed our way through a maze of wagon wheels, bodies, shafts, and prongs, feeling sure that here the brakemen would never find us and unmindful of the fact that it wouldn't take much of a bump to shift this mass a little and make hash out of both of us.

After the coal, sitting on the floor of the car seemed a luxury. Soon the passenger train passed by, and then we began moving. We fell asleep and didn't waken till our train slowed down for Toyah about eight in the morning, the last division point before El Paso, some 190 miles further west.

Extricating ourselves from the maze, we made a dash for a small restaurant nearby; and again I had coffee and doughnuts. This left me with ten cents for eats at El Paso. We had caught up on our sleep; so we strolled around the small town of Toyah, always keeping one eye on the railroad yards. About noon we spotted a train being made up nearby.

Since this was really way out in the wilderness, the brakemen weren't a bit watchful. We had plenty of time to choose a nice private car, a boxcar filled halfway up with bags of Pillsbury flour. This was too good to be true! We quickly jumped in through that same little back entrance and went to the opposite end of the car to build a low wall of bags, behind which we lay and hid in case the brakemen peeked in. In this luxury we reached El Paso, uneventfully, at about 8:00 the next morning.

We had been on the road (617 miles) for three days and four nights, suffering extremes of heat and cold, lack of sleep, hunger, and much discomfort; yet we emerged from the ordeal in perfect health and buoyant spirits.

* * *

Now let me interrupt this narrative and skip to a time some thirty years later when I had a diverting exchange relating to the adventures I have just described. My wife and I were invited to dinner at the Webbs' summer place at Shelburne Point on Lake Champlain. Our hostess's maiden name was Lila Vanderbilt, a daughter of William H. Vanderbilt. Since we were intimate friends of Mrs. Webb's daughter Frederica, we were frequent guests at the house.

One evening there was a dinner for about fifteen of us. Among the guests was William Church Osborn, father of Aileen, who had married Mrs. Webb's youngest son, Vanderbilt Webb.

After dinner Mr. Osborn and I took our long corona cigars and our coffee into a corner and began talking of ships and shoes and sealing wax. Knowing that he had been president of the Texas and Pacific Railroad at the time of my first hoboing expedition, I surprised him by saying, "Mr. Osborn, it has just come to my mind that I owe you some money." He looked at me in astonishment and, after scratching his head for a moment, said, "Why, Jaro, it can't be. I can't remember anything about that. How come?" I replied, "Well, it happened this way, Mr. Osborn. Back in 1907 I hoboed my way from Fort Worth to El Paso on your railroad and never paid the fare."

I told him the story just as I have here, careful to include the exact mileage between each freight division. From that time on, every time we met he had a mischievous smile on his face.

* * *

Now back to our arrival in El Paso. We looked like chimney sweeps. Shaving was no problem, because even fuzz hadn't started to grow on my chin. One thing we were sure of, though: if a job was to be found, we had to look more presentable. With this in mind, we walked the mile into town straight to a pawnshop, where I hocked my watch for five dollars. Then on to a cheap Chinese restaurant for breakfast.

I ordered ham and eggs at twenty-five cents. While these were frying, the waiter brought in a plate of sliced bread piled about eight inches high. The whole pile was wolfed down in about two minutes, long before the ham and eggs arrived. After breakfast we found a cheap rooming house where we could bunk in for twenty-five cents a night.

After showering, I immediately went to a haberdashery and bought a shirt for fifty cents, a pair of socks for fifteen cents, and a tie for twenty-five cents. Back at the rooming house, I cleaned up my coat and pants as well as I could in preparation for going out to look for a job.

Bick, whose original intention had been to go on to California, made up his mind to spend the night and then leave town on the first freight. He was no friend of long standing; so, although he was a genial companion, our separation was no disappointment to me. I had come to realize that this business of looking for jobs together was a handicap. Now I was free to take the first job that came along without having to consider someone else.

It was about one o'clock when I started out to look for a job.

19

Luck was with me. The first place I applied was at the general office of the El Paso and Southwestern Railroad, now a part of the Southern Pacific system. As I addressed the employment manager, he told me, "Yes, we have a job we have been trying to fill for over a month. It is not in El Paso but in a Godforsaken place 117 miles west of here called Hachita, in New Mexico. The only reason for the existence of the place is that it is the first division point west and a switching point for trains running to Clifton and Morenci, a branch line. I must warn you that there are only about ten white men and six Mexican families living there, all working for the railroad. There is a small general store and what calls itself a hotel, with about twenty rooms. The crews coming in from the east and west sleep there while changing trains. The job is that of yard clerk, working twelve hours a day, seven days a week. You would live in a small shack with attached kitchen, alternating every week with the other yard clerk, working nights and days, sleeping in the one bed when off duty. There is also cooking equipment, all of which is furnished free by the railroad. Of course, there is no entertainment and it's a desolate place, but the salary is good—sixty dollars a month."

"I'll take it," was my quick reply. "When does the first train leave?" I couldn't say it fast enough.

"The first one gets there at midnight," he said, "but you might better take the one getting there at noon, which leaves here at eight tomorrow morning."

With that he handed me a pass and wished me luck. I was so excited that I made the journey back to the hotel in nothing flat. Bick was not there, but I soon found him strolling about town. We kept strolling until suppertime, when we went back to the Chinese restaurant and had twenty-five cent suppers. Then early to bed, where I slept badly, all the while thinking, "How exciting this all is!"

We rose early the next morning and had fifteen-cent breakfasts at the Chinaman's. Having paid our combined expenses in El Paso, I still had about a dollar left from the five dollars I got when I hocked the watch. I felt sure that I could get an advance on that monumental sixty-dollar-a-month salary waiting for me; so I gave Bick all that was left and we parted good friends, never to see each other again.

20

3

HACHITA, NEW MEXICO

I arrived at Hachita about noon. Looking through the window of the railway car, I could see nothing but sand with mesquite bushes eking out a parched existence on the desert. The railroad tracks ran parallel to the border of Mexico all the way; moderately high mountains were visible on both sides.

We passed through only one town, Columbus, which Pancho Villa had the audacity to raid some years later. The population could not have been more than twenty souls. It was desolate, but to me it looked beautiful because it was the Wild West I had heard so much about.

Stepping from the train at Hachita, I saw a high water tower, a small railroad station, and four small houses on one side of the track. I noted a small general store and a twenty-room hotel, plus about five Mexican shacks, with railroad yards about half a mile down the tracks.

In the railroad station I introduced myself to the stationmaster. His first query was, "Haven't you any baggage?" I told him that I had slept in a hotel in El Paso the night before and that someone had entered the room while I slept and stolen my purse as well as my baggage.

This didn't seem to surprise him at all. "Aren't you hungry?" he asked. "Very," was my quick reply. So after telling me what kind of work I would be asked to do, what the pay would be and the number of work hours, he handed me ten dollars. "Here is an advance on this month's pay," he said. "Go across the tracks to the hotel, have a good meal, and come back later to meet the others in the office."

21

I went in, passing about twenty cubbyholes before I found the diningroom. There I ordered steak and potatoes, coffee, and a double portion of ice cream, all for fifty cents. While I waited for the meal, the Mexican waiter told me that their clientele was composed almost entirely of train crews which brought in trains from both east and west. Here they ate and slept between runs.

Finally, after an everlasting wait, the waiter brought in an enormous platter of steak and potatoes. To me, not having had a decent meal for a long time, it looked like a feast for four people. Thought I to myself, "Evidently these train crews are very hearty eaters; this is something unbelievable." The double portion of ice cream was equally enormous, but I ate everything. On leaving, I could hardly rise from the table.

Back at the office, I was introduced to the staff: the stationmaster, a bookkeeper, a telegrapher, and a yard clerk. Two more, a telegrapher and the yard clerk whom I was replacing, were not present because they were on night duty and were sleeping in small houses nearby. Finally I was asked to stay at the hotel, at company expense, for several nights until I learned the routine, so that the man being replaced could leave, and to report for work at 7:00 the next morning.

It was about four o'clock by this time. I strolled toward the railroad yards and took note that they comprised eight tracks, about a mile long, beside the main line. Walking the length of these and back, I returned to the hotel in time for supper. After consuming another enormous meal, I went to my room, climbed into bed, and slept like a log till 6:00 the next morning.

I arrived at the office early. Refreshed by the hearty meals and ten hours' sleep, I exuded get-up-and-go. My first work was to sweep out the office. By the time I had done that, it was seven o'clock and the day telegrapher and yard clerk arrived. The latter took me in hand and proceeded to teach me the job, as follows: "As soon as a freight train arrives, the cars are shunted off onto a track in the yards. The conductor then makes a list of all the cars, with information about each car as to origin and destination, consignee and consignor, and contents. He gives this to the yard clerk, who is then required to go out and check the list to ascertain its correctness, also to check all seals on all cars to be sure that they have not been tampered with and the cars broken into."

22

Returning to the office, the yard clerk then made out a new list, according to priority, for the local switching crew, from which they picked out cars that became the nucleus for the new trains traveling either east or west, or north up the branch to Clifton, Arizona.

Aside from a few minor chores, such as selling one or two tickets a week for passenger trains, two of which stopped at our station from the east and the west in the daytime, and two at night, and the wheeling out of a baggage cart to receive whatever arrived by express, my whole twelve hours' work seven days a week consisted of taking down car numbers in the yards and then reassembling them according to priority for our switching crew for their further travel.

This didn't really require too much intelligence. At the end of the second day my instructor reported to the stationmaster that I was capable of carrying on alone. Since the man whom I was replacing was anxious to leave as soon as possible, it was arranged that he should depart the midnight train. My instructor would work twenty-four hours, thus taking over the night shift. And I would move over to the little house with my instructor and take over the day shift next day.

Did I say "move over"? This was somewhat of an anomaly, since I had absolutely no possessions but the clothes I had on and shoes with soles so worn that I expected my bare feet to touch earth any minute. Moving was no problem. During the day my roommate and I had discussed arrangements for baching it together. He agreed to buy the food supplies and do the cooking until I got oriented. That he could cook was good news to me, since I had never tried my hand at it. Of course, all expenses would be split fifty-fifty.

That evening I walked over to the store and bought a pair of shoes, khaki pants, two pairs of shorts, and two shirts, on credit. With no rent to pay, it looked as though with my sixty-dollars-a-month salary I would be a rich man in no time.

Actually, after about three months, even with nothing else to spend money on, my food was costing thirty dollars. Just remember that Hachita was out in the middle of the desert with temperatures running in the nineties daily, and there was no ice to be had. We were dependent almost exclusively on canned and sun-dried beef, antelope, and rabbits.

Fresh vegetables were nonexistent. Once, when a car of watermelons from California came through and I was on the night shift, I couldn't resist breaking the seal and stealing the biggest melon. I took it back to our house, where I woke up my roommate and the day telegrapher. I cut the melon into four pieces, three of which we ate with great relish, not only because it tasted good, but also because nothing ever happened there and it broke the monotony. After carefully burying the rinds, I carried the fourth piece over to the telegrapher on duty. His eyes sparkled when he saw what was coming his way.

Next day the conductor, in checking the train he was about to take out, discovered the broken seal and reported it to my roommate, who remarked, "It must have been those Mexicans. You can't trust them any further than you can see them."

* * *

After I had bought those few articles of wearing apparel and had eaten supper at the hotel, I moved into what would be home for the indefinite future. It was a wooden house with one room, about twenty feet square, with plastered walls and ceiling. There was a small lean-to-attached in which were shelves for storing food and dishes, plus a kitchen-style kerosene stove. Furnishings in the main room were a double bed, four kitchen chairs and a table, and two small closets for clothes.

Though simple, it was all neat and clean and, to me, looked like the Waldorf-Astoria compared to those railroad cars I had been sleeping in, especially the one loaded with so-called soft coal.

It didn't take long for me to settle in those nice clean sheets. I soon fell asleep, only to be awakened occasionally by the noise of some animal outside our back door trying to pilfer the contents of our garbage can. Eager to get going my first day on the job, I rose early and, having been informed that a pot of coffee was always kept filled on the stove, as well as a big pot of oatmeal, I was soon eating my breakfast.

I tried very hard to leave the bed as neatly made up as my roommate had left it for me. After all, he and I would be alternating weekly, sleeping in it by night and day. Arriving at the office at six, I swept it out; and soon it was seven o'clock, when the work of the yard clerk was turned over to me alone. It wasn't difficult work; so with the two days' training, it wasn't necessary to trouble the stationmaster to help me even once.

Crews kept bringing in and taking out trains from the east, west, and north all day and all night long. It was customary for the crews to carry rifles on these trips, for the engineer and fireman were always on the lookout for antelope to shoot, if possible. If they were successful, they would stop the end of the train close to the spot where the animal lay and the conductor or trainman from the caboose would go out and pick it up. Many an antelope was brought into the office with the request that I store it in the baggage room until their return trip, usually the next day.

Except for the weekly shift from day to night, which entailed working a twenty-four-hour stint, the routine never varied. Life would have become very monotonous except for the periodic coming and going of trainmen, bringing in problems and a lot of kidding.

I grew to know them well. I made two trips to El Paso sitting in the cupola of the caboose, knowing then that they wouldn't put me off the train. Being so much younger than they, I was joshed a lot, but never enough to make me angry. We got on famously, especially since it was within my province to stick them with a lot of switching, which they hated. Their objective was to get a train that would go straight home with the least amount of work.

I also got along well with my roommate; maybe because we hardly ever saw each other except at seven in the morning and seven at night, when we exchanged jobs. Then, along with discussing problems left over from our work, we would also plan our food and marketing for the house. Since the man on the night shift would want a good meal in the morning and the man on the day shift would want breakfast, we never ate together; each of us got his own meal. I eventually could fry up a can of hash with the best of them.

The man on days would clean house once a week, and a Mexican woman would do the laundry on Saturday. Working twelve hours and sleeping eight and allowing one hour for house chores left three hours of free time. I usually spent it reading books or the El Paso newspaper.

Best of all, I liked the trips into the yards, taking down car numbers. There were at least three trains a day coming into the yards, each of which meant a walk of two and a half miles round trip. But it was fun meeting the many desert animals, such as chameleons and other lizards, armadillos, tarantulas, rabbits, always worth a slight pause to watch along the way.

Most fascinating of all were those trips in the dead of night. Often I would climb to the top of a freight car with my lantern hanging from my elbow and look in all directions in awe and wonder. The immensity of it all should have made me feel very small indeed, but—quite the contrary—I felt that I was king of it all. That's exuberant youth for you!

Since it hardly ever rained, there were the stars and moon above, loose desert sand under foot, and except for the water tank and the few buildings visible in Hachita a mile and a half away, nothing but uninhabited desert and cactus for a hundred miles in all directions. Excluding an occasional yelp from a coyote or roar from a mountain lion in the distance, the absolute stillness was eerie. Those who have experienced this void of sound will know what I mean. It's really spooky.

I used to stand there and wonder what my parents would think if they could see their sixteen-year-old son standing there like Diogenes with a lighted lantern hanging on his elbow in this vast wilderness and solitude in the black of night.

Then again, it was hell going out there in the thick of the March sandstorms. That sand really stings when it hits you in the face at velocities of fifty to sixty miles an hour. Regardless of the weather, I was obliged to make those trips every time a freight arrived.

Not having protective glasses, I would arrive back at the office almost blind, with my hair, eyes, nose, lungs, mouth, and clothes full of sand. It was hard to tell which was worse, the sand blinding my eyes or that grinding between my teeth. All of this I took in stride, apparently none the worse for wear, but much wiser in experience, though not in manners, since all contacts were with rough-and-ready railroad men and no women.

Along about May the weather was getting progressively hotter, so that those trips out to the yards became almost unbearable in the daytime and sleeping at night was impossible without wetting the sheets to cool off.

I hadn't been there long before it became apparent that there was no future in this place for me. I began to save every cent possible, which was no hardship, since there was nothing to spend it on except food and clothing.

After the third paycheck. I sent our kind landlady in Fort Worth enough money to pay my debt to her, plus five dollars. She very soon returned the violin and suitcase with my belongings. The violin was the cheap one which my father had bought in a pawnshop for three dollars, but I loved it dearly. I began almost daily practice, thereby regaining most of the proficiency I had lost during my neglect of it.

At the same time I resolved that when my savings reached a hundred dollars I would leave and try my luck in El Paso. So it was that, after six months' sojourn, I left Hachita on a freight train, never to see it again.

In the meantime I had given the station agent a month's notice. At my departure he handed me my paycheck with a fine recommendation to the general offices, and a pass on the passenger train. I turned this down, saying I preferred to ride with my friends in the cupola of the caboose on the freight train.

4

EL PASO, TEXAS

When I arrived in El Paso, my first job was to check into a rooming house, deposit suitcase and violin, and head straight for the pawnshop to retrieve the watch which I had pawned there six months before. Next, I took the streetcar across the Rio Grande to Juarez, Mexico, where I went on a spending binge and sent curios to my parents and friends back in Cleveland. Without my even realizing it, fifty dollars vanished as if by magic. Oh, well, who cares! I thought. I was having a good time and was free of that twelve-hour-day-seven-days-a-week straightjacket. So, after having a supper of enchiladas, I returned to the United States and went straight to bed.

The next few days I spent loafing and getting acquainted with the town, after which I presented my recommendation at the general offices and was given a job on the spot. It was a clerical job, which meant sitting at a desk doing paperwork from eight to five, six days a week, at fifty dollars a month. After the hours I had been keeping, such a civilized job, in a modern office building, seemed the height of luxury. When I was asked, "How soon will you be ready to start?" (it was still early in the day), I answered, "Now," and that was it. The job was mostly book-keeping; so the breaking-in period lasted only four or five hours.

That night, on returning to my rooming house, I searched the newspaper want ads for a place to room and board with a family, made a note of several, and immediately set out to look them over. The first place I came to appealed to me. I went no further and moved in the following day. It proved to be a very happy choice since they treated me like one of the family and I remained with them during my whole stay in El Paso.

Besides the father and mother, there were three boys and two girls. One girl and a boy were slightly younger than I; the other three were a little older. Their father operated a bookstore. Why he would want a boarder puzzled me until I saw the run-down condition of the store. It was evident that, at sixty-five, he simply couldn't keep up with the work. But the meals were very good and the room was comfortable. (However, one morning I awakened to discover a tarantula sleeping under the sheet with me. Since it was good enough not to bite me, I didn't have the heart to murder it; so I rolled up the sheet and shook it out the window.)

My job was a pleasant one; yet I longed to devote more time to my first love, the violin. Hence, evenings were spent in getting acquainted with the musicians of the town; and when, in the course of time, I heard the man who was considered the best fiddler in town, I said to myself, "Hell, I can play better than that!" This gave me the courage to enter into competition.

At the office, after about three months, I was so good at the job that it took me about two hours less than the allotted time. I wasn't about to tell the boss (he'd only find more work for me). So I went through the motions and loafed. Inevitably, this led to mischief. One day when I was feeling more bored than usual, the idea struck me to roll up small pieces of paper and shoot them with a rubber band at my fellow employees, then quickly pretend to be hard at work.

A few days later the head clerk called me to his desk and said, "You're fired. Go and get your pay." At the cashier's office I was paid in scrip. Because of the financial panic at the time, all money was withdrawn from circulation. The panic, however, was no great inconvenience to me because I had saved a little over a hundred dollars, which I carried in my pocket. (The scrip, which amounted to about twenty dollars, was paid as my parting salary.)

By this time I already had joined the musicians' union and was playing at one or two dances a week, waiting for the day when I could quit railroading and support myself exclusively with the violin. In retrospect, this dismissal proved to be a blessing in disguise, because it gave me the added push I needed to find out whether I could make a living with my violin.

In spending part of each day at the union headquarters, I soon became acquainted with all the musicians in town as well as all the places that hired these men. Soon I heard a rumor that the Elks Club had become dissatisfied with a Mexican orchestra, which had been playing in its diningroom for dinner, because they played nothing but Mexican music.

I hurried right over to the Elks Club for an interview with the manager. He asked me, "What kind of combination do you have?"

I replied, "A trio—piano, violin, and cello, a combination well suited for peaceful dining." "Just what we want," he replied. "Our members are getting tired of listening to that Mexican music. It all sounds the same. When can I hear you play?"

"Give me a week to organize this properly and to buy a repertoire that is suitable; then select an evening when we will come over to play for your dinner free of charge. Then you'll be able to tell how we go over."

"Fair enough," he said. "Let's make it next week. Sunday— that's our biggest day."

So off to the music store I hastened, walking on air. I bought twenty dollars' worth of popular music—Victor Herbert, George M. Cohan, etc.—and presented the proposition to the best pianist and cellist in town. Both were delighted.

We rehearsed diligently for three or four hours every day that week. When Sunday came, we were well prepared and received most enthusiastic applause from the diners, after which the manager approached me with a broad smile on his face. "The job is yours," he said. "Come tomorrow and we'll talk terms."

The next day we settled on seven dollars an evening. That meant three dollars for me and two for each of the others, including a supper equivalent to that which was served to the diners.

The Elks and Country clubs were the two ritziest in town; their members were among El Paso's most important and influential people. The trio was a big hit, and gossip had it that a new and very good violinist was playing there. Business in the restaurant increased considerably, and I was getting some free publicity.

About a month later, one of the diners approached us in an

ecstatic mood, complimenting us on our beautiful music. During the course of the conversation, he remarked that he had just returned from territory between El Paso and Los Angeles, mostly silver- and copper-mining towns. While listening to our music, he realized that, with so few musicians in these parts, the people must be starved for good music. Would we consider making a concert tour? He would do the managing and would split profits and expenses equally four ways. This looked to the three of us like the start of something really big, and we readily agreed.

The next two weeks were spent making preparations for the trip, selecting a program in which each of us would play a solo and the rest of the time would supply light, popular music such as we had played at the Elks Club. The only thing I knew from memory was Schumann's "Traumerei"; so down it went. None of us, except the manager, who could sing a song, owned a dress suit; and since the business of renting hadn't yet been born, there was nothing to do but try to borrow them from friends. Not knowing many people, I had great difficulty in finding someone my size. But with the help of the others, I finally succeeded. Then we gave notice to the Elks Club that we would be out of town for an indefinite period. The manager was so angry, he replied, "Don't ever come back here again."

Other than a few dance dates and one or two lessons, I wasn't losing much. But the cellist and pianist, who had full-time employment at two theaters, were sacrificing a great deal— especially the pianist, who had a wife and three children to support.

Our first concert was at Silver City, New Mexico, where we played at the United States government hospital for tubercular soldiers. There we had a big audience of several hundred patients, who were admitted free, since the fifty dollars we received was paid out of their entertainment fund. We slept there on cots in a big dormitory along with about fifty patients.

Nothing much happened in the next four or five towns. Instead of standing-room-only signs, we could have put up sitting-room-only signs. Audiences averaged about twenty, so that our ticket intake didn't even cover the cost of the hall. But we kept hoping that the next town would be *the* one.

Arriving in Globe, Arizona, we were delighted to learn that the concert was to take place in the enormous armory there. "Oh, this may be it," thought we. It hardly ever rains in Arizona, but that night it came down in torrents. When we appeared on the stage, the sight of some twenty people who had braved the storm seated in an enormous auditorium was just about as dreary as the weather outside. But nothing daunted, we proceeded with the concert. To add to our misery, the roof was of sheet metal. With the heavy rain pounding throughout the performance, we could hardly hear each other. What the audience heard aside from the rain must have been almost nothing. At least no one left until the end—perhaps because they were afraid to go out in the rain.

Our next stop was Tucson. There we learned that there was some mix-up in communications between our manager and the local manager, with the result that the public had not even heard of the concert. This was the last straw. I was flat broke; so we decided it made no sense to continue. The other three had money in the bank at El Paso. Our manager wired for enough to get us all home.

In the meantime, we discovered that a theatrical company was giving shows at an open-air theater in town. Our manager conceived the idea of announcing during an intermisson in their program that the famous Euterpe Trio of New York would give a concert after the show. Anyone wishing to stay could do so for twenty-five cents. This resulted in our biggest audience of the tour—about fifty people.

After several days delay awaiting the money, we returned to El Paso a bedraggled, forlorn, and disheartened crew, forced to admit that our trip had been a complete fiasco. Well, there was nothing to do but try to get back into the swim of things. For the pianist and cellist, it was not difficult. They had been replaced by inferior players and were gladly welcomed back to all the work they had had before. I, on the other hand, was a new boy in town and had created a certain amount of distrust in my reliability. Since the Elks Club had rehired the Mexican orchestra, there remained nothing for me to resurrect but two pupils at a dollar per hour a week, and one evening dance date to play from 8:00 until 2:00 at three dollars.

5

NEW CHALLENGES

About the first of May life in El Paso began to slow down for the summer. Half the population of whites left for points north, mostly for Cloudcroft, New Mexico, where the elevation was about 9,000 feet. Since the weather was already unbearably hot, dancing had ceased, and my two pupils didn't want lessons because they were leaving for the summer.

I owed our manager about twenty-five dollars. My rent while we were away, plus what I had to borrow from my landlady (bless her, she trusted me), all amounted to about seventy-five dollars. During this time, from May first to June fifteenth, I ate only one meal a day—usually a big dish of pork and beans at noontime.

June fifteenth was a turning point in my fortunes; I was never again reduced to such poverty. On that date, my landlord made arrangements to move his bookstore. He asked me if I would give them a helping hand at fifteen dollars for a six-day week. Since the prospects of getting any musical work were practically nil for the summer, I jumped at the chance.

Resuming board with the family, I soon regained my usual weight. The first week we worked very hard from sunup nearly till midnight. I haven't any idea how many thousands of books had to be sorted out and shelved. Finally at the end of the month, we wound up with stacks of books that had been lying on shelves for years and were out of date or had damaged covers. For these I built display shelves. They were placed on the sidewalk in front of the store at much reduced prices and were disposed of quickly.

I also waited on customers as occasion required. This I

33

enjoyed, because it helped cure me of my shyness in meeting people. Thus the very hot summer passed quickly. By October first, all my debts were paid. Those to my landlady were a special satisfaction to both of us: to her, because I had worked harder and longer hours than required; to me, because I had fulfilled her trust in me, a total stranger.

Suddenly, on October first, my fortunes unexpectedly turned from rags to riches. An urgent message arrived from the manager of the two biggest theaters in town asking that I come to his office posthaste. No one needed to tell me that this must be something big. I dropped everything and rushed over. He informed me that he had just received word that the man who, up to that point, had the reputation of being the best violinist in town and had charge of supplying the music and musicians for the two theaters was not returning to El Paso. My heart stopped beating but quickly rallied as he asked, "Would you be available for this job?" After some hesitation, I replied, "Could I bring back a definite answer tomorrow morning? This is quite a responsibility. I would like to consider it overnight."

"That's okay with me, but remember, the season starts on October fifteenth; so you'll have only two weeks to get things ready," he said. Of course I had no intention of letting this windfall slip by, come what may, but it seemed necessary to act important and play hard to get in order to strengthen my bargaining position when the question of salary came up. Back at the bookstore I told my landlord the good news and that I could work only a week longer for him. His face fell. He said that I had seemed so happy there he was hoping I would stay on indefinitely.

With solutions to all problems suddenly in sight, and with the excitement of all my new prospects, naturally I rolled and tossed all night without a wink of sleep.

Next morning I appeared at the manager's office at nine o'clock and signed a contract to supply the music for the two most important theaters in town. One seated about 400, at which a stock company performed and at which we used a five-piece orchestra—piano, violin, cello, cornet, and drums. The other theater was a 2,000-seat building used principally for road shows with Broadway casts. They would usually stop to play a matinee and two night shows at irregular intervals, averaging about once a week throughout the season. For these shows we had to keep an orchestra of twelve men available at all times.

This is how it worked out. By adding a cornet and drums to our ill-fated trio, we had the five-piece orchestra for the small theater. Nearly all the musical road shows carried an orchestra of fifteen to twenty men with them. To these they would add the local orchestra, which in our case was twelve men.

For a play such as *The Music Master*, our usual twelve men played between-the-acts and incidental music. When both theaters were booked, we would leave our piano player behind at the little theater to play the shows alone, while we four moved over with the addition of eight men to play the road shows.

It was not difficult to secure the best men for this work. Here it was considered a status symbol comparable to that of being a member of the New York Philharmonic in New York. Besides, we were being paid to see famous shows that others had to pay high prices to see.

When I say "best men," that doesn't mean that they were really good musicians. I was pretty poor. The pianist was the best of the lot, having played with the New Orleans Opera. Unfortunately, he was sober only when he was broke, and that was two days after payday until the next payday. (He had a wife and three children.) In the interim he was forever borrowing from me money which he never repaid. I simply couldn't fire him for three reasons: first, he had a family; second, he was the best man in the orchestra; and third, he was a nice person who seldom got so plastered that he failed to play his part well or became objectionable or unreliable.

Our cellist was a good player, too. (Both were much better than I was.) He was single, and his real ambition was to be a balloonist. Most of his money was spent on books on the art of flying a balloon and plans for flying machines. He played his part well and was dependable and cooperative, but his mind always seemed to be up in the clouds with his balloons. Since none of the rest of us wanted to do any high flying, he became a loner, apparently to his satisfaction, since not one of us was as scientific as he.

Two men, the cornet and trombone players, were about on a

35

par with me in ability. Let's make one word of that and say *inability*; it comes closer to the truth. From here on down, proficiency diminished to the flute player, who was willing but unable to play the more difficult passages. This presented no problem, since these passages were always cued into my part. I played them without anyone's being the wiser. All the men were much older than I; most were in their thirties.

At this time the population of El Paso numbered about 25,000, half white and half Mexican. It was a typical frontier town. There were saloons on every corner and cowboys from outlying districts roaming about all liquored up, wearing revolvers in holsters hanging from their hips. Several streets were lined with houses of ill repute, the girls sitting in doorways in negligees, soliciting customers. Indian territory had recently been linked up to Oklahoma and admitted to the Union as a state.

Man was just learning to fly. I remember going to one of the parks to see what was planned as an exhibition of flight by one of the first planes ever built. It proved unsuccessful because the air at El Paso's altitude was too rare. Many attempts were made to get the biplane off the ground, but the best the pilot, who sat right out in the open with two steering sticks in his hands, could do was about six feet. More successful was a similar demonstration, when a flyer sat in a contraption consisting of a cigar-shaped balloon with an understructure made of bamboo poles, at the rear of which was anchored a motor with a propeller attached to drive the balloon forward. To gain elevation, the flyer moved back a foot or so on his trestle of bamboo, which tipped the nose of the balloon up; and of course it was done vice versa to descend.

It was still the Wild, Wild West when all too many men found it more satisfactory to shoot an opponent than to convince him by argument. No wonder, then, that the cultural aspects of a more civilized world were only in their infancy here.

* * *

After signing the contract, I had two weeks before the show opened. Since everything had happened so quickly, I was tempted to quit the job at the bookstore at once, but realized this would be unfair to my landlord. I begged him to find my replacement as soon as possible.

This he did within a few days, so that I had a full week to make all arrangements necessary to get going, such as buying some decent clothes and a library of orchestra music, as well as hiring and rehearsing the orchestra. There was so much running around involved that the week passed very quickly, but still not fast enough for me. It had been known for some time that the famous "Fatty Arbuckle Show" would open the season and would remain for an indefinite period.

Rehearsal was scheduled for noon, just before the first performance at two o'clock. We met Arbuckle. He was a facsimile of Jackie Gleason in size, but even more agile on his feet. Comedians are notorious for having dispositions opposite to the roles they portray on stage; not so with Arbuckle. He was always full of beans. It was great fun working with him.

The shows were what might be called mini-musical comedies, with a cast of four or five actors plus a dancing chorus of about ten girls. The program was supposed to change twice a week; but, as it turned out, Arbuckle was such a master at ad-libbing there was an almost complete change with every performance. Only the rehearsal and first show were performed as planned. With all the singing and dancing, the orchestra was kept busy most of the time. I had to be on the alert every minute listening for the cues to start the orchestra playing. With such freedom with the dialogue, the cue often was not given. Arbuckle, however, was so clever with his patter that sooner or later I'd get the point and start the orchestra off without the audience's being any the wiser. The first few times I felt guilty for having missed the cues. Then I learned that, even if it were my fault, the free and easy manner in which the shows were run was just what made them delightfully funny.

After the first week, the show was playing to full houses at almost every performance and Arbuckle and the manager complimented the orchestra on its proficiency. We were all very happy—all, that is, except the drummer. Because Arbuckle was doing so many pratfalls, and he had to come in with a big bang on every one of them, the drummer had no time to relax his attention for a moment. After the second week, the manager included in his advertising a statement to the effect that $100 reward would be paid to anyone who could prove that his theater didn't have the best orchestra in town.

Shortly thereafter, the manager of the Elks Club called to ask if our trio wouldn't like to resume playing at their suppers every night. Of course I agreed saying, "But it's going to cost you a little more." He agreed to my price without any argument.

Gradually pupils began applying for lessons; and after several months, a singing teacher, a pianist, and I joined forces and rented two studios, where we taught and gave joint student recitals.

Then there were the dances, which usually started at 8:00 p.m. and lasted till 2:00 a.m. A pianist would play for them alone until about 10:15. Then I would come marching in with my violin to the accompaniment of great applause and finish out the evening with her. You can be sure I timed my entrance in between dances when all eyes would be focused on me.

So there we have my daily schedule—one which kept me busy from nine in the morning until two the next morning every day except Sunday. On Sundays there were no lessons and no dances, only the two shows and the Elks Club. So I joined a foursome at tennis, which met every Sunday morning at six in order to avoid the severe heat of the day. We usually played three sets. Occasionally, when none of the players were able to come, I would still arise at daybreak, hop a streetcar on Montana Street, ride to the end of the line, and climb Mount Franklin, seldom meeting anyone along the way and returning about noon very thirsty and hungry. I would have a light lunch at a restaurant and go home to bed for about an hour's nap, being sure to set the alarm clock so as to be at the theater ready for the matinee at two o'clock.

I regretted very much not taking meals anymore with the family I was rooming with. My landlady was so kind and a fine cook. But my hours were far too irregular for that.

It would seem that with a daily schedule of seventeen working hours I would be suffering from lack of sleep. Occasionally I was, but with my upbringing, my fibre was tough. And since I could fall asleep at the drop of a hat, I found opportunities during the day, such as between lessons, when I could take catnaps.

Best of all, I liked playing for the road shows that came to town, usually for three or four performances. At the theater, the musicians' room and the actors' dressing rooms were located along the corridor under the stage. This gave us musicians a good chance to hobnob with them.

I had to discuss musical arrangements with David Warfield, George M. Cohan, and many other stars. They were a friendly lot of worldly people. The chorus girls, as soon as they got their costumes on, would come out into the corridor and start monkeyshining around. It was great fun to watch them and sometimes take part in the tomfoolery.

It happened during the stay of the Montgomery and Stone production of *The Wizard of Oz* that the whole company was laying over on a Sunday for a day of rest. The thing for all visitors to do on Sunday was to go to Juarez, across the Rio Grande in Mexico, and watch the bullfights.

Just before the Saturday night performance, about ten of the girls cornered me and pleaded that I take them to see a bullfight. Wouldn't I please be their guide and show them around? The next day I took them over by streetcar and showed them the town, then on to the bullring.

We arrived a bit early and got very good seats. Everybody was in a gay mood; and I was happy, too, to see the girls having such a good time. That is, until the first bull, on entering the ring, got stuck with two banderillas. All the gaiety suddenly ceased. When the picador entered on his mangy horse, the antics of the bull charging the horse and the picador stabbing at the bull with his long lance made the girls look pale around the gills. But the last straw was when the matador dispatched the bull with the unkindest cut of all—thrusting his sword right to the hilt between the shoulder blades. That did it. Four of my girls keeled over in a dead faint, and most of the rest looked white as corpses. Fortunately, one of them had a bottle of smelling salts in her bag. When all were revived, it was generally agreed that one bull was quite enough. We returned to El Paso in a very somber mood, but they all seemed glad that they had had the experience.

Since it was only about four o'clock, I suggested we all go to a small Mexican restaurant where they served the best tamales and beer in town. This seemed to perk up spirits all around. We sat eating and drinking beer till 5:30, when I had to bid them good-bye in order to be at my job at the Elks Club by 6:00.

This, then, was the pattern of my life from October to June, when schools and theaters closed and a goodly portion of the population left for cooler climes.

6

BACK TO CLEVELAND

In spite of the fact that I kept lending my pianist money, with never a repayment, I still was able to save around three hundred dollars by June. Never before had I possessed more than fifty dollars; so I felt rich. With several months of free time on my hands and the realization that my sojourn in Texas was now of more than two years' duration (add a touch of homesickness), I made the decision to go home for the summer.

"Why not make it as pleasant as possible?" said a little gremlin at my ear. Taking the train to New Orleans, I boarded the S.S. *Comus* there for what was advertised as "100 golden hours at sea" to New York. In those days there was still some truth in advertising; so what with a first sea voyage, good weather, flying fish, porpoises, and congenial passengers, along with good food and accommodations, I thoroughly enjoyed the trip. (Except, that is, for one episode when I was enticed into a friendly poker game and lost twenty dollars before I wised up to the fact that the friendly game was crooked.)

In New York I visited some cousins who took me sightseeing for a few days. The hustle and bustle of the big city, the tall buildings and the steamer trip up the Hudson to West Point were most exciting.

Then, too, the titles such as "Forty-five Minutes from Broadway," which had been referred to in the traveling shows I had been playing, made it all the more interesting.

After the train trip to Cleveland, the long-lost son was welcomed with open arms by father, mother, and sister. It was quite a contrast with the past to be treated by my father like a grown-up son and with much kindness. Here I spent the summer, mostly loafing, catching up on my sleep, and visiting with relatives and friends. Two and a half months passed quickly. And so back to El Paso.

The rail journey took two and a half days, the latter part so hot that we had to keep the coach windows closed because the breeze coming in off the desert was hotter than the air inside. For a whole day and night, just before reaching El Paso, it was insufferably hot.

In El Paso, my room had been kept for me. So, with the return of the summer population, my pattern of life returned to what it had been.

Pupils kept drifting back, new ones came, and soon there were more than I had time for. But I had come to the conclusion that the hour from 9:00 to 10:00 in the morning would be more beneficial to my health in sleep than in teaching; so I accepted few new ones.

By October first the Elks Club was in full swing. That meant playing for dinner from 6:00 to 8:00. The theater opened at about that time also, but we received the sad news that Fatty Arbuckle wasn't coming back. He was operating in Hollywood and just becoming famous in the silent movies. Instead, there would be a succession of stock companies, which would put on plays, with a change of program twice a week. Few of these were musical comedies; so our work became very easy. We played only during intermissions, with incidental music to heighten suspense during climactic moments. How sick we got of playing "Hearts and Flowers" during the sob scenes!

The dances also began about this time. The road shows didn't begin coming until about November first. I couldn't wait till the next one came—it was so exciting meeting all those fascinating people. (I can still hear the voice of the immortal Sarah Bernhardt.)

The action in the theater when the companies moved in or out was like a beehive, and it always got under my skin.

* * *

Such was my life during the next four years. Through the summers I played along with a pianist from 2:00 to 5:00 p.m.

and 7:30 to 10:00 p.m. at the theater where silent movies were shown.

I was so busy and liked the work so much, since I was in close contact with many stimulating people all the time, that for the first time in my life I was really happy.

By this time the scrip we had been using was being cashed in for real money at the banks. Dollars were all in silver. Anything above that was in greenbacks with an occasional five-, ten-, or twenty-dollar gold piece.

During this time Halley's comet, with its very long tail, made one of its rare appearances; and, of course, the whole town got up in the middle of the night to observe it.

Then President Taft and former President Teddy Roosevelt came to town to commemorate some historic events and shake hands with President Diaz in the middle of the bridge crossing the Rio Grande into Mexico. This warranted a parade and big celebration, at which I played the bass drum in the El Paso band as we paraded by the reviewing stand. Teddy was a great favorite of mine (and still is): so I made sure that he noticed me.

Then there was the Mexican Revolution in 1911. Madero's troops had the town of Juarez surrounded on all sides except the north, which, of course, was the Rio Grande. It was several weeks before they attacked the city. During this interval people from the American side were fording the river, which was very low, carrying supplies of all kinds to the revolutionaries. And, of course, I had to be one of them.

The insurgents were scattered all over the hillsides, drying fresh beef in the sun, and greeting us visitors like long-lost friends. I happened to fall in with a group of about fifty mercenaries, of whom one was the son of Garibaldi, the famous Italian patriot.

The atmosphere was that of a big picnic. The revolutionaries were lounging around, relaxed, and joking with an almost equal number of visitors from across the border.

I spent a most exciting afternoon roaming about talking to the men, and left reluctantly when it came time to report for work at the Elks Club.

In El Paso all activity had been disrupted. Under the cover of darkness the traffic fording the river became enormous. There were war supplies of every description. Even the Civil War

43

cannons which had been scattered in parks around the town disappeared one night. It was easy to guess who got them, because the whole population, both Mexican and American, was strongly in favor of the revolutionaries. Later, when we heard the first shots being fired across the river, all normal work ceased and everybody ran to the river's edge to watch the bombardment.

I was fortunate that my room was on the second floor of a two-story house on a bluff about a hundred feet from the river bank. A door from my room opened onto an upstairs porch which faced the river. From here we could see a panorama of the city of Juarez and the surrounding hills.

In two days I had more friends (about twenty) visit me than in all my stay in El Paso. We could see the flashes of cannon fire from the surrounding hills and the shells exploding in the city. We had a perfect vantage point from which to watch the spectacle— everybody stayed throughout the first day, and most of them came back on the second—until suddenly, about noon, a bullet crashed into the roof of the porch about a foot above my head. For a moment we stood there looking at each other, pale as ghosts, and then, just like runners at the starting line in a track meet, we made one concerted jump through the door of the house. There we congratulated ourselves that no one was hurt and agreed that if Madero were going to take Juarez, he would have to do it without our help. Madero did take the city in a few days of fighting, but it took El Paso over a month to get back to normal again.

7

ADIOS, EL PASO—HELLO, WORLD

Up to this point I had been an immature and thoughtless kid. I had learned everything the hard way, through experience. My parents, living in a neighborhood of foreigners, didn't understand the ways of life in this country beyond their own district. They couldn't give me any advice on matters of education, customs, manners, or future outlook. And I, pigheaded as I was, wouldn't have paid much attention to their advice anyway. Every move I made was dictated by my own instinct and judgment.

As I look back, it seems to me that this stubbornness was a blessing, because it concealed a dogged determination to excel at everything I attempted, along with a never-say-die spirit.

Shortly after I returned from my visit to Cleveland, I perceived that in El Paso I was considered the best violinist in town. I had more work than I could handle, no competition, and no challenge. Yet my knowledge of the violin was actually most elementary.

The more I thought about it, the more I was convinced that there was no future for me and my violin in El Paso. Since the career of a violinist was the only life I cared to pursue, it meant leaving town and taking up the study of the violin in earnest.

At this time Kubelik was considered the greatest violinist in the world. Therefore I set my sights on studying with his teacher, the famous Otakar Sevcik. Once I had made that decision, nothing could swerve me from it.

From this point on I became miserly in my expenditures. I saved up every penny possible until, at the end of three years, I had saved almost three thousand dollars, a sum I thought would be sufficient to pay all my expenses abroad for some years.

Once I had outlined a new future, my mind kept returning to it, concentrating on it, more and more. More and more my work bored me; so my departure from El Paso, when it came, was joyous instead of sad. There was a double reason for this. Even though I had enjoyed my work and my life there, the fact that I was masquerading under the name of Henry Miller had always been a subconscious irritant. The minute I left town I resumed my own name and felt much relieved. This was an easy matter, since I had never had it changed legally. Actually, the chief reason for changing it was that I had always felt embarrassed that people, except Slavs, of course, found it difficult to spell and pronounce. Now, having spent over four happy and instructive years in the Southwest as Henry Miller, I was escorted to the train early in June 1911 by a group of well-wishing friends, and departed from El Paso, never to return.

I, as Jaroslav Siskovsky, again spent the summer at home with my parents, who received me with great joy. The news of my intention to perfect my violin playing studying abroad with the great Otakar Sevcik, plus the fact that I was resuming my own name, made them very happy indeed.

They were enthusiastically in favor of my project and offered to help me in any way they could. Fortunately, I didn't need any help at that time, a fact that gave me great satisfaction. With a full realization that my playing was not nearly advanced enough to be accepted by Professor Otakar Sevcik, I laid plans to study with one of his best pupils, named Suchy, who taught at the Prague Conservatory.

The summer soon passed as I practiced diligently three to four hours daily and otherwise enjoyed myself among relatives and friends. With a brand new life and the whole world to look forward to, I departed from New York on the S.S. *Vaderland* of the Red Star Line on October 28, 1911. I landed in Antwerp about nine days later.

8

EUROPE

On the pier in Belgium the small size of the railroad cars immediately caught my eye; and, in my ignorance, I stood there laughing and ridiculing them with the stupid remark that in America children played with toy cars that size. Fortunately, this derision was addressed to other Americans just as green as I. Some years later it dawned on me that this size was much more practical in the small countries of Europe than our large cars, built for long hauls, would be.

Soon the laugh was on me. Walking along the streets of Antwerp, I noticed people staring and children laughing at me. It took me some time to discover what was so funny about my appearance. It was that pair of peg pants I was wearing, the latest style in the United States, which I thought would be just the most fashionable thing for the trip.

Realizing that Europeans considered them ludicrous instead of stylish, I soon discarded them. For the benefit of those who do not know what peg pants looked like, let me explain that they were baggy at the top and tight around the ankles, something like riding breeches.

It was a revelation to see how clean and free of litter the streets were kept and how clean and sparkling the windows of the houses, with freshly laundered lace curtains. Even the street and railroad cars had clean windows. Everything and everybody looked well-groomed and orderly—especially in Germany. I have never seen anything like it before or since. Remember, this was only three years before World War I, when Kaiser Wilhelm II ruled the land.

Siskovsky (*left*) and Gilfillan (*right*) on an outing with two Czech girls one Sunday in 1912 in the environs of Prague.

Arriving in Prague by train, without a change, from Antwerp, I stopped at a hotel for a few days while I searched for a room via want ads in the newspaper. I found one that suited me on one of the heights called Vinohrady.

Prague, like Rome, is a city built on hills, and universally acknowledged to be one of the most beautiful. It is also one of the most ancient in central Europe. Some of the buildings date back to the year 1000.

I called on Professor Suchy and made arrangements to take one lesson a week from him. Now I settled down to the serious business of practicing six to seven hours daily. On days when it was going very well, I would do even more, sometimes up to fourteen hours.

A continental breakfast would be brought in by my landlady at about eight, after which I would practice about three and a half hours, then go to a restaurant for lunch, then practice another three and a half hours, then go to a restaurant for dinner and next to a coffeehouse for coffee and reading the London *Times*.

On days when my interest was at a really high pitch, I would practice straight through from 2:00 to 10:00 or 11:00 at night without going out for the evening meal. At such times I would climb into bed dead-tired but with nerves so taut that sleep was difficult; next morning I would arise completely exhausted.

The first few months, before I had made some friends, I spent Sundays reading up on and roaming about the streets of the oldest parts of the city. After all, my father and mother were unadulterated Czechs; the surroundings and their history were close to my heart.

Just before Christmas, Professor Suchy had a recital at his house at which I and six other pupils played. This gave me an opportunity to compare my proficiency with others', and it awakened me to the fact that the violin was a very difficult instrument. Although most of the other participants were younger than I, my playing was the least advanced of all.

No wonder. This was the first time in my life that I had had competent instruction. Since my lessons had been started only two months before, this evaluation did not discourage me. Quite the opposite—it made me more determined, especially because I sensed the fact that even though the other pupils were more advanced in technique, I seemed to feel the music more deeply than they.

The recital gave me the opportunity to meet these other pupils of Professor Suchy. To my surprise, among a majority of Czechs, there were five Americans and a Britisher. After the recital, I had a conversation with one of the Americans and the Britisher. The three of us planned a walking trip of about ten miles along the banks of the Moldau for the following Sunday. This was a happy development, for up to this time I hadn't had a chance to make any friends and my life was a lonely one.

The country around Prague is beautiful in all directions, much like our Berkshires. The rapport among the three of us was such that when we arrived back in Prague in the evening, happy and tired, we resolved to make the event a regular one every Sunday, weather permitting. Since all three of us enjoyed hiking so much, we were disappointed when the weather spoiled our Sunday excursions.

Soon a very solid friendship developed between the American and myself. Frederick J. Gilfillan was about ten years older than I. His father had been a banker in St. Paul, Minnesota, and with Mr. Weyerhauser he founded the Weyerhauser Timber Company. Let's call my new friend Gil from now on, since that's what I always called him. Gil's father had died and left him a fortune. Gil immediately left the employ of the Weyerhauser Company and settled down in Prague in a modest four-room apartment, with maid in attendance, and devoted his energies to the study of the violin, which he loved, and swearing at business, which he hated. He practiced faithfully and became quite a good player. He was college-bred, well traveled, and I thought very shrewd and logical in his conclusions. For some reason he seemed to take a fatherly interest in me.

I, on the other hand, valued his opinions because for the first time in my life I had someone with whom I could discuss my problems, someone who understood what I was talking about. I mention this because his judgments were always sound and of great help to me.

It was a great comfort to have someone with his knowledge and worldly experience agree almost 100 percent with the plans I had made for my future. We saw each other on an average of twice a week, when he would invite me to dinner. After dinner a violist and cellist came, and we would play quartets till a very late hour. We always attended concerts together. And we practiced diligently.

Thus the winter passed pleasantly and quickly. In June we had another recital. In comparison with the others, I was agreeably surprised to see what progress I had made. This, plus Gil's encouragement, gave me the heart to hazard a trip to Písek, a town about seventy miles from Prague, to see if the famous Otakar Sevcik would accept me as a pupil.

Arriving at Písek, I had to wait several days before Sevcik could find time for the audition. This was very short, because it didn't take him long to assess my capabilities. I recognized him as a simple, kind, and sincere person. So when he said, "You may come and be my pupil," I felt like throwing my arms around his neck and hugging him.

Returning to Prague at once, I stayed just long enough to pick up my baggage, say good-bye to my few friends, and eat a last supper with Gil, at which I drank too much port wine and felt very sick.

I caught the early morning train for Písek with that hangover feeling everywhere but in my thoughts, which were buoyed up. Here is what I had been shooting for. Let's hope it turns out well! I thought.

In Písek, with the assistance of a city official, I found a room in a house with a couple. The husband was some kind of government official. They turned out to be very good to me and we became friends.

I had my first lesson as soon as the professor could find the time. It was supposed to be an hour, but it turned out to be closer to two. I had never been more inspired by anyone.

My instructions were to practice not less than four hours daily and not to come back for another lesson until this one was well in hand. I practiced anywhere from six to twelve hours daily, depending on my assignment. Everyone experiences days when no matter how hard one tries nothing goes well. On such days I would limit practice to six hours.

Breakfast—a bun and coffee—would be brought to my room at eight. For lunch, groups of us would gather at different restaurants for a light meal and much discussion, principally about music and politics. By two o'clock we would be back at our practicing until 6:00 to reassemble around 7:00 at the same restaurant for a heavier meal and a stein or two of that delicious Pilsener beer. There we stayed on, just talking till 10:00 or 11:00, then going home to bed. While there was always a lot of jesting going on, we learned almost as much from one another as we did from our teacher. The close contact with people from so many different countries was a priceless education in itself. It made us humble and gave us broader vision. The list of pupils studying there at the time of my arrival reads like a list of the delegates to the United Nations: two from Africa; thirty from the United States; five from Russia; one from Argentina; four from Australia; six from Austria; eight from Britain; one from Czechoslovakia; two from Bulgaria; two from Canada; one from Yugoslavia; one from France; four from Germany; one from Greece; two each from Holland and Hungary; two from Italy; one from Malta; one from Mexico; two from Poland; one from Scandinavia. We all got along like a happy family. Of course, when we Americans conversed with Britishers, Canadians, or Australians, we spoke English. But, interestingly enough, mix us all together and the language would be German. A person was judged by his or her behavior and intelligence, not by nationality, race, creed, or color.

An example of just the opposite was Hitler's convincing the German people that they and their country were superior to all others. Look at the atrocities they committed in the name of patriotism! Yet there is hardly a chamber of commerce or Rotary Club in the United States which doesn't try to brainwash its people with the same brand of hogwash. "My town is the best town in America; our country is the best in the world; and, of course, we are the finest people." The Hitler spectacle doesn't seem to have taught them anything. We should have learned long ago that a braggart is a pest and therefore to be shunned by others. Your opinion of yourself doesn't count nearly as much as what others think of you.

After much travel all over the world, my experience has been that no matter what country you're in, if you're nice to people, they will be nice to you; look for trouble, and you'll find it posthaste no matter where you are.

By September our big colony began to decrease in number. Many were teachers who came just for the summer for a refresher course or for the honor and prestige of being able to say when they got home that they had been pupils of the great Otakar Sevcik.

Then, too, there were those who preferred to study with Sevcik in Vienna, either at the Master School (a postgraduate course of two years after graduation from the Royal Conservatory of Music) or privately, because of the added advantage of being able to participate in the musical life of the most musical city in the world.

In the wintertime Sevcik commuted between the two cities weekly, leaving Písek by sleeper on Sunday night and returning by sleeper early Friday morning. It was about an eight-hour journey. Thus he spent three days in Písek and four in Vienna.

By October first only ten of us chose to remain in Pisek for the winter. This situation, of course, united the survivors; we met daily for our noon and evening meals and held nightly bull sessions in the same restaurant. In time we really felt like a group of brothers and sisters.

About this time the professor received a request from the magazine *The Strad* asking for an article describing the life in Písek the previous summer. This was a London magazine devoted to news of the violin world. For reasons of his own, Sevcik asked me to write it. I had never written anything for publication, let alone for a magazine published in so famous a center as London; so I demurred. Finally I gave in to coaxing and after much effort through sleepless nights, I wrote an article which appeared in the October 1913 issue of *The Strad*. The following is a condensed version.

The Summer Colony in Písek

A great lover of nature, Professor Sevcik spends part of every day, rain or shine, tramping in the almost endless chain of forests surrounding the town. His favorite walk is along the banks of the Otava River, where one often meets him in shirtsleeves, walking along at a brisk gait.

He leaves home some time before daybreak, returning in time to have breakfast and start teaching at 6:00 a.m., continuing till 10:00 p.m. He never sleeps more than four hours. During the daytime very few of the students are to be seen anywhere; but take a walk down almost any street and you will hear some very fine violin playing pouring from a great many windows. On Saturday nights, there is a general get-together with Professor Sevcik at the Hotel Dvoracek, very like a tea party, only here we had mostly beer or coffee.

Since there were almost a hundred of us present in the summer-time, including parents or other relatives, the object of these parties was to get better acquainted. Concerts are held at the hotel every fortnight to which the general public is invited. The students participate in many of the local benefit concerts, especially one in the neighboring town of Prachatitz, where Sevcik was born. This is an annual event for the benefit of needy schoolchildren.

As for recreation, walking in the woods seems to be most popular with the students, though some find pleasure in boating, swimming, bicycling, and tennis. Very often trips to the various castles in the vicinity are arranged, and it has to be something very important to keep the professor from coming along on every one of these trips.

Every summer a banquet and dance is held to which many of the local inhabitants are invited. On the whole, our life here is most enjoyable, for which we owe many thanks to the citizens of Písek, who do all in their power to make it just so.

I chose not to go to Vienna that winter because I became aware that I was making tremendous progress under my new teacher. This inspired me to try even harder. And the place to accomplish my purpose was right in Písek, where there weren't the distractions of a big city and where the professor would not have to keep an eye on his watch.

As it turned out, it was the most fruitful period of my life. It seems that with a lot of hard work and with the guidance of a super-teacher, the progress I was making was astonishing even to me. A talent that had been lying dormant needed a man like Sevcik to bring it out.

Much as I hated speaking Czech as a child, I realized now what a blessing it was to be able to mingle with the citizens of the town. By this time I was speaking it fluently. Professor Sevcik taught me in Czech, though he spoke English well.

I played tennis and billiards with a number of college professors, and I was concertmaster of the local orchestra of about sixty pieces. Thus I became integrated with the life of the town without deserting my colleagues.

I had a head of bushy hair, and one day the idea struck me, "Why wear a hat?" I tried it in all kinds of weather and liked it, and since then I have never worn a hat. With this departure, I unwittingly started a lot of talk about town. First they were concerned about my health. Teachers were warning their classes that it was a dangerous experiment and that there was danger of pneumonia or what not from this practice.

What started out innocently on my part now became a dare and I had to prove they were wrong. None of their predictions came true. I remained hatless and healthy throughout the winter, through the most inclement weather. Thirty years later I returned to the town and couldn't find a single man wearing a hat.

The winter passed and June came, with the same influx of students from all over the world. Life was a repeat of the past summer, with one exception. That was a big Fourth of July party that we Americans organized. All the foreigners came, and we invited the important citizens of the town.

At the dinner I was chosen to make two speeches—one in English, the other in Czech—welcoming our guests and explaining what we were celebrating. The whole town was out to watch the display of fireworks. They hadn't seen anything like this for years, and it created great excitement.

It had long been my intention to spend the next winter in Vienna. At the end of September in 1913, I joined a group of my colleagues to make the trip there.

9

VIENNA

Vienna was such a beautiful city that I immediately fell in love with it. After a one-night stay in a hotel, I found a room in a six-story building which suited both my taste and my pocketbook. It was owned by an elderly widow with two teen-age children, a boy and a girl.

The first night I couldn't sleep a wink because of itching all over my body. The next night the same thing happened. Suspecting bedbugs, I quickly got up, turned on the light, and there they were—five or six of them in plain sight against the white sheets and running in all directions.

I murdered all I could catch and then sat up the rest of the night pondering what to do. I liked the room, and the landlady seemed pleasant enough. Also, from the looks of the modest furnishings, it was apparent that the room rent was important to her. I had been warned by colleagues that bedbugs were common in Vienna because of the very old buildings.

Moving meant perusing the want ads, tramping the streets again, and who knows how many times I might have to move before finding a room without bedbugs? So I decided to stay until I had tried out a certain plan of attack on the pests.

This decided, and knowing full well that I wasn't going to fall asleep sitting up, I wrote to Gil in Berlin, letting him know that I was in Vienna.

The next morning I told my landlady about the bedbugs. She was most chagrined, of course, and couldn't understand how it was possible. Then I asked permission to try out my plan of attack. She beamed all over and replied, "Oh, bless you, do anything you like that won't ruin my furniture."

56

I went out and bought half a kilo of putty, a pint of kerosene, and a small brush. I hauled the bed into the center of the room and tore it completely apart. Then I filled every hole and crack in the wood with putty, and painted all inside corners with kerosene. I did the same with all the furniture. Then I stacked everything in the center of the room in order to get at the moldings. There were so many interstices between floor and wall and molding, I felt sure that there was where most of the culprits found refuge. All these I carefully puttied up. Finally, after replacing the furniture, I took a sheet from the bed and spread it on the middle of the floor. Standing in the center, I took my clothes off and examined every seam carefully, along with the few other clothes I had.

The operation took all day. So I went out to supper, then straight home and to bed, and slept like a log till late the next morning.

I was getting nicely settled and well started on practicing when along came a letter from Gil saying he had just bought his first auto, a Benz. He was contemplating a trip to Italy to visit a young lady whom he was courting and would I care to keep him company. He asked me to wire an immediate reply. This was an opportunity I couldn't afford to miss! The answer was a strong affirmative.

In two days a letter arrived with a railroad ticket to Berlin enclosed, along with a request to come at my earliest convenience. Professor Sevcik would not start teaching for several weeks, and I was free to catch the first train.

We stayed in Berlin for a few days while Gil learned to drive. The roads outside the city were unpaved. Ninety-five percent of the traffic was horse-drawn, with very few autos in sight. We started out doing about fifteen miles an hour in the city, but on the country roads we had to slow down almost to a walk because the horses were auto-shy and would start to panic when they saw us coming.

Some drivers had great difficulty controlling their animals, and we got plenty of cursing as they passed us. In some places where no traffic was visible, Gil would open up the Benz to thirty miles an hour, and we thought we were speeding.

Stopping along the way for sight-seeing, we proceeded without incident till we got to Czechoslovakia. One afternoon as we tried to pass a balky team drawing a farm wagon, the horses panicked, ran off the road out of control, and slammed into a tree. Of course we stopped and started to walk back to see if we could be of any help. A small group of peasants were stacking hay in a field next to the roadside. When they saw what had happened, they came at us like hornets, waving their pitchforks and cursing. Fortunately, we had not gotten far; so we dashed for the car and were off.

Gil would have liked to go through Switzerland, but it was against the law to drive autos in that country. Instead, we went through Bavaria. In negotiating the passes over the Alps, we had to make two changes of cartridges, stuck into the carburetor, to adjust the mixture of gas to the density of air we encountered. Thus we reached Lenno on Lake Como and put up at a hotel near the villa on the shore of the lake where Gil's sweetheart was living.

What a beautiful spot it was! He spent the days at the villa while I practiced the violin and rambled around the quaint villages and countryside. One moonless night Gil got an idea. "Suppose we get a rowboat? You take your violin, and I'll row you over under Hilda's window and you serenade her."

Knowing that her father was the most famous cellist in the world, I wasn't enthusiastic; but since Gil was so excited about it, I consented. The lake was quiet as a mill pond. Gil rowed to a spot in front of Hilda's balcony, I took the violin out of its case and started to play romantic music.

I had played for about five minutes when suddenly a powerful search light was turned on us from far up the lake. Gil said, "Keep on playing. It's the Italian customs searching for smugglers from Switzerland." They kept the light on us for what seemed a long time, switched in another direction and back to us several times, while I, like Nero, kept on fiddling. When they gave up, we rowed back to our hotel.

There had been no sign of life at her window, except a light, while all this went on. But next morning Gil learned that the whole family had come to her room in much amusement.

We stayed at Lake Como three days, then started a round-about journey back to Berlin, with stops at Florence and Venice and other cities along the way. Munich had about ten famous breweries. We decided to celebrate and go to all of them, having just one stein at each. I barely made it to the fifth. After that, bed looked better than all the famous beer in the world.

We got back to Berlin without incident after a three-week trip. It was my first sight-seeing tour and my first auto ride, as well as the first time I had lived in quasi splendor. It was also my introduction to the masterpieces of Italian art and to the grandeur of Alpine scenery.

But I was anxious to get back to work in Vienna. There I settled down to regular morning and afternoon practice; and through my colleagues from Písek, I joined a group of students of both violin and piano whom we met in one of the coffeehouses at 6:00 every evening, where we had coffee and discussed problems musical and political.

Here, English newspapers kept us up-to-date on happenings elsewhere. On Sundays we would ride to the ends of the various streetcar lines and hike in the beautiful Vienna woods to some country inn, where we would rest a while and have a lunch of cheese and bologna on large slices of rye bread with a stein of Pilsener. It was a meal fit for a king. These outings became regular Sunday events, rain or shine. In good weather we would walk about ten miles; in rainy weather, only a few miles to some inn, where we would sit and discuss things. I can't remember a time when someone didn't have something of interest to talk about.

These outings were lifesavers for us who spent all week indoors practicing. Then there was the abundance of operas and concerts for which we students were often able to secure free tickets. There were some ten concerts by first-rate artists taking place every night; it was sometimes difficult to make a choice. The opera was sold out every evening; but by standing in line for a few hours, we were able to buy standing-room tickets up in the third balcony for about thirty cents.

*   *   *

Someone convinced me that a vegetarian diet was best for keeping strong and healthy; so for about six months I had all my meals in a vegetarian restaurant. Then Gil arrived for a one-day visit. Looking at me, he said, "What's the matter, aren't you well? You look pale; you've lost weight." When I told him that it might possibly be due to the diet I was on, he said, "Some people thrive on it, but it doesn't seem to be your dish. Try going back to meat and see if you don't look better and feel better." This I did, with immediate beneficial results, and the vegetarian restaurant lost one customer.

It can be seen that my time was fully occupied with a weekly lesson added to some unusual tasks. For instance, my landlady saw how well I rid my room of bedbugs and begged me to help her fix other things around the house. She seemed forever to have something that needed repair. Still, it was an opportunity for me to show her I appreciated the extracurricular things she did, such as asking me to dinner on special holidays.

The heating stove in my room was of the tall ceramic type common all over eastern Europe, which stands in a corner and reaches from floor to ceiling. I would estimate the climate to be on a par with Richmond, Virginia. On cold days the landlady would put a couple of handfuls of kindling wood into the grate at the bottom and light it. From then on I would watch it and, when the wood turned to red hot embers, I would screw the door tight shut. That would hermetically seal it and preserve the heat for quite a long time. If the door was a tight fit, the stove would still be warm the next morning.

The damp night air was considered injurious to health. No one ever opened windows unless he wanted to commit suicide. To be sure, the room never got very warm—not over fifty degrees. But that's the way Europeans like it. At first I felt cold, but gradually got used to it. When I got back to the United States I also thought we kept our houses overheated. My greatest difficulty, at first, was to get my fingers warm enough for practicing, until one of my British friends told me to soak them in a basin of hot water. Why couldn't I have thought of that?

This, then, is a slight idea of what my life was like in Vienna that winter. Now to the Easter holidays—the most important days of the year in Europe, more important, even, than Christmas. Anyone who can will go off on a spree. Thus one evening when our coffeehouse group was discussing what each of us was going to do over the holidays, one of the girls announced that she was going home to Budapest; if there were any two in the crowd who had nothing better to do, she would like to extend an invitation to visit her and her parents for a few days.

Of course there were a lot of takers; so we had to pull straws. A pianist pupil of Godowsky and I won the draw. His name was Schluer. In discussing our plans, we decided that since we were invited for only two days and we had a week to spare, we would make it a walking trip.

By going a bit north we would be in mountainous country, more beautiful than the more direct route along the Danube. It would be a walk of about 200 miles. Since we were both good hikers, all went well till the end of the second day, when, after a long hike of some 35 miles, and dead-tired, we registered at a country inn and had just entered our room, thinking how nice it was going to be to get washed up, have a good country dinner, and get to bed early, when two gendarmes entered our room and asked to see our passports. Schluer and I had been in Austria about two years. Never once had either of us been asked to show his passport; so neither of us carried one. We tried to explain this, but the gendarmes said, "That's just too bad. You are under arrest on suspicion of being Russian spies. Come with us." So off to jail we went.

From here on let me copy the story as we told it, on our return to Vienna, to Vic Winton, a reporter for the *Musical Courier* and one of our coffeehouse gang. It was printed in the April 23, 1913, issue of that magazine.

Our American colony was not aware of the fact that it sheltered such dangerous elements as Russian spies, but it seems that such is the case. In our midst during the last couple of years, two young Americans have been pursuing their respective studies: The one, Carl Schluer, a pianist with Godowsky, and the other, Jaroslav Siskovsky, a violinist with Professor Sevcik. Now, we had looked upon these two boys as well-behaved and diligent students; so it was with the fondest of wishes that their many friends bade them good-bye and wished them a good time when they left Vienna armed with their knapsacks and cameras, headed for a tramping trip down through Hungary with Budapest as their final goal. Nothing very exciting happened to the pair during the first stages of the joureny, and it was not until the two footsore and weary adventures arrived at a little village called Rajec, near the Galician border, that their troubles (or fun) began.

It took the super-ingenuity of one of the Slavic gendarmes to discover and inform the boys of their calling, and he would have it that they were Russian spies sent in probably to get the lay of the land, for the boys had been seen about town busily taking snapshots.

Mr. Schluer and Mr. Siskovsky did not quite agree with this brave officer of the law, but as no satisfactory means of identification was at hand, there was nothing to do but go along and take a little sojourn in the village lockup.

Considering the dangerous makeup of their prisoners, it was thought necessary to strengthen the guard over them; so two special detectives were brought into service. It was not until the two boys could get word to our Vienna consul, Mr. Denby, that they were allowed to go free; and then, to top the bargain, they had to pay their friends, the detectives, for the kind service rendered in watching over them.

We sat there in jail three days and nights. We were pestered by a constant procession of interrogators and men with stacks of photographs comparing our faces with their photos. I had about five rolls of film, which they developed and printed. This work they charged me for, but returned only six pictures.

We had slept very little in all that time. When we were freed, we walked as far as a country inn in the next village and slept for a day and a half.

Continuing our walk to Budapest, we arrived at our friend's house four days late. They had been worrying about us, of course; but when they heard our story, everyone laughed heartily and we were forgiven. We spent two idyllic days there, being entertained and touring the beautiful city, which reminded me of Prague because of its similar layout. We returned to Vienna by train. It was months before the gang quit ribbing us about our misadventure.

Incidentally, I forgot to mention that these daily meetings of the gang would last only about an hour. By 7:30 p.m there wouldn't be a soul left. I wouldn't have missed a meeting of this discussion group for anything; we learned so much from each other, especially how dramatically manners and customs can vary around the world. What is polite in one country can be silly and even rude in another. As an example, all over Europe it is customary when meeting a lady to say, "Kuss die Hand, gnadige Frau" (Kiss the hand, gracious lady), and then proceed to do so. Altogether, I lived abroad eight years, and though my strict motto was "When in Rome, do as the Romans do," not once could I gather up enough courage to kiss the hand. Of course, all the foreigners thought I had no manners, which was true in that case.

Among Vienna concertgoers, Brahms fans were forever feuding with Wagner fans. They booed each other after certain of their favorite compositions were played, and sometimes ended up having fist fights. Only on one occasion did I see anyone get hurt. It happened when Schoenberg conducted one of his own latest works, precipitating a real brawl, in which several did get hurt. It was too modern for orthodox ears. About 75 percent booed it with great disdain, while the other 25 percent cheered and applauded so fervently that a lusty brawl erupted.

The one forever-ingrained lesson I learned from these dissensions was "Keep an open mind. It is a new concept and the chances are the reason you don't like it is that you don't understand it." I have always been amazed at the numbers of people who are allergic to change, especially as they grow older. To me, change has been rejuvenation, something exciting, even if it did not turn out well.

In the light of hindsight, take the case of Schoenberg just mentioned. He and his compositions are now accepted as among the greatest. It stands to reason that an outstanding person must have thoughts on a higher plane than the average. If he didn't, he wouldn't be outstanding. I am mentioning all this because at all the concerts there were generally a few from our gang present; and whenever any unusual composition was played, we would assemble afterwards and learnedly discuss the happenings of the evening.

About this time I received a postcard from Professor Sevcik to come to see him as soon as possible. We always arranged lessons via postcards because very few telephones were in use at that time. When I arrived, he informed me that he had just received a letter from one of his best friends, a lady, considered one of the best pianists in Prague, stating that she was planning on giving a joint concert with one of his better pupils about a month hence and would he please recommend one. He would be required to play a concerto of his own selection and a Schumann sonata with her. Sevcik then asked if I would care to do it, all expenses paid. I replied that my playing wasn't good enough as yet, to which he quickly replied, "Don't be silly. If I didn't think you could do it, I wouldn't be asking you." What else could I do but go?

After a whole month's hard work and extra coaching by the professor, I was prepared to the limit of my capability on the two big numbers as well as several encores to be played. Arriving in Prague two days earlier than the concert, I was met at the railroad station by Mme. Cermak, who was giving the concert, and we spent most of that time rehearsing. What free time was left we spent making personal calls on all the newspaper music critics imploring them to come to the concert. This I found a bit nauseating, but Mme. Cermak assured me it was a local custom and that if we didn't do it, hardly any of them would attend; so I tagged along, not too happy about the whole thing.

To make a long story short, the concert took place in a lovely hall seating about 2,000 people, with every seat taken by great admirers of Mme. Cermak. It was easy to sense that she was very popular locally. All the numbers were applauded enthusiastically, including my solo, to which I had to add an encore.

Criticisms in the papers the next day praised Mme. Cermak highly and in my opinion deservedly so, since she was a great artist. To me they were kind, saying that I played with much feeling from the heart and not feeling for the notes ending up with the standard old cliché, "This young man shows evidence of a promising future." Personally, I didn't feel completely satisfied and now in my old age, after some 4,000 to 5,000 concerts, I can't remember a single one after which I did feel entirely satisfied.

* * *

Back in Vienna, I soon returned to the routine of life. Kreisler was my favorite violinist at the time; I went to every one of his concerts. Although he played to sold-out houses all over the world, here in his home town he attracted only small audiences; so I had no difficulty getting tickets. At one concert, when he opened with the E-major Bach Praeludium, his memory failed him. Being unable to get beyond a certain point in three attempts, he apologized to the audience and substituted a number. I recalled this incident thirteen years later in New York City when a friend of mine, also a violinist, told me that he was living in an apartment in the Wellington Hotel directly under the one where Kreisler lived. He spoke of hearing Kreisler drop his shoes when retiring at night, of hearing him composing at the piano, but seldom practicing the violin. This could explain why Kreisler's left hand fingers were not as facile as those of many competitors. But his uniquely subtle interpretation, which many a violinist tried to imitate without success, more than made up for that deficiency.

Again, there was an unfortunate incident at a concert in Vienna which Professor Sevcik and I attended. Daisy Kennedy, a star pupil of his, had chosen a very taxing program of three concertos. Everything was going along famously when, in the middle of the Tchaikowsky concerto, she fell to the floor in a faint, holding her violin above her head. Of course, attendants rushed in to carry her off the stage and a doctor in the audience hurried up to lend a hand. Sevcik at my side was visibly shaken and went home, but the rest of the audience remained seated. In about five minutes it was announced that Daisy was recovering and hoped to continue with the program shortly. She reappeared amidst a thunderous ovation and finished the program creditably.

In El Paso I had learned to take pictures with a Kodak, but it wasn't until Prague that I became an avid photographer. The old cities are picturesque; one finds a beautiful composition around almost every corner. I became so enthusiastic about this hobby that I learned to do my own developing and printing.

After one of our regular Sunday outings, when I had taken an unusually large number of snapshots, one of my colleagues asked, "When are you going to develop these? I would like to come over and watch."

"Come ahead," I said. "I will do them after practice tomorrow, at four."

I had a wash basin in my room and around it I had improvised a dark room which could be dismantled. Working away at the job, we completely lost track of time. Suddenly he said, "How late is it?"

"Take a look at the clock out in the room," I replied.

I heard him shout, "My God, I am supposed to play at a concert at the conservatory at eight o'clock. It is now seven-fifteen." He lived at the opposite side of town. It would take him at least an hour and a half to make the round trip by either streetcar or horse-drawn taxi. (There were no auto taxis as yet.) As the conservatory was close to where I lived, this was a pretty how-do-you-do.

After some speculation, we decided that the only possible way he could make it was to outfit himself in my full-dress suit, ludicrous as it seemed, for he was a slim six-footer with narrow shoulders and long legs and I was a chunky, broad-shouldered five-foot-nine. He was a sight going out the door. It took a long time to stop laughing. The coat and vest hung on him like bags, and the trouser legs ended up six inches high off the ground. The only part of the whole outfit that fitted him was my violin case.

Returning after the concert, he told me that the suit was unnoticed, once he got into the mass of players and was sitting down. What had seemed like a serious predicament turned out well.

* * *

Shortly thereafter we returned to Písek, and old-timers like myself fell right back into the idyllic life of previous years. Soon the town filled up with the hundred or so pupils from foreign lands, and the sound of violin practicing was heard from windows in every direction.

I was particularly happy that summer, possibly because of my recent success in Prague; it felt like returning home to a place I loved dearly. This elation came to an abrupt end when news of Archduke Ferdinand's assassination—June 28, 1914—struck the town like a bombshell. Not that the Czechs had any great love for the archduke, but everyone knew it could have cataclysmic consequences.

There followed a whole month of apprehension, with endless rumors going around; then on July 28 the axe fell and Austria declared war on Serbia.

I was playing tennis at the club that afternoon when someone brought the news. We hurried over to the main hotel, where the foreign colony usually foregathered. There most of them were already milling around excitedly, discussing what to do. The result was that they departed on the first trains which could accommodate them.

Russia began mobilization July 30. Germany declared war on Russia August 1, on France August 3, and then invaded Belgium and Luxembourg. At that point England declared war.

In a few days our colony was decimated. About twenty diehards remained, of whom ten were Russian, French, or British, who simply couldn't leave town on the already overcrowded trains because of their instruments and baggage. They were soon rounded up by a gendarme and taken off to an internment camp.

There remained only about ten of us from countries not involved. I might have been one of those leaving at the first opportunity had it not been for the fact that I had my sights set on a try for the Master Class. This was a postgraduate course of two years at the Royal Conservatory of Music in Vienna. It consisted of a select group of twelve, six entering each year, from all over the world. A conservatory graduate could enter this class, but others were required to take an examination on a par with exams for the class graduating from the conservatory.

I had made my application about six months before and had just received notice to appear for exams on September 1. Naturally I wasn't leaving for home if I could help it. There didn't seem to be any danger of the United States' becoming involved in the foreseeable future. So back to Vienna I went toward the end of August.

This time I found a room in a more modern apartment, and—to my joy—it was free of bedbugs. Soldiers in uniform were everywhere and crack German troops were on the march on some main streets, evidently to stir up war fervor. Foreign name signs such as "London Restaurant" were being torn down and burned in the gutters. Otherwise, everything seemed to be operating as before.

The day of the examination came. When applying for entrance, we were given an instruction sheet which informed us that at the examination we would be required to play one Bach unaccompanied sonata, one Paganini caprice, and one concerto. All of these I had prepared well; yet I was so nervous that my memory failed in two places. My feeling was that I had done badly. As a nightcap, they gave me a difficult unknown piece to play at sight. Thanks to my theater experience in El Paso, I was a pretty good sight reader, and in this I gave a good account of myself.

Since there were some fifty applicants for the six places in that year's class, I was quite sure they wouldn't accept me. It was three long days before notice arrived by mail that I had been accepted. I can't describe what this meant to me and what a satisfaction it was.

Soon after, the professor informed me of a vacancy in the first violin section of the famous Tonkunstler Orchestra. Why didn't I go over and audition for it? He would give me an introduction to the conductor. I thanked him and went and got the job.

Now I was really busy. What with orchestra rehearsals and concerts, plus classes at the conservatory, there was very little time for recreation. There was no time on Sunday for the walks in the woods, only the hour from 6:00 to 7:00 when four survivors of the old gang still kept up the discussion group. Later on, this had to be stopped, because customers complained that we spoke English.

Then, too, the United States was more and more displaying its sympathies for the Allies, and the local newspapers were bitter about that. The men in the orchestra, knowing that I was American, wouldn't speak to me and kept showing their resentment. Even my landlady blamed me because my country was siding with Austria's enemies. By the end of November I became so disgusted with this treatment that I would have left, but my tuition was paid to January, the beautiful new music academy had just been finished, and the dedication was to take place on December 20.

I had been chosen to play first violin in a string quartet which would play Haydn's *Kaiser* Quartet at this dedication. Since we had been rehearsing for some time, and it was such an honor, I decided to stick it out till then.

Even though my sentiments were strongly pro-Allies, I made it a point never to express them to local people, realizing that it was only natural for them to be patriotic citizens. So, not blaming them at all, I departed for America the morning after the concert.

Wishing to say good-bye to my many friends in Písek because I might never see them again, I made a stopover there. The pace had always been slow, and now it was even slower. Písek had an unkempt appearance. People kept whispering in my ear, "Tell them in America that we hope the Germans get a good licking." No wonder; the Czechs had been under the German heel for centuries. There was a time in the nineteenth century when they were almost extinct.

One evening one of my friends broached the idea of my giving a concert for the benefit of the widows and children of the fallen heroes. It appealed to me very much. What a nice way to say good-bye, I thought. After sounding out various people and finding so many in favor of it, we quickly organized a committee. The concert took place ten days later! The papers were full of it during that time, and an enthusiastic audience filled every one of the 1,000 seats in the hall. Even Professor Sevcik came—as though he hadn't heard me play before!

A small delegation saw me off on the train for Berlin a few days afterward. I wanted to say good-bye to Gil, whom I hadn't heard from since the war started.

My, what a change in appearance! Remember my remarking on how orderly and well-kept the German cities were? Now everything looked neglected and dead. Traffic was negligible, and many businesses were closed for the duration.

I left my baggage at the railroad station and took a tram to Charlottenburg suburb, hoping to surprise Gil, only to be informed by the janitor of his apartment house that he had departed for parts unknown immediately after the war broke out. This was quite a blow. Neither of us had an address for the other except our latest European one; so it looked as though we might never see or hear from each other again.

Since nothing could be done about it, I hastened back to the railroad station and caught the first train for Rotterdam. The next day I was able to depart on the S.S. *Rotterdam* for New York. Because this was a Dutch ship from a neutral country, we were supposed to be relatively safe from German submarine attack. But since the English Channel was mined, we had to proceed up the North Sea around the northern tip of Britain, where we had to stop and pass inspection by the British navy. Traveling on a much more northerly course than the usual shipping lane, we arrived at Halifax without incident, though we did have one death with burial at sea and we did have daily lifeboat drill.

Proceeding down the coast on our way to New York, we almost ran over the small boat of a lone Portuguese fisherman on the banks of Newfoundland who had gotten separated from his mother ship. We picked him and his rowboat up and took him with us to the port.

I spent two days in New York visiting cousins and sight-seeing. Then I went on to Cleveland for a hearty welcome from family, relatives, and friends after an absence of over three years. Since favorable reports about me had been filtering into our Czech newspapers from the Písek papers, everybody was anxious to hear me play. This suited me to a T because I was dreaming of giving another concert for the benefit of the widows and orphans of the fallen heroes of Czechoslovakia. Hatred of the Germans was at high pitch, and most Czechs were looking for an opportunity to be of some assistance to their fatherland; so here was a chance to fulfill two purposes at one stroke.

One of the many clubs took hold of the project and tickets were being sold in no time. The concert was given in a large hall in downtown Cleveland to a packed and enthusiastic house. The event was a huge success, and it received laudatory comments from both the English language and Czech press. I was talked about all over the city and overnight had more friends than ever knew me before. Of course, all the excitement soon cooled down. The problem of what to do next became uppermost in my mind. Had the war not started, I should have remained two more years at the Master School in Vienna. I felt I needed that much study to reach the peak of my capabilities.

In Vienna I had heard the young Heifetz play and was tremendously impressed by his style and sense of nuance. His teacher, Leopold Auer, was as famous as Sevcik. I broached the subject of studying with him to my parents. They said, "If that is what you would like to do, go ahead; we will back you." (I forgot to mention that the funds I had saved up ran out and I had to fall back on their support during the last year.)

With this encouragement, I wrote to Professor Auer to ask if he would accept me as a pupil, to which he answered, "Yes, if your playing is advanced enough. I will be at the Voksenkollen Hotel in Christiania (Oslo), Norway, from June 15 until September."

So back to Europe I went, leaving Cleveland for New York in time to board the S.S. *Oscar II* of the Scandinavian-American Lines for Christiania on June 10. By this time the Germans were torpedoing ships in great numbers. There was always the chance that our ship, even though from a neutral country, might be mistaken for the enemy. Therefore, the trip might be classified as a hazardous one. Most of my friends in Cleveland thought I was a nut for attempting it. But then, most of my friends were not as ambitious as I was; so all that talk went into one ear and out the other. Again we took a very northerly course; and again there was daily lifeboat drill; and again we made it safely to the Orkney Islands, where we were stopped and boarded by a British patrol boat whose crew examined all the passengers and crew, as well as the cargo, for four days. The result of this inspection was that some ten persons were taken from the ship. We surmised that they were Germans. We were allowed to proceed the next day. That night the captain's dinner was combined with a concert for the benefit of the seamen's fund, at which I played.

After dark, as we were sailing north up the fjord toward Christiania harbor, we were privileged to witness a sight which has remained imprinted on my memory all these years.

It was June 22, a bright clear night, at about eleven o'clock. Remember that this was one of the longest days in the year and we were at a latitude so far north that the sun disappears below the horizon for at best an hour at that time of night. Looking north, we saw the sun, a great ball of orange fire about to set just above the horizon. Then, turning and looking directly south, we saw another great ball of orange fire in just the opposite location. It was a full moon seemingly about to rise.

We all stood watching, enthralled, until we docked in Christiania about midnight. Because of the late hour, we were given the choice of debarking or staying aboard until after breakfast the next morning. I chose to stay aboard.

10

NORWAY

I checked into a hotel the following morning and called Professor Auer. Mme. Auer answered, and we arranged for an audition at four that afternoon.

The professor had scheduled the audition between lessons. After listening to me play a few minutes, he said, "All right, when would you like to start?" I explained that I had just arrived from the United States and hadn't found a room yet. That started a long conversation, mostly about the dangerous trip across the Atlantic. A young man of about twenty, waiting for his lesson, soon joined in. He turned out to be a local boy, Christian Thaulow, son of a famous Norwegian painter.

During the conversation, Thaulow offered to help me find a room. I promised to call Professor Auer as soon as I was settled, and Thaulow promised to meet me at my hotel the next morning at 9:00.

We looked for two days, first visiting the places advertised in the papers. Then he called up several friends without success. Either the rooms were too expensive, or they wouldn't allow practicing. You see, the city was overcrowded with war refugees; rooms were scarce and inflation rampant. Finally, since Professor Auer and about twelve of his pupils were living at the Voksenkollen Hotel, and Thaulow knew the owner well, he said, "I'm going up there to explain your predicament and see if they can't arrange something at reduced rates."

The hotel was a large wooden structure set on a hilltop about ten miles from the city, to which it was connected by express trams. The view of the fjord and surrounding hills was magnificent. As a result of Thaulow's efforts, I got a simple room with meals, just like all the other guests, at half price. I shall never forget this kind deed done by a Norwegian for a complete stranger.

I moved to the Voksenkollen in a hurry and soon was part of the happy colony of Auer's pupils. Lunch and dinner we had at one long table with the Auers, who sat at the middle. Professor Auer was such a clever raconteur that he had the table in stitches most of the time. Not only could he tell a story well, but usually he acted it out. Those seated next to him had to be on the alert not to get a fork or a knife poked in their eyes. He had a never-ending string of tales about the famous musicians of his time; and, since he was court violinist to the czar, he told of many incidents occurring inside the palace—all of which was instructive as well as entertaining.

After dinner everybody retired to the big lounge, where we had coffee and discussed various topics of the day. Patrons of the hotel were mostly elderly people from Denmark, Sweden, Norway, or England who came for a respite from the humdrum life at home. The newspaper rack in the big hall displayed papers from Paris, London, Copenhagen, Berlin, Stockholm, and other cities. It was an education to compare reports from the battlefields in the papers of opposing countries. For instance, I got into the habit of reading an account in the Berlin paper and then comparing it with one in the London *Times.* You couldn't believe they were talking about the same war. Of course, the other side was committing all the atrocities. "They" were always wrong, while "we" were always right. Now compare the two accounts with what the local papers carried, and you would arrive at something approximating the truth.

One evening someone suggested we give an after-dinner concert for the guests. This proved such a success that we took turns giving concerts twice a week. Up to that time there had been some complaints made to the office about our practicing. The concerts stopped all that; in fact, we became the most popular guests. Everyone went out of his way to be nice to us. Since we never charged for our music-making, the management rewarded us in many other ways. As an example, I went back for two more summers at half rate.

For exercise, we played tennis and took walks in the forests. In the long bright evenings we often sat on a rock where we had a panoramic view of Christiania Fjord, and watched the sailboats flitting through the water.

There was only one handicap to this idyllic life. All summer I found it difficult to fall asleep in broad daylight even with the shades down. Nonetheless, my work on the violin was proceeding with zest and a resurgence of interest. Professor Auer's personality was so dynamic that each lesson was an inspiration.

Every so often Thaulow would invite me to his house for dinner to meet a few of his friends. In this way I came to meet Edvard Grieg's niece; she remains one of my closest friends to this day.

And so the summer passed. Among Norwegians the talk was all about the shipping business and people making money in it because of the war. Even so, life was so idyllic that, except for the newspapers, we would never have known what a brutal war was going on close at hand.

By the middle of September, the weather had become quite cold, especially the nights, which were now about twelve hours long. Professor and Mme. Auer departed for St. Petersburg, and most of us followed soon after.

Ordinarily, we would have traveled by train to Stockholm and then by ship to St. Petersburg. But, because of a stoppage of all shipping in the Gulf of Bothnia, we were obliged to go around it by rail. This necessitated going as far north as the arctic circle and then south through Finland, a journey of over two days. Thaulow and I had become such good friends that we decided to make the trip together and try to find rooms with one family in St. Petersburg where we would be near each other, but would not interfere with each other's practicing.

A Swedish girl from Stockholm, one of our group studying with Auer, invited us to stop over in her city to see how beautiful it was. This we did; and after an all-day sight-seeing tour, we wound up at her house, where her mother had prepared a most delicious meal.

This was my first experience with Swedish punch (a rather sweet liqueur), which tasted so good that I drank it like wine. About an hour later it hit me like a ton of bricks; and so, on wobbly legs with a wobbly stomach, I made a dash for the bathroom, and there went that delicious dinner along with the punch. Of course, the rest of the party knew what had happened; so I was very ashamed, but there was nothing much to do about it except apologize profusely. For many years after that, whenever mention was made of Swedish punch, my stomach would shudder, and just the thought of drinking it almost made me sick.

The next morning we left Stockholm and arrived at Happaranda, where we had to detrain and be ferried across the river to connect with another train in Finland which would take us to Petrograd.

This was Lapland, just five degrees south of the arctic circle; and we were fortunate enough to strike it at just the time when the Lapps, for some reason or other, were herding hundreds of their reindeer. Since it took several hours for about one hundred passengers to be ferried over and processed through two customs stations, we had plenty of time to observe a most exciting sight.

The rest of the journey into Petrograd was mostly through birch forests. Even though no snow had as yet fallen, the trees were barren and a bleak sight almost all the way. We found Petrograd crowded with refugees; so rooms in hotels were very scarce. After spending all morning looking, Thaulow again saved the day by appealing to the Norwegian ambassador, whom Thaulow knew very well. We were invited to have dinner that night with the ambassador, his wife, and his charming daughter, who was a schoolmate of Thaulow's in Norway. The next day the ambassador was able to locate two beautifully furnished rooms for us in an apartment house in the center of town just three doors away from the Nevsky Prospect, the main street of Petrograd. The apartment itself was on the fourth floor and was run by a German widow (with two young daughters).

That the family had once been affluent was evident. Rich Persian rugs were all over our two rooms, even on the walls. Neither of us could have afforded the rent she asked but for the fact that the ruble was so greatly devalued on the world's money markets. For example, normally the ruble sold two for a dollar. At this time, it was selling twenty for a dollar, and later on even more than that. As I remember it, the room cost twenty dollars a month. Thaulow's kronen, too, were as valuable as the dollar; so we were sitting on clouds.

With all the particulars settled, we moved in at once and started to lead a very cozy life. My big brass bed was comfortable and bug-free. The furniture looked as though it had come from a museum. The ceiling was at least fourteen feet high, and so was the handsome ceramic heating stove standing in the corner. To me this was the height of luxury which I had never dreamed of experiencing; so I settled down to enjoy it.

Both of us started practicing in earnest. Since we had adjoining rooms, we were able to hear each other which at first was annoying; but by keeping our fortissimi down to forte, we soon learned not to be distracted.

Going for weekly lessons was always a harrowing experience, because Professor Auer lived a good hour's street-car ride from us. You rarely saw one of these trams without people hanging all over it. Imagine trying to get on one with a violin case and music satchel in your hand. I did it every week (don't ask how), often arriving at Professor Auer's with torn clothes.

11

TWO WINTERS IN RUSSIA AND THREE SUMMERS IN NORWAY

By December the days were so short that there was only about one hour of daylight on a sunny day. The weather got bitter cold, most of the time ranging from zero to forty degrees below.

There were the Russians in felt boots, fur coats almost to their ankles, high collars covering mouths and noses, and fur hats on their heads. There was I without a hat, earmuffs on my ears, a light black overcoat down to my knees, cotton socks, and ordinary leather shoes. People used to stare at me, figuring that I was a loony foreigner who didn't know any better. It didn't bother me in the least. The overcoat was one I wore at home, and if I didn't have to stand outside for a long time I was never really cold. It was rare to have a thaw before April. One snowfall after another piled up; and all traffic, except for streetcars, changed to sleighs.

When an especially heavy snowfall blocked traffic, the Russians brought out big metal boxes on runners. Under these they built wood fires, which melted the snow; and the runoff was channeled down sewers. Because St. Petersburg was built on many low-lying islands, it was a very damp place. On the coldest days, it was a sight to see the people going about their business covered from head to foot with hoarfrost.

In the winter it was customary to putty up all the cracks around the windows. They were usually double French windows; the outer pair opened up into the street and the inner pair into the room. This left a space about a foot wide between the windows. At the bottom of the inner doors, a pane some ten inches square was made into a little door opening on a space which could be used as an icebox. That is where I always kept a one-pound can of that delicious caviar which I loved.

It was my habit to read until after midnight, since I slept till about nine. Then, first thing, I went to the landlady's kitchen for a couple of handfuls of kindling wood to get a fire going in my stove. It was really cold in my room at that time of the morning. Any water left standing overnight was iced over.

Breakfast consisted of two glass tumblers of hot tea (the most delicious I ever tasted) and a bun. This kept my body temperature up until the room warmed to its maximum, which was seldom above forty-five degrees because of the high ceiling. Of course, we all wore long underwear and heavy sweaters. By soaking my hands in hot water, I was able to start practicing. This in itself kept me comfortably warm for a long time. It was a Russian custom to keep a samovar with a teapot standing on it all day long. Everybody could help himself to hot tea, always drunk from a glass tumbler. This, of course, was stimulating, too. It was so delicious I had a glass about every two hours. Some people liked to hold a lump of sugar between their teeth and drink their tea through it.

The first week or so after our arrival, Thaulow and I went out together to places of entertainment in the evenings, but gradually we went our separate ways except for occasional visits to the Norwegian ambassador. His daughter enjoyed playing bridge. So by inviting me and a girl friend of hers, we had a foursome. I enjoyed these parties, for it meant a good dinner with Mr. and Mrs. Ambassador; and we heard the latest inside news of the war and the underhanded machinations of the various nations.

It developed that Thaulow was a gregarious playboy who loved nothing better than going out every night to nightclubs and cabarets and drinking a lot. As these didn't really get going until midnight, he seldom got home before five in the morning. This kind of living bored me; and, what's more, I couldn't afford it. Besides, it just isn't possible to do any decent practicing after nightly binges.

It so happened that one of Auer's pupils who had stayed with us at the hotel in Norway during the past summer was the daughter of the richest banker in St. Petersburg. The whole Berson family was artistic in one way or another, either as musicians, painters, or sculptors. They held monthly soirees to which top artists were invited. I frequently participated in chamber music groups. Often I was invited to dinner as a sole guest, especially on opera or ballet nights at the Marinsky Theatre when all of us would ride in their luxurious troika to be seated in the family loge. These people took their opera and ballet very seriously, much as Italians do. I listened without doing much talking on those subjects.

To get a little exercise, I joined the Y.M.C.A., which was called the lighthouse, where we did calisthenics and played basketball with Britons and Americans living in St. Petersburg. At that time there was a large British colony there.

At Christmas Thaulow surprised me with the news that his sister had invited the two of us to spend the holidays with her and her husband in Dubrovka, a town about eighty miles east of St. Petersburg, where her husband was manager of a paper mill. This was a chance to get out into the country, and I accepted gladly. It involved a train ride of some four hours on a rickety local, which stopped every ten minutes or so; then a troika would take us to the mill, a drive of two and a half hours. A few days later we got up early to catch the train, which was scheduled to leave at 7:00. Due to a heavy snowfall and a sharp drop in temperature to forty degrees below zero, it was difficult for wood-burning locomotives to build up steam; so we sat in the railroad station all day, wondering if the train would or wouldn't move. Inquiries to the stationmaster were met with, "It will go, but I don't know just when yet."

Finally at 4:00 p.m. the train was announced, and there was a rush to get aboard. Thaulow and I were the only passengers with suitcases; the rest were peasants carrying cages of pigeons, chickens, rabbits, and that sort of impedimenta. The coach we sat in was like a circus all the way. I hadn't laughed so hard for a long time.

Arriving at our station, we were greeted by the driver of the troika, who had been waiting for us all day. The horses were three beauties, with the traditional Russian yoke over their shoulders. The driver handed each of us a long bearskin coat and fur cap. "It's very cold tonight," he said. "You had better put these on. When you seat yourselves in the sleigh, I will bundle up your feet and knees in this bearskin lap robe."

It was a fabulously beautiful night. Not a cloud in the sky and a full moon shining, with stars so bright and close you felt like picking a few. When we arrived at our destination, I was sorry the ride was over. With every inch of our bodies, including our noses, packed inside those bearskin coats and fur hats, only our eyes were exposed, and we were comfortably warm all the way.

Arriving at 10:00 p.m. instead of at noon, we were warmly greeted by our host and hostess. In the process I noticed him looking at me with anxious eyes. I began thinking, "Now what have I done?" when suddenly he grabbed me by the arm and led me outside. He picked up a handful of snow, bade me close my eyes, and then rubbed the upper part of my nose with the snow. Feeling it numb, I realized it must have gotten frozen without my being aware of it. A few minutes of vigorous rubbing restored the flow of blood, and we joined the rest of the party for a hearty dinner. It being Christmas, we sat around the enormous fireplace drinking and telling stories until five in the morning.

All week we played games and much music. They treated me as one of the family and made it a memorable Christmas for me. We stayed until after New Year's Day, returning to St. Petersburg the same way we had come. This time the train was almost on time.

By now I was feeling perfectly at home in Russia. Oddly enough, the twenty-three hours of darkness out of every twenty-four didn't depress me at all.

Along with the frequent invitations from the Bersons to the ballet and opera, I attended many concerts. Getting home late involved a procedure that was peculiar to Russia. All over Europe, it was customary to lock the front door of apartment houses at nine o'clock. Anybody coming home after that would have to ring the doorbell, and the janitor or one of his family would come to unlock the door. Of course, a small tip was mandatory. Here in Russia, the door was closed at nine, but the janitor, instead of waiting inside, would sit on the doorstep in every kind of weather, cuddled up in a bearskin coat, fur hat, and felt boots. He would sleep there the whole night through, being awakened when one of his tenants tapped him on the shoulder with a request to open the door. Often I would come home to find him buried under a foot of snow.

I now attended classes at the conservatory two mornings a

week, walking a distance of about ten blocks and back. It was here that I met Jascha Heifetz and his father, who attended every lesson. Jascha was, at fifteen, a child sensation all over Europe. Many managers from the United States were trying to sign him up for a tour. This meant a quantity of mail in English, most of which Papa Heifetz brought to my room from time to time for me to translate and answer.

The submarine war was going full blast by now. Naturally, the Heifetz family—father, mother, son, and two daughters—were apprehensive about crossing the Atlantic. It wasn't until two years later that they finally got to America, via the Pacific.

Walking to the conservatory twice a week gave me a chance to mingle with the people and learn more about them. Contrary to public opinion in the United States, most of them were tender-hearted. Let me mention two incidents out of many that I experienced on these walks.

I was passing one of the busiest corners in the center of the city when I observed a big crowd. Inching up closer, I saw about fifteen Austrian prisoners who were evidently waiting to be transferred to another streetcar line, of course under guard. Their uniforms were threadbare and they looked underfed. People were pitching money to them from all directions and making friendly remarks, which brought smiles to their faces. On another occasion I saw a cabdriver beating one of his horses unmercifully. Quickly a crowd gathered and the cabdriver got a good licking in return.

After the holidays my life got busier than before. A girl refugee from Riga, a niece of our landlady's moved in with us. She was about eighteen, taking typing lessons, and eager to learn English. I offered to exchange English for Russian lessons with her. This we did three times weekly. For the first time, I became aware of how unpredictable English spelling can be.

There was a large English department store which specialized almost exclusively in English products. I used to visit it occasionally just for the fun of browsing around. On one such occasion my eyes lit on a book entitled *Card Tricks by Sleight of Hand*. This intrigued me; so I bought the book and began to practice card tricks as religiously as I did my violin.

Soon it was Easter. The Russians go all out to make this the biggest event of the year. Our landlady spent days making goodies of all kinds to last throughout the week. On Good Friday I went to midnight mass with the family, after which we were each handed a cornucopia in which there was a small lighted candle. The object was to carry your candle home without letting the light go out. The sight of several thousand people streaming from church, protecting their lights from the wind with their hands, was very moving. If you got home without mishap, you were supposed to have good luck for the coming year. If your light went out, you would have bad luck. My pity was for those who didn't make it, for if you keep expecting something it usually comes to pass.

Shortly after this, I attended a concert by the young composer Prokofiev. He had graduated from the conservatory only a few years prior to this, and now he was to conduct the finest orchestra in all Russia in a program of his own compositions. It turned out to be the most pitiful fiasco I ever witnessed. There were no fights, as in Vienna, to liven things up. Instead, those fine musicians in the orchestra kept laughing their heads off as they played. The audience sat silent but respectful. The music sounded mighty queer to me, too. Mind you, this was early Prokofiev. Let us look at this in the light of hindsight. Now, fifty years later, Prokofiev is accepted as one of the all-time greats. Why did the men in that orchestra find his music so hilarious? They didn't understand it. It was a completely new concept, and their training hadn't reached that point.

On June 1, I left St. Petersburg for Christiania, my pal Thaulow having left a few weeks earlier. As I bade good-bye to my landlady, she voluntarily promised to reserve my room for me in the fall (my reward for ridding her kitchen of cockroaches!). This was a great relief to me, because I was already worrying about a room, knowing how jammed St. Petersburg was with refugees.

Arriving at the most northern point, where we had to cross the river to change from a Finnish train to a Swedish one, I unexpectedly witnessed the saddest sight of my life. There stood a long train from which the Finnish Red Cross personnel were carrying German and Austrian prisoners. They were so badly mutilated that most had to be carried in baskets to sleighs, which would ferry them across the still frozen river to Sweden. Another train was waiting there with equally mutilated Russians, who would then be exchanged for the Germans and Austrians. Some were without legs, some without arms, a few without either legs or arms, but all hopelessly disabled. Yet they seemed cheerful.

I spoke to quite a few of the Austrians, who were thanking God that they would soon be seeing their families. The Finnish Red Cross couldn't have been nicer to them.

When the Germans and Austrians reached the Swedish side of the river, they were unloaded and the Russian prisoners put into the sleighs for the trip back. They were jubilant because they were coming home. Again, the Swedish Red Cross couldn't have been more solicitous. The Russians were equally happy to hear Russian spoken, even if not well, by a foreigner. This experience haunted me for weeks.

Many times since then have I thought that if only those who had voted against the League of Nations had seen this sight, they might have voted for a world governed by law and order instead of might and murder.

Back in Christiania, I wasn't sure whether I would be allowed to stay at the hotel at half rate again but, as all the hotels in the city were crowded, I decided to go there anyway, if only for a few days.

The lady manager of the hotel greeted me with open arms and a big smile. Yes, I could have my old room and at the same price. This was a great relief to me because I dearly wanted to be with the old gang, most of whom would be returning shortly.

Professor Auer was already in the vicinity. He and Mme. Auer had decided that the hotel was not peaceful enough. So they rented a cozy villa a short distance down the mountain, and we went there for our lessons.

Within the week, most of the other students had arrived. We were again a happy family of about ten, although we did miss the professor's humorous tales at the dining table. To make up for this loss we had a prestidigitator in the group by the name of Siskovsky, who often did card tricks to the amazement of all at the after-dinner coffee table. So we settled down to our regular routine of practice and amusement.

Our weekly recitals of the previous year had proved so popular that many of the other guests returned this season just to hear them; they enjoyed the intimacy.

One afternoon Professor Auer telephoned to ask me to come to his villa. A small group was there, and he wanted me to take snapshots. I hastened down to find Jascha Heifetz, Max Rosen, Toscha Seidel, and Margo Berson waiting. We spent the rest of the afternoon taking pictures.

Being of an inquisitive nature, Jascha asked if I did my own developing and printing. When I told him I did, he said, "I would like to see how it is done; may I watch?" So I invited him to the hotel to have dinner with the rest of the gang, and then the two of us hurried into the completely equipped darkroom in the cellar and developed three rolls of film. We hung them up in front of a fan and had them dry within a couple of hours.

The negatives looked so good that we couldn't resist the temptation to continue with the printing; so we didn't get to bed until four in the morning. Correction, please—he got into my bed and I slept on the floor.

We awoke too late for breakfast, at 10:00 a.m.; so we had to go without. Actually, we were more interested in our pictures than in eating, and went at once to the darkroom to discover that the results were exceptionally good and sufficiently dry for Jascha to take his share home. He was quick to catch on to the whole procedure. As for me, I had more fun from the thrill he was getting out of it than from the pictures.

Incidentally, these pictures proved very useful a year later when I returned to America where the Wolfsohn Bureau had just signed a contract for Jascha to make a ten-concert tour. His manager was waiting for me to disembark, with the plea that I help him out since he didn't have a single picture of Jascha. I supplied him with about a dozen, almost all of which appeared all over the country as the first Heifetz publicity.

A little later Toscha Seidel and Jascha gave separate concerts in Christiania; of course, we all went. Both were successful and were well attended. Toscha received such an ovation that the king and queen sent a royal coach with a request that he and his mother come to the palace after the concert. The students, seeing what was happening, unhitched the beautiful team of white horses and pulled the coach themselves up Karl Johanns Gade (the main street) and up the hill to the palace. We felt very proud to have one of our own honored so highly.

For me, however, that triumph was dwarfed by what took place some fifteen years later at Town Hall in New York City. At a concert for some charitable cause, Toscha Seidel played first violin in a string quartet next to a second violinist whose name is recognized as the greatest of twentieth century physicists, and an all-time great, Albert Einstein. One does not have to be very old to remember how his theory of relativity revolutionized the cosmic thinking of the scientific world.

Unfortunately, I do not remember the names of the cellist and violist, nor do I remember the compositions played. But I do remember that the program was a difficult one and that Town Hall was sold out. I sat with my ears glued to that second violin part, every note of which I knew well, and was amazed to hear how well it was played. How Einstein found time enough for practice to reach so high a state of proficiency is still an enigma.

By this time, through my friend Thaulow—and through one contact leading to another—I had gotten to know and like many of the people of Christiania. Just the mention of Norway makes a sweet feeling of nostalgia rise within my heart.

Another idyllic summer passed, October arrived, and the days shortened rapidly. The conservatory had opened about the middle of September (remember, the Russian calendar was thirteen days behind ours), and we all had to think about getting back to St. Petersburg. The news that Thaulow wasn't going to be able to go back was a great disappointment to me. Even though we went our own ways, our friendship was a close one and it was nice to have him nearby. Since most of the others had started out earlier, I was making the trip alone this time.

We traveled by day train to Stockholm, where we changed to sleeping cars. These cars are built differently from ours in that the aisle runs along the outside wall instead of the center. From this aisle you enter compartments, each with two long upholstered seats spanning the width where two people on each side sit facing each other. Overhead on each side is a folding bed, which disappears into the wall. Thus, by making up beds on the seats and the overhead bunks, there are sleeping accommodations for four people.

The other three men in with me were a Frenchman and two Italians—father and son. The father was a famous musician who was conductor at the Petrograd Opera, also famous for having written a waltz very popular at the time, his name was Drigo. His son was about sixteen years old. It was obvious that none of us were either Swedish or Russian. So, as was customary amongst foreigners, the conversation started in German, which we all knew; so we stuck to that without further exploration.

We had dinner together in the dining car, and the food was delicious. I ate much more than usual and felt some discomfort therefrom. About 10:00 p.m. our beds were made up. I was allotted a lower, and Professor Drigo got the other. Above him was the Frenchman, and above me was the son. Lights were turned out and I fell soundly asleep.

Sometime during the night I had a horrible nightmare. I dreamed that as our train was crossing a bridge, the bridge gave way and we fell into the water. Fortunately, the car remained upright but was filling with water so rapidly that the only air left to breath was up close to the ceiling; so I started climbing into the upper berth with the son, who in turn started hollering his head off. This awakened me and the rest of the occupants. I was in such a stupor that it took some time for me to come to. Fortunately, no one turned on the light; so I slunk back to bed with a very guilty feeling.

The next morning I overheard the father and son discussing the episode in Russian. They thought I didn't know the language. When the father asked what happened, the son replied, "I haven't the slightest idea. All I know is that he was trying to get into bed with me." On hearing this, I decided to play dumb and not mention it if they didn't, so we proceeded on to Petrograd without their being any the wiser; but, of course, they must have done a lot of speculating.

At the railroad station money exchange office I was given enormous sums of rubles for just a few dollars. Even small change in coins had disappeared and postage stamps were being used instead. How wonderful for me, I thought, but what about the poor people? Riding to my room in a one-horse cab, I was depressed to notice how run-down everything looked. The streets were full of refugees from the front, soldiers on leave or drilling to the beat of their famous marching songs.

At my apartment I was welcomed like a son coming home from the wars. Yes, the landlady had saved my room and I could have it for as long as I wanted at the old price. This was practically nothing at the new exchange rate.

After making calls on my old friends, I soon settled into the old routine of lessons, practice, concerts, opera, and ballet, the latter two through the courtesy of the Bersons, who invited me to sit in their box almost weekly. He was the J. P. Morgan of Petrograd.

Wherever you went, the general topic of conversation was the war and what a drubbing the Russians were giving the Germans on the western front. But I, having read the London *Times*, the Berliner *Tagblatt*, and the Norwegian newspaper, knew that the Russians were not getting the truth. For that matter, neither were the British, Germans, and Norwegians. You might ask, "Why should the Norwegians want to lie about it?" For the simple reason that their sympathies were almost 100 percent pro-British. Their Queen Maud was a granddaughter of Queen Victoria. They were getting rich supplying ships to the Allies; indeed, almost every Norwegian owned stock in at least one ship.

No one had much faith in the newspaper reports about the war. More intriguing were the juicy tidbits of gossip going the rounds about a monk by the name of Rasputin who practically lived at the palace, where he held sinister sway over the Czarina, who in turn dominated the weakling Czar to the detriment of the country. Stories continued for some months. Just before Christmas, my landlady, bringing in my breakfast of tea and a bun, reported that at the bakery, she had just learned that Rasputin had been murdered during the night and that his body had been dropped into the Neva River through a hole in the ice. Prince Felix Yussoupov and a few of his cohorts had invited Rasputin to the prince's palace to play cards. During the game they spiked his drinks with poison; but the monk, who was a notoriously heavy drinker, kept right on playing without showing any signs that the poison was taking effect. Finally they bashed his brains in with a bottle. Not a word about this appeared in the newspapers for almost a week. When it did appear, we were surprised to learn how true to the facts the rumors had been.

Everybody seemed to be glad that the old scoundrel had been disposed of. Now, they said, maybe something would be done about the disorder and shortage of food. There was a lot of speculation as to what would be done about Yussoupov. He was a relative of the czar and overnight became a hero of the people. Would they execute him? Would he go scot-free? Would they try to hush it up? Then, when the people had almost forgotten about the whole affair, a short account appeared in the newspapers. Yussoupov had been tried and banished to Siberia.

During this time Papa Heifetz was a frequent visitor to my room. Both Professor Auer and I kept urging him to make the trip to the United States via Siberia and the Pacific Ocean. With conditions in Europe getting worse and concert managers in the United States making ever more tempting offers, Papa's resolve not to hazard the journey was weakening. The managers sensed this and sent imploring letters in a steady stream; but until Papa Heifetz decided what to do we could only politely stall.

I spent a wonderful Christmas at home with the "family." We all went to midnight mass Christmas Eve and I got a terrific kick out of hearing those remarkable Russian basses sing so low with such purity. Our landlady had cooked so many goodies for Christmas dinner that we had a real feast, even though food was beginning to be scarce. They made me feel perfectly at home, and I loved it.

Due to the demand for war supplies at the front, the distribution of food and other supplies at home became disorganized. Too many perishables were sent to one place, while elsewhere there were shortages. People had to stand in line in the bitter cold for certain commodities. Refugees from Poland and the border countries were selling their diamond jewelry for very low prices and hoarding food with the proceeds. Hotels were so crowded that people were sleeping on cots in the hallways and ballrooms, and even in the bathtubs.

The government was corrupt from top to bottom. Everybody was heartily sick of the war and close to despair. Sporadic riots broke out which, for a time, the police were able to break up. But on March 12 it was different.

I had been invited to a large dinner party of some fifty guests at the Bersons. The usual time to arrive for these affairs was ten o'clock. I took a one-horse cab to their house. Along the way we kept passing large groups of women shouting, "We are hungry. We want bread!" all the while being chased by the police. In several places we drove right through the crowds, but there was no shooting; so I arrived safely.

By the time we had finished a seven-course dinner with five different kinds of wine and the usual hygienic cleansing of the teeth at the table (using the index finger held in a piece of the napkin and dipped in a finger bowl of hot scented water), we were beginning to hear sounds of shooting from the streets below.

We settled down to a fine vocal concert. But those gunshots from the street kept me painfully aware of the paradox of the situation. Here we were, in surroundings of splendor, surfeited with food and wine, listening to music sung by the finest artists of Russian opera; and there they were—those uncounted thousands out in the bitter cold streets crying for bread and being shot down.

Ordinarily, these soirees lasted until 4:00 or 5:00 in the morning. But tonight everybody was in a nervous state of apprehension, and we started dispersing by 2:00. Out in the street there was utter confusion. People were running in every direction in fear of the spasmodic bursts of machine gun fire coming from the rooftops where the police were stationed. One thinks quickly in a situation like this. By slinking from door to door, I managed to reach a back street, and ran the twenty blocks home in less time than it took to get there by cab. The street was practically deserted, the temperature a bitter thirty degrees below zero, and I still wore only that light overcoat which I had brought from Cleveland.

I reached my doorstep breathing hard and perspiring freely, and awakened our janitor. The disorders hadn't reached that part of the city yet, but you could hear the firing in the distance. After telling him what I had just been through, I went up to the third floor to my cozy, comfortable bed, and he to his hard seat on the marble steps.

Occasional bursts of machine gun fire resounded throughout the night. Sleep was fitful; I kept wondering how many of the protesters got hit each time. By midmorning the din of shooting and hollering was right beneath my window.

I swigged two big glasses of tea, dressed hurriedly, and went out, unmindful of the landlady's pleas and warnings that it was too dangerous.

We lived only three doors from Nevsky Prospect, where most of the action was. In no time I was swallowed up in a dense crowd of hungry human beings. They were milling up and down one of the widest avenues in the world crying, "We want bread!" It is so easy to be swayed by the excitement of a mob! I got right in among them and marched along.

Every so often the police on the rooftops would spray us with machine gun bullets; then the crowd would disperse into side streets and courtyards, only to reassemble when the firing ceased. Many would lie down on the pavement to present less of a target, thereby making it difficult to tell the injured from the uninjured. I felt pushed around by waves of humanity, with no sense of direction.

I had been in this atmosphere of hysteria for some hours when a shout went up—"Cossacks!" The mob scattered in all directions. I could see the Cossacks in a wide column charging at us at full gallop, swinging nagaikas or waving their spears. (Nagaikas are leather straps about two feet long with lead balls sewn into the free-swinging ends.)

There was barely time for a mad dash out of the way. Of course, many did not escape. I, along with what seemed like thousands of others, made a run to the side streets where archways led to courtyards behind the buildings. I still do not know how all those people vanished so quickly. I was lucky to find a space where I could lean my back against a building. The first wave of Cossacks charged right by us, trampling on any who were in their path. Then came other waves of Cossacks on the trot, their duty to keep us from reassembling in the street.

One of these men posted himself so that his horse's nose was almost touching mine. His spear was pointing straight at my breast, only six inches away. My whole attention was riveted on the point of that spear. After a time that seemed like forever, I dared to look up into his face. Imagine my relief at seeing him smiling at me! I told him that I was an American and he replied that he had never met an American before and was sorry it had to be under these circumstances. While I patted his horse, we had quite a chat until he was called off.

The arrival of the Cossacks broke up the demonstration, and I was able to proceed home without incident.

Having had little to eat all day, I was very hungry. With some bread and tea, I ate an enormous helping of that super-delicious black caviar which I kept between the double windows.

That night Jascha Heifetz was to give a public concert, for which I had a ticket. One might think hearing him play twice a week in class sufficient, but it was always more thrilling to hear Heifetz play from the stage of a large hall. Things outside had quieted down, and it seemed reasonable to assume that the concert would take place; so I started out. It was eerie to be walking up Nevsky Prospect, always a very busy thoroughfare, but now deserted except for an occasional human being on foot. The sounds of distant shooting and rioting became louder. As I approached the concert hall in the big Winter Palace Square, I realized that there would be no concert that night. I had had my fill of rioting for the day, and I walked right back home.

The janitor was fast asleep on the marble steps in the bitter cold. It always pained me to have to wake him; yet it was good to know that our tips helped support him and his family.

The next morning it was easy to tell from the sounds of firing that the fighting had increased in intensity. Not only was the rat-a-tat of machine guns almost continuous, but now heavier artillery was being used. The night before I had made up my mind that it would be foolhardy to get into the midst of it again. So, since this intense fighting continued for the next three days, I restricted myself to occasional quick trips to the corner to try to bring back news for the family.

By a bit of judicious peeking and inquiry, I learned that a regiment from the army had deserted overnight and had joined the workers. Regiments sent in to quell the riots soon deserted, and the fighting spread to all parts of the city until the police and Cossacks were wiped out or had surrendered.

Oddly enough, it was the police whom the populace hated most. After the fighting had ceased and I had begun to roam the streets again, I saw many a troika loaded with police corpses being carted away, followed by angry mobs clubbing them even in death.

About the third day after the shooting, one of the most impressive funerals possible took place. Starting around nine in the morning, the procession marched down Nevsky Prospect,

91

twenty abreast, shoulder to shoulder. Bands played slow funeral music. A regiment of Cossacks carried on their shoulders about a hundred coffins containing the remains of their fallen heroes. Services were held at a mass grave in a park in the center of the city.

The procession was so long that it took over twelve hours for it to file past the grave. I was so entranced that I stayed there all day watching it. By the time I returned home I was half starved and half frozen with the thermometer at zero. Six glasses of hot tea were a lifesaver. By this time, you may wonder what I did about the necessities of life. Here we were, living in an apartment house five stories high with two apartments to each floor. Our apartment housed four people: a widow of about sixty, two teen-age daughters, and me. Because of the danger of looters, the men in the building were organized into pairs to do two-hour shifts of night watch. I stood the 4:00 to 6:00 a.m. shift. Shortly after the uprising started, every service stopped. Shops closed— and in Europe that means metal shutters were pulled down over the glass windows. All modes of transportation disappeared from the streets. Electricity and water were shut off.

Fortunately, Mme. Matusova, my landlady, had had enough foresight to fill the bathtub with water. Fortunately, too, there was about a two-week supply of kindling wood to keep the kitchen warm if used sparingly. My room and the rest of the apartment would have to go unheated.

Food had been scarce for some time, and now all she had on hand when the shops closed was a five-pound bag of wheat grits, about ten heads of cabbage, and a few leftovers, which soon disappeared. Add a plentiful supply of tea and my one-pound can of caviar, and that is what the four of us subsisted on for about ten days—grits, caviar, and cabbage soup. Tea was our lifesaver because it was the most stimulating and helped to keep us warm. We each drank about ten glasses a day.

The most boring part of the ordeal was sitting around the kitchen stove all day trying to keep warm. But it was the middle of March and close to the equinoctial period. Had the crisis come a few months earlier, we would have sat in cold and darkness all day long. I kept thinking that everyone should live through an experience such as this to realize how many things in life we take for granted and don't appreciate until we lose them.

My room was so cold that practicing was out of the question. Time hung heavy except for frequent excursions into the street to get a peek at the rioting and pick up some rumors.

In about a week the fighting died down and people began to appear in the streets unarmed. Trucks distributed one-page newspapers for which a news-hungry public scrambled. Many a dive into the snow did I make to get one.

Bakeries, the only shops that opened, rationed out one-pound pieces of rye bread to people in queues many blocks long. This situation lasted for weeks. Often we stood for five or six hours in that bitter cold, finally to be told, "That's all we have today; come tomorrow."

Can you picture me in that long line of human beings, some well dressed, some in tattered clothes, but all muffled in furs, while I stood in my light black overcoat with no head covering? To be sure, I did have on two suits of long underwear, a sweater, two pairs of woolen socks, and heavy shoes and earmuffs.

The teen-age girls in the family came and stood with me every day so that we could get three handouts. We always returned frozen to the marrow after standing in line sometimes for four hours.

Now we entered a period of great uncertainty and anxiety. The daily paper was thrown to us from a truck; it was apparent that things were in a state of total confusion. One day the czar was abdicating; the next day he wasn't. The Duma was called into session, but no solutions were coming from that sector at the moment. Orators were haranguing the people from the tops of buses. A crowd would gather about the bus and, after hearing a man speak, would start purposefully up the street as if bent on some important mission. At the next corner another orator would stop them and send them scurrying in another direction. That is the way it went—they were blown around just like the leaves in autumn.

I learned another vital lesson; watching, I saw how helpless and useless great numbers of people are without leadership. I spoke to many; they were all imbued with the loftiest idealism. They had the naive notion that their revolution was taking place all over the world. "Now the exploitation of the workers will stop, and we will be paid a proper share of the profits. Now the war will end because the German soldiers are deserting just like our own."

Then came news of the czar's abdication. There was great jubilation but even more confusion, because the government had collapsed. Shopkeepers were reluctant to open their shops because no one knew what value, if any, the Russian ruble had.

Gradually more people ventured out, but only in the daytime. At night the streets were deserted except for students who were recruited to travel on foot in pairs to prevent looting.

I befriended one pair assigned to our neighborhood and roamed the streets several nights with them. One night we encountered a looter who decided to be nasty and draw his gun. One of the students quickly shot him, thereby triggering the gun of the looter, whose bullet whizzed by inches away from my ear. The student had fired his shotgun at such close range that it severed the looter's arm at the elbow. There was the arm lying at our feet. The sound of the shot brought many other students on the run. They tied a tourniquet around the culprit's arm and led him away. This incident cured me of my inquisitiveness, and it was many weeks before I ventured out at night.

This I wish to put on record, to the everlasting credit of the Russian people. In the nights that I roamed the streets with the students, that was the only case of looting we encountered, though the police were non-existent and the military hadn't taken hold. Later, I learned that looting throughout the city was almost negligible. The students deserve high praise.

The Duma was in session around the clock; yet nothing seemed to come of it until Kerensky was elected leader. Now people began to have some faith in the monetary system. Some shops opened up for business, but supplies were so scarce that one had to stand in line for hours to buy the bare necessities.

Now came a period of street brawling. The city was full of soldiers who had deserted their regiments and were just loafing. Attempts by officers to organize them met with scorn and complete failure. Kerensky was in favor of continuing the war; so there were continual clashes between those in favor and those against.

Before long, news got around that Lenin and Trotsky had

arrived in the city and were organizing the workers. Soon it became apparent that real pros had taken charge. All the indecision on the labor front had changed to positive action, with protest demonstrations all over the city and accompanying riots. I decided that it was high time for me to be leaving, especially since the United States had just declared war on Germany.

It took a few days to get my passport processed for departure. During this time I dwelt on the many things I was going to miss—a symphony played on church bells every Sunday morning (the likes of which I had never heard before); those Russian basses; that delicious tea and caviar; and, last but not least, an Egyptian brand of cigarette which I didn't see how I could do without. I bought 2,000 and packed them in among my clothes in the bottom of my trunk.

The day of departure was a sad one. I felt like a member of the family; and they couldn't have been nicer to me. I could have been born into it. We parted in tears, never to see or hear from each other again.

Though it was early May, snow still lay on the ground. All of Finland was covered with a white blanket. Traffic across the Tornio River into Sweden was over the ice by sleigh. When I reached Christiania, I telephoned the Voksenkollen Hotel to find out if it was open. To my delight, I heard, "Yes, come ahead, we have a wing open."

Again, it was like coming home, especially when I learned that one of my best friends had been staying there all winter. He was a Russian citizen named Koenig, whose father, a German, started the sugar industry in Russia and made a fortune at it; he had earned the title of sugar king. The son was living in Norway to avoid service in the war.

He was preparing to go on a hunting trip and was looking for someone to go with him. There I was, just as if he had telephoned for me. There was one drawback. The only things I enjoyed killing were fleas and bedbugs. "Never mind," he said. "I'll do the shooting; you come along because it will be an interesting trip." Little did I think crossing the Tornio River a few days previously that I would be back that far north again. We took the railroad over the mountains from Christiania to Bergen. The tracks were covered by snow sheds a good part of the way. From Bergen we traveled to Trondheim by boat, then to Snaasa, about one hundred miles by rail, and then three days by stagecoach, stopping overnight at spotlessly clean little inns. In a charming cluster of five farmhouses, not even on the map, called Agle, we put up in a farmhouse. The family consisted of the owner and his wife, about fifty, his father and mother, in their seventies, his brother, and two children in their teens.

This far from rail or water transportation, one would expect to find people leading primitive and austere lives. Quite the contrary. Everywhere one looked there were signs of modest affluence. Grandma was sitting in a corner pumping away at an old spinning wheel, and right beside her (I couldn't believe my eyes), stood a modern Singer sewing machine. The furniture, in good taste, was mostly in the green and red that is typical of Norway.

I learned that these people lead an almost self-sufficient life. They have herds of cows which in the summertime they drive high up into the mountains to pasture, and from whose milk they make cheese. This is their money crop. They have sheep from whose wool they make much of their clothing. In addition, they have some goats and pigs, a plentiful supply of fish and wild game, and all the meat they can possibly use. In a soil that rests nine months of the year, they can grow almost any vegetable— and some fruits that usually grow in more temperate zones. This leaves them with only a few items, such as salt and sugar, to spend money on.

My good friend Koenig was anxious to get started with the hunting, so we got busy with preparations. The plan was to go to the *saeter* (cabin) up in the mountains where one of the family drove the cows and stayed with them all summer. It was some ten miles away, the last two of which were very steep terrain.

This was the middle of May; snow was on the ground everywhere. I had never been on skis and, while Koenig assembled supplies for the two-week stay, I practiced on them. By the next day I was doing well enough to hazard an attempt with a knapsack on my back. Along the level road I had no difficulty, but when it came to climbing some three thousand feet up the mountain, I found it very hard going. Still, with a few assists from my friend, I made it to the cabin without accident. I was so tired that the little log cabin looked like a palace. The snow was hip-deep around it and we had to do quite some shoveling to get in.

Plenty of firewood was stacked up in the corner, and we soon had a fire going in the stove. We cooked a supper of ham and eggs and went to bed early. The bed was made of saplings covered with straw and was hard as a rock. Koenig snored like Mount Vesuvius erupting. I didn't sleep a wink.

At four in the morning he awakened refreshed. I felt like an old wet sock! "Up and at 'em," he called. "We've got to get a few of those woodcocks around here." After coffee I explained that I hadn't slept all night and felt miserable. Since I wasn't going to do any shooting, would he mind if I stayed in to get some sleep? "Why, of course not. Do just as you feel," he said.

The next three days were spent sitting in a very cold blind trying to imitate the mating call of woodcocks. During all that time he shot five birds.

Nights I spent in misery because I was so wrought up I couldn't fall asleep. One night I got up at about eleven, just in time to see the sun drop below the crest of a mountain and soon after rise again in a spot that seemed only a few feet away. Finally I explained my plight to Koenig. He suggested that I return to the farmhouse and await his descent in three or four days.

Next morning I started down the mountain with a knapsack strapped to my back and five woodcocks strapped around my body. This was the most difficult part of the trip. After many falls and much sliding on my back, I got down to the farmhouse by afternoon without any broken bones.

The family, seeing me return alone, were apprehensive about Koenig. My Norwegian wasn't good enough to tell the whole story, but I did manage to make them understand that he was all right and would be coming back in a few days. They were just having their afternoon snack of coffee and buns, and shared it with me, after which I went right up to bed and slept straight through until the next morning, when I awakened feeling like a new person.

After breakfast I put in about three hours of practice on the violin. The afternoon was spent skiing in the countryside. That night (if you can call broad daylight night), after a delicious meal similar to a New England boiled dinner, the family begged me to bring in my violin and play for them. How could anyone refuse these gentle people? There they sat at the uncleared table—the whole family. I stood in a corner playing my violin, at first lulling them with simple tunes, then progressing to some of the most difficult numbers in my repertoire. The faster my bow and fingers wiggled, the wider their mouths seemed to open. When I stopped, after about two hours, they sat there speechless.

When Koenig returned a few days later, we were having a concert almost every night. It gave him great joy to be instrumental in bringing an event of such great satisfaction to these isolated people.

He brought back seven more woodcocks, which made this a truly successful hunting trip.

Now the spring thaw set in. With twenty-four hours a day of sunlight, nature works fast in these latitudes. In the next two weeks the snow in the fields melted, the ice on the rivers broke up and flowed out to sea, and everybody worked twenty hours a day plowing, harrowing, and seeding the soil. There was no time for concerts, but I continued to practice. By the time we left, the new spring crop was already visible.

There was plenty of small game in the vicinity; so I tagged along while Koenig hunted. One day, when the ice had just flowed out of the river, we took a fast jump in and an even faster one out.

During all this time none of the farmers got much sleep. I have a snapshot of one of them plowing a field at eleven at night, with the sun just above the horizon. Koenig and I didn't help much with the farm chores, but we did quite a bit in the kitchen. These people worked long and hard in the short growing season; but during the long winters they would have plenty of time to rest.

For me it was a great pleasure to live with such kindly, simple people, and I am sure they must have spoken about that violinist for some time. So we returned to Voksenkollen in the same manner in which we had come, which took about a week.

It was now around the middle of June, and our hotel was full. It was a good thing we had kept our rooms while away.

Professor Auer was in Stockholm and not teaching, having departed from St. Petersburg financially ruined and with only a few possessions which could be carried. Fortunately, his Strad was one of them. He wanted to come to the United States, but because of the submarine menace was considering settling in Stockholm.

As for me, I had wanted to study with the two finest teachers in the world until I was as close to perfection as my natural ability would permit. I had now reached this point, and it was time to go home. Also, the United States was now at war and I would be obliged to serve.

I spent the last few weeks enjoying myself with many dear Norwegian friends while I waited for the Norwegian Line steamer, the *Bergensfjord*, to depart, on July 20, 1917. As we steamed down the Christiania Fjord, I kept looking back in tears at the country I loved so dearly.

By this time I had become quite a seasoned traveler. It was interesting to watch, at the beginning of a voyage, how birds of a feather flock together and separate into congenial little groups of their own.

The English Channel was heavily mined, and all shipping had to proceed around northern Britain. The number of ships being sunk by the Germans was now staggering. I think in this respect it was the peak of the whole war. Once we reached the open ocean, there wasn't much that we could do about it except attend the daily lifeboat drill and trust in the good judgment of our captain and the skill of the Norwegian crew, who, in my opinion, are unsurpassed by any sailors. We steamed on in a state of apprehension, waking up each morning thankful that we were still in the land or, that is, on the water of the living.

One night we put on an entertainment for the benefit of Norwegian seamen, during which I played, accompanied by the wife of the first secretary of the United States embassy in St. Petersburg, who was a good pianist. Thus we proceeded in perfect comfort and peace without even sighting another ship, let alone a German U-boat. Had it not been for the telegraph, we wouldn't have known what a murderous war was going on. All this peace and comfort was too good to be true; so to even things up, just before we got off the banks of Newfoundland, we struck what the captain called the worst storm he had ever experienced. In one way it was a blessing, for it lasted three days and nights; and we all felt secure that no U-boat would be out on the prowl in that weather.

Attendance in the dining room dropped to about 10 percent.

The ship pitched and rolled so violently that it was hazardous to stand up, let alone do any walking. The few of us who had cast-iron stomachs and an appetite made it to the table at risk of life and limb by making leaps and bounds from one stationary object to another. Once there, we found table and chairs anchored to the floor, a guard rail surrounding the outside edge of the table and the table cloth soaking wet to prevent the dishes from sliding around and falling off.

Now imagine the cooks down in the galley trying to cook, and then the waiters doing a ballet up the aisles balancing trays in one hand, and you wonder why so few dishes—and bones—were broken. Those of us who could eat lived almost exclusively on smorgasbord for three days. But, may I ask, who can make better smorgasbord than the Scandinavians?

For three days the foghorn blew at regular intervals. With that noise and the tossing about of the ship, very few of us got any sleep; yet spirits were high when we arrived in New York, for now we knew that our safety was relatively certain.

At quarantine, after being questioned by the attending doctor, I was surrounded by eight people. Six were newspaper reporters who wanted to know all about the Russian revolution and how matters now stood there. There was Jack Adams of the Wolfsohn Concert Bureau, with whom I had been corresponding for Papa Heifetz regarding a tour of the United States for Jascha, and Carl Fischer of the music publishing house, for whom I was bringing back manuscripts which Professor Auer had asked me to deliver and which would be published by this firm.

Mr. Fischer hurried away with the manuscripts, but Jack Adams asked me to take on the reporters, since he was anxious to hear about it himself. Between telling my own story and trying to answer questions coming from six directions, I became somewhat confused; but I did my best to please, because I was feeling very important at the moment.

By the time the reporters finished with me, we had already docked and were about to go through customs. I started to worry about those 2,000 cigarettes in my trunk that I was smuggling in; so I asked Jack Adams to wait until the customs examination was finished. Even though the officer did a fairly thorough job, he didn't discover them. Now I felt very happy. Would you believe that my trunk went through customs five times, in and out of four countries, and not one of the examiners found the cigarettes?

Back to Jack Adams. He informed me that they had just received a signed contract from Papa Heifetz for a tour of ten concerts the following year. He hoped I had some pictures of the lad as he had absolutely no publicity material. I gave him a dozen or more snapshots, for which he was very thankful. As I was anxious to get home as soon as possible, he helped me get my baggage to Grand Central Station; and I caught the first train for Cleveland.

I left New York before my experiences in Russia were published in the papers, and I never did see what the reporters wrote. But having had hundreds of interviews with reporters since then, I am sure there were six quite different versions of what I said.

On August 3, I was home in Cleveland after an absence of two years and two months. I had lived through and seen so much that would go down in history, it seemed like a lifetime.

My trunk arrived a few days later. After distributing some of those precious cigarettes in miserly fashion, and thinking what a treat my friends were getting, I became involved in an enigma. Reports came drifting back that nobody liked them. To make matters worse, I tried smoking them again; and, believe it or not, I didn't like them either! It was a great disappointment. I finally threw the remainder into the trash.

When I tried to register for the draft four months after the rolls had closed, no one in state or city officialdom seemed to know where I could do it at this late date. So, what with the uncertainty of being called into the service at any time, my hatred for the Prussian German, my ignorance and inexperience —I believed the slogan being fed us, that this is the war to end all wars—I decided to enlist.

Knowing that the center of musical activity in this country was New York, I planned to settle there after the war. Thus, I returned to New York City and wound up at Fort Slocum for induction into the army in October.

12
YOU'RE IN THE ARMY NOW

Fort Slocum, a recruiting station on an island in Long Island Sound, was about thirty miles northeast of New York City. Cannon emplacements bristled at strategic locations around the fort to help protect the city. Men were sent here to be exaimined, outfitted, and sent on to other camps.

On my first night there, about a hundred of us were put to bed in a cantonment with upper and lower bunks. My patriotism shrank to zero while I listened to vulgar talk only hoodlums could mouth. Some of them kept it up until the wee hours. My nerves were on edge all night, until, at daybreak, as I was beginning to relax, all hell broke loose.

Cannons suddenly started booming all over the island. Glass was flying in all directions and so were soldiers. Confusion reigned. Later we learned that those cannons hadn't been fired in some fifty years and were being tested that morning. The result was that practically every window on the post was broken.

After breakfast, about eighty of us novices were lined up on the parade ground by a bunch of rough, tough, and gruff sergeants. Apparently their purpose was to break our spirit so we wouldn't question why but would go in to do or die.

It took three or more days to complete the induction routine, which included thorough medical, intelligence, and occupational exams, as well as the distribution and fitting of uniforms, swearing-in ceremonies, and, finally, allocation to the branch of the service of our choice. After being lined up and checked off at roll call, we stood for at least three hours, first on one foot and then the other. What you do more than anything else in the army is stand around doing nothing, waiting for somebody to tell you what to do.

Finally a sergeant announced that we wouldn't be inducted into the service here. There would not be time. The next day we would be taken to Fort Dix, New Jersey, where a troop ship was waiting to fill out a contingent already aboard, shy eighty men, which was to sail for France. Induction would take place either aboard ship or overseas. Of course, all of us expected to land overseas sooner or later, but not as quickly as this. On top of all the early morning cannonading, this was just too much.

The sergeant departed and left us standing there, and standing still can be punishing when there's no end in sight. Finally another sergeant appeared; and everybody pricked up his ears, thinking, "Now what?" Reading from a slip held in his hand, he shouted my name, badly mispronounced. My intention was to shout, "Here," but what came out was a whisper, and I had to raise my arm. Up to this time that sergeant had made himself out to be one of the toughest of the tough guys; so he gave me another shock when in a gentle voice he said, "Follow me, please."

As we walked across the long parade ground, the only words spoken were his remark that the bandmaster would like to speak to me. He knocked on the bandmaster's door, and I noticed that the name on the plate was Petersen. Aha, I thought, he is either a Dane or a Norwegian, Swedish names end in "son." When he greeted me, I knew from his accent that he had been born abroad. My curiosity got the best of me; and I asked, "Mr. Petersen, excuse me, but which are you, Danish or Norwegian?" He replied, "Norwegian." "Which town or city?" I asked. "Christiania," he said. After I had told him that I had returned only two months before, that the country was booming because of war profits, that Grieg's niece was one of my best friends, and what have you—a conversation that was like old home week—we finally got down to business.

He said that his attention had just been called to a report in my induction papers that I had high qualifications in the music field. At the moment Fort Slocum was in great need of a man like me, especially since I had also had experience in the theatrical field. He went on to explain his overall problem; he had a permanent

103

band of eighty, composed mostly of Germans born abroad. There was also a reserve of about a hundred and fifty men, who needed further training.

Mr. Petersen's immediate problem was that Broadway shows were being sent to the fort twice a week to entertain the boys, but his German assistant band leader and the orchestra leader just couldn't play jazz or get the hang of accompanying the actors. Many of the show companies were refusing to return, claiming that the orchestra ruined their act. Would I be willing to become a member of the permanent band and did I think I could direct the men and music to the satisfaction of the actors? After two days as a nonentity in the mob, I felt like an individual again as my morale rebounded.

I said that I wished to do what would be most useful. The bandmaster immediately dispatched a message to my sergeant that I was not going to leave with the rest of my group. He told me that he would have me transferred to the band barracks as soon as possible. In the meantime, I was to return to my barracks to await further instructions. I did, just in time to see the rest of our contingent departing for Fort Dix.

Lying in my bunk that night in a barracks almost deserted and peacefully quiet, I marveled at how mob psychology can change your personality so quickly. It made me callous and indifferent to what would happen to those boys. I only felt jubilation because now I would get some sleep.

It was different as the next morning I awakened refreshed from a sound sleep. I had something to look forward to. Instead of a hundred, there were now only about ten of us to stand reveille at five o'clock. Starting right after breakfast and continuing until five that evening, we were processed through the induction routine. By the end of the day I was a full-fledged soldier, even if I did have the silly look of a new recruit whose uniform didn't fit properly. The last move was to sell my new civilian suit, which I had recently purchased for $25, for $3.

When I had finished the routine, I found my orders to move into the band barracks. There I was assigned to a cot in a room with some fifty other snorers. With no upper bunks and plenty of space between the cots, the place was agreeable and had a clean look.

The ordinary soldier's life is a very dismal one. If he has any brains or initiative, he is discouraged from using them, and with good reason, for since he is always acting in great numbers, it is important to act with concerted power, and therefore obeying orders is of utmost importance. So the average GI cannot make plans for himself, stops using his head, and amuses himself as best he can sitting around awaiting orders.

Next morning I was called into the office of the bandmaster for a long talk. The result was that I was given carte blanche to form an orchestra as soon as I became familiar with the proficiency of the men available. There were some two hundred of them. When in doubt about anything, I was to consult with the assistant band leader. It would take at least a week to get acquainted and size up the situation.

Also, I had to learn to play a band instrument. Did I have any choice? Knowing that, except for the drums, the saxophone was easiest, I chose the alto sax.

After mulling over the situation for most of the night, I decided that I must find out how the assistant band leader felt about the orchestra's being taken over by a brand new buck private. It seemed only natural that he would resent it; if not, he could be of great help. So this was the first man I looked up the next morning.

He was a German of about forty who had a nice room of his own in the barracks but lived with his wife and child in an apartment in New Rochelle, a town close by. He invited me into his room, and I told him that I had just returned from five and a half years' study abroad. He asked me about events and conditions there, and after we had talked for about an hour, we were like old buddies.

The conversation had come around to the orchestra when he jumped up, took his violin out of its case, along with some sheet music, and said, "Here is a piece I've been trying to learn how to play all my life, and I am still unable to play it. Would you play it for me, so I'll know how it really sounds?" It was a difficult arrangement of operatic airs which I had never heard of, let alone played. This I told him, with the reminder that it would be sight-reading. I played the number with the greatest of ease, along with a few really difficult ones of my own. The result of this was we became good friends, and he helped me in every way possible to organize the orchestra. Who said miracles don't happen?

Since he wasn't sleeping in his room, he invited me to move in. In addition to this, I was given a permanent pass, which gave me the right to leave the post at any time my services were not required. All this seemed too good to be true. Everything seemed to be falling into place nicely by my doing what came naturally.

The first two weeks I spent meeting men through introductions by either the band leader or his assistant; then, with advice from the latter, we produced an orchestra of eight from the permanent band and seven from the unattached recruits. We eliminated all but one of the Germans who had been in the former orchestra. They were older men who had been in the service for some time. I feared they might be offended, but was reassured by the assistant band leader, who said, "When you have been in the army as long as they have, you don't do any more work than you have to."

After a week of daily rehearsals, we took on the task of playing for the Broadway shows which came to entertain our troops.

When I moved into my private room, I was not obliged to get up to stand reveille. Since my high school days, when I had had to get up at three in the morning to drive the milk wagon into the country, I had been accustomed to going to bed at a late hour, and this reveille business was very repulsive to me. Aside from the wearing of canvas leggings and a stiff stand-up coat collar, which I never did get used to, my life was a relatively happy one— certainly much happier than the average doughboy experiences. I have never stopped being thankful to the bandmaster and his assistant, who helped make it that way.

I bought a saxophone self-instruction book for seventy-five cents and within a month I had learned to play well enough to join the band. My army pay was eighteen dollars a month from which life insurance, laundry and a few other deductions were withheld.

The martial music on parade thrilled me. I rarely missed participating, although I had the regular excuse that the orchestra had been out playing the night before.

The government had set a date after which no more volunteers would be accepted. This was within a month or two. Now they came flooding into our recruiting station in such numbers that our facilities were overwhelmed. After the drill hall and every other building had been filled with cots, tents were erected on every inch of space available. Even this wasn't sufficient. Entry onto our island had to be cut off, and the overflow of volunteers flooded the town of New Rochelle. All the schools, churches, parish houses, and even many private homes were filled with recruits.

Winter came early that year, and it was the most severe one in a long time. For weeks the thermometer hovered around zero and below. The boys sleeping in the tents almost froze, since there was a shortage of blankets and they had to be rationed.

It was heart-warming to see how the citizens of New Rochelle cooperated in such an emergency. It always has been a mystery to me why humanity needs distress to make it rise above the ordinary yet becomes lethargic when it comes to working for peace.

All work at the post was concentrated on processing the newcomers and moving them on to less crowded locations. Any thought of entertainment was out of the question because of lack of space; so I took advantage of the lull in my work to accept an invitation from a cousin in New York to have Thanksgiving dinner with her and her family.

When the day came, the lines of boys waiting for the ferry to the mainland stretched in all directions over the island. I stood from 9:00 in the morning until 3:00 in the afternoon in the below-zero cold before my turn came. By this time I was numb from head to foot, and decided to go to a hotel in New York City for a hot bath before proceeding to my cousin's.

Lying in that tub, it took me about fifteen minutes to thaw out. On emerging, I was surprised to see that my body was covered with a red rash. Realizing that this could be something serious, I called my cousin to say that I would have to return to the post immediately. Since I had not had anything to eat since breakfast, my hunger was at high pitch. I ate a good meal and, feeling a little better, decided to go to bed and return to the post first thing in the morning.

At the post hospital, the doctor diagnosed my case as measles and sent me to the isolation ward. There I idled for three weeks, along with a changing population averaging about fifteen boys, whom I often entertained with my violin and card tricks in the evening.

Returning to duty and finding that the post was still over-crowded, with the consequent lull in my work, I began to realize that any advancement for me at this post would be dependent on some higher-up's dying. I asked our bandmaster if he had had any requests for a bandmaster lately. "Yes," he said. "Here is one from an outfit at Fort Dix just getting ready to sail." Would he mind if I went over and applied for it? "No," he said. "What's more, I'll give you a good recommendation. But do be cautious; there are many commanding officers who have low opinions about bands. Also, talk to the men themselves to gauge their intelligence; otherwise, you might get into a most unhappy mess." Next morning I started out early and found the company already on shipboard, due to depart at any moment. I found the commanding officer to be a pleasant person; he informed me that this was a completely new outfit without any training whatsoever. They were being rushed over to boost the morale of the French, and the men in the band were there only because they had expressed a desire to be in it. It was uncertain how much any of them could play. It would be up to the bandmaster to make musicians of them.

After that he introduced me to the assistant band leader, who told me that they hadn't had any rehearsals because they hadn't received any music; many of the men didn't have instruments; and, finally, nine of them were in the brig for various mis-demeanors. This last remark did it. Up to that time I had been thinking, "Here is an opportunity to start something from scratch. It will be a challenge." But this was a situation requiring a strict disciplinarian. It wasn't in my nature to be one, and I gave the commanding officer this reason for not accepting the job. Back at my post that evening, my bandmaster fully approved of my decision.

Several months later I went on a similar expedition to Fort Jay. This time the commanding officer proved to be such a dis-agreeable tough guy that I ended our talk at the earliest convenient moment.

During this time, when Fort Slocum was so overcrowded, the band made intermittent excursions into New York City to play at rallies at which famous actors like Charlie Chaplin, Elsie Janis, and others were selling Liberty Bonds.

Now and then I dropped in to visit the Heifetz family. On one occasion when Papa Heifetz opened the door, it was immediately apparent that he was in a great stew. His hands were simulating the tearing out of his hair, which was practically nonexistent, while he uttered curses about that son of his not wanting to practice. This was at a time just after Jascha had made one of the most sensational debuts in Carnegie Hall history and just three days before he was to give a third concert. Now quoting Papa: "Can you imagine it? He hasn't touched the violin in a week; in three days he is playing a completely new program including that most difficult "Il Palpiti' of Paganini, which he hasn't played for at least a year, and five minutes ago he had the nerve to tell me, 'Don't worry, Papa, everything will be all right.' " I didn't linger long that day, and I could not go to the concert; but I waited impatiently for the newspapers the next day. Jascha was right. Again he was acclaimed a sensation.

The orchestra was becoming popular off the post. Almost every night we played at entertainments or dances. Often we would be gone three or four days at a time without returning to the post, and would have to sleep in a dormitory in a hotel (rented by the government) where soldiers, many of them drunk, would come to get a few hours' sleep. The way they robbed each other was scandalous. We soon learned that the only way to wake up in the morning with any clothes to put on was to make a bundle of everything around our shoes and use it as a pillow. We would have to check our instruments at the office.

While we are on the subject of thievery, I soon learned that there is something about it which is endemic to soldiers. For instance, when we arrived in cities and towns for parades, we usually were several hours too early, in which case we would be allowed to sit in a schoolhouse until parade time. Invariably there were those who would start searching for small objects which could be concealed in their pockets. Chalk and erasers were the most visible things lying around loose. They would disappear as if by magic. Once I asked one of the boys, "Why, when you know very well that you have absolutely no use for what you have stolen, do you take such things?" His reply was, "Oh, I don't really know; maybe it's some kind of urge within me; anyway, I get a kick out of it."

Long Island Sound had frozen over, and, mind you, this was salt water. Now spring arrived and another bit of luck was dropped into my lap. A civilian friend of one of the German boys in the band had a sixteen-foot motor launch which he had been using for fishing in our area for a number of years. He had received notice from the government that since he was not a United States citizen he would not be allowed to fish in or travel on the waters of Long Island Sound, and he was looking for someone who would use and take care of his launch for the duration. I jumped at the chance. Although I was not an enthusiastic fisherman, I did spend many a delightful hour just cruising.

At about this time I began having an occasional meal at one of the canteens in New Rochelle set up for servicemen. One of the volunteers there was named Eunice Ball. She struck my fancy. One thing led to another; my visits got more frequent; and before long I was seeing her at her home, where I enjoyed many a good meal in a congenial atmosphere.

In the beginning Eunice would go boat riding with me properly chaperoned by her mother or sister. Later we were allowed to go alone. I built five or six lobster traps, which we set out in the sound, and soon the Ball family was being supplied with five to fifteen pounds of lobster twice a week. They had so much lobster that they were canning it.

With these developments, I lost all interest in trying for a bandmaster's job; I was more than comfortably situated, even though the pay was miserly.

From the foregoing you might get the impression that I had very little to do. Quite the contrary. In the summertime the orchestra had Broadway shows four times weekly. Other nights we played for dances and block parties. Although we didn't have to get up for reveille, we had to go out with the band in the afternoon when occasion demanded. It was rare that I had a night free; so most of my recreation was in the daytime. There was great variety in the work; boredom was out of the question.

Considering the hell that our boys were going through in France, our life here was a picnic.

But wait a minute. Soon we were involved in a terrible catastrophe. The great flu epidemic struck us like a lightning bolt. It had already made its appearance in other cities, which gave our commanding officer of the Medical Corps the opportunity to lecture on precautionary measures. He himself set us an example by carrying a roll of toilet paper and always tearing off a sheet for protection whenever he touched door handles and other objects.

Would you believe it? He was the first one to catch the flu. Of course, the ribbing he got was most embarrassing. With overcrowded conditions, the epidemic spread like wildfire and the death rate became appalling. One of the first to succumb was our assistant bandmaster. He fell ill and died at his home in New Rochelle. By this time our post had been quarantined and we couldn't even attend the funeral. His death was a blow to me because we had become such good friends. I will never forget him and his many kindnesses.

Now I was chosen to be assistant bandmaster over the heads of all the other members of the band. Of course, many non-commissioned officers who outranked me didn't like this, but there wasn't anything they could do but gripe. Actually, I had made no effort to get the job and felt no guilt about it.

Thanks to my predecessor, I was already living in the assistant bandmaster's room and didn't have to move; but it did throw more band work on my shoulders because I often had to rehearse and conduct them on parade and in concerts.

Normally our recruiting station was equipped to handle about 4,000 men, but at the height of the epidemic there were some 10,000 on the island. The hospital, drill hall, and other available spaces were filled with bedridden patients. Deaths were averaging 100 and more a day. With only fifty horses and fifty caissons at the post, the band had to escort two or more funeral processions of flag-draped coffins the quarter mile from the hospital to the ferry every day.

One day there were exactly 101 coffins. The first 50 were duly delivered. The problem was what to do about the fifty-first in the next batch so that we wouldn't have to make a third trip. Before

111

long, someone found a wagon which could be transformed into a caisson. Another suggested, "Why not borrow the mule from the garbage route?" No sooner said than done, and the procession was off.

The route was in the rear of officers' quarters. This was the regular garbage route, and the mule had worked on it for years. Luckily, he was at the end of the procession, because at the first garbage can he stopped and no amount of persuasion could make him budge. Finally the driver had an inspiration. He got off the wagon and rattled the cans about a bit, and the mule moved on unconcernedly to the next cans, where the driver had to go through the same procedure, and so on down the line. They arrived at the ferry a half hour late.

I haven't any idea how many men succumbed to the flu at our post; the number must have been in the thousands. The great majority were farm boys from upstate New York and New England who hadn't built up the immunity to germs that the city boys had. It came as a shock after the war, to learn what a large number of boys from those areas were illiterate.

Quarantine confined us to the island for at least two months. During that time our only activities were rehearsals and funeral processions to the ferry. We did have one bit of joy in all that gloom—the news of the armistice! Now we looked forward to being discharged and to making plans for the future. For me, the most disagreeable aspect of army life was the uncertainty. I gradually acquired a fatalistic frame of mind and lived only from day to day.

After the first of the year, the government put on a special effort to sell Victory Bonds, and we again participated in New York City concerts and parades. With our elderly bandmaster ailing, much of the directing was transferred to me.

When spring arrived, the drafted men were being discharged at such a rate that our work was cut to a minimum. This gave me the opportunity to spend much time on the water in my motor launch before returning it to its owner. Eunice again accompanied me on many an outing, often with members of her family, when we would gather mussels, swim, or just cruise.

Because I had volunteered and was therefore in the regular army, and since draftees were given priority, it seemed ages before my discharge was processed. Finally it did arrive, on August 12, 1919; and I was a free man again. It didn't take long for me to bid good-bye to my friends in the band, most of whom were permanent enlistees. Then I removed myself and a few belongings to a room with a family in New Rochelle.

13

THE NEW YORK
STRING QUARTET

I was a civilian now and felt like a displaced human being. Away for six years in Europe and two in the army, I had become disassociated from the stream of life in the United States. The problem of finding a niche where my talents would be sought after and where I would be happy seemed enormous. (Fort Slocum was a principality with a government all its own, and I never felt there that we and the civilians were of the same nationality. We had circulated among them almost daily, but it was as though we were visitors in a country with which we had no particular connection.) It was a frightening period of great uncertainty and loneliness.

Realizing that the whole field of concert violinists was limited to four or five exceptional talents who had to have strong financial backing, I considered the next step down—chamber music. But no American quartet up to this time had been successful; so that was out. I had to earn my living. The next possibility was a position with one of the more prominent orchestras. Franz Kneisel once told me, "A violinist in an orchestra can play like an angel and nobody hears him, but let him play a wrong note and everybody would like to murder him." However, I reasoned, one always plays the highest type of music in an orchestra and the opportunities for a job are relatively plentiful for qualified men. I had already had six months' experience with the Tonkunstler Orchestra in Vienna and enjoyed the work; so the decision to try for an orchestra job seemed logical.

I wrote to the business managers of the Boston, New York, and Cleveland Symphony Orchestras, as well as to the New York

Philharmonic. Replies were as follows: from Boston, "No vacancy"; from the New York Symphony, "Mr. Damrosch is at Bar Harbor, will be back in New York early October—apply then"; from the New York Philharmonic, "Mr. Stransky is in Europe, will be back in New York early October—apply then"; from the Cleveland Symphony, "The conductor (I forget his name) will be in New York in several weeks—come (to such-and-such a hotel at a specified time) for an audition."

While I was in the army I had neglected violin practice because it was almost impossible to concentrate with so much going on. As soon as I was discharged, I resumed practice with a vengeance, and I was slowly getting back into shape again.

My audition with the Cleveland conductor went well; he was anxious to have me sign a contract on the spot. But I was aiming for New York, where the finest musicians in the country were concentrated and musical standards were highest. I thanked the conductor, saying that I had other opportunities to explore before making a decision.

Damrosch returned in early October and asked me to come to his house for an audition. After we had finished, he said, "There is one vacancy in the violin section and there are six applications for it. You are the first I have heard; until I have heard the other five, I can make no decision. My secretary will tell you within a couple of weeks what conclusion we come to."

Then a letter arrived from the New York Philharmonic. Mr. Stransky would like me to come for an audition. Thank goodness it was destined never to take place, for in the same mail another letter arrived—this from the cellist of the New York String Quartet. He wrote that they had organized the quartet about six months before, that their second violinist was proving unsatisfactory, and that I had been recommended by a colleague. Was I available? Was I!

The chances against this happening to anyone were about a million to one. Now my future took on a much brighter outlook. The only question was, would I be accepted and fit into the group? After a sleepless night, I decided that writing was too slow; I took the train into New York and called on Mr. Vaska, the cellist. We agreed that I should attend their rehearsal the following morning. The address turned out to be the town house of Joseph Pulitzer, publisher of the New York *World* and of Pulitzer Prize fame.

I went back to New Rochelle and practiced for some six hours. Next morning at the rehearsal everything went splendidly. It soon became apparent to them that I could fill the slot. They must have noticed how thrilled *I* was.

They told me about Mr. and Mrs. Ralph Pulitzer. He was Joseph's eldest son and had been president of the New York *World* since his father's death. Frederica was the daughter of Dr. and Mrs. W. Seward Webb. (Mrs. Webb was born Lila Vanderbilt, a daughter of William H. Vanderbilt.) The Pulitzers had founded the quartet to fill a need for chamber music in this country. Actually, it was Ludvik Schwab, Kubelik's accompanist for many years and an excellent violist, who had become a friend of the Pulitzers and had interested them in the project. He got in touch with Bedrich Vaska, cellist of the Sevcik Quartet, known throughout Europe, who had recently come to this country. They brought in Ottokar Cadek, the first violinist, and another violinist who had proved unsatisfactory. They believed it was important to have four Czechs or Czech descendants. (Their feeling for the music would be sympathetic.)

Now that I was accepted by the group, I was told that Mr. and Mrs. Pulitzer had given us three years to perfect an ensemble before making our debut. In the meantime, we would appear only for private concerts at either of the two Pulitzer houses—in the winter at 17 East 73rd Street, New York City, and in the summer at Manhasset, Long Island.

The quartet was to be a democratic one; all players were equal in authority and would share future proceeds equally. Monthly salaries were to be paid until the quartet established itself. This seemed too good to be true, and it took time for me to become convinced of its reality. I was especially happy that finally I was back on my own feet and didn't have to depend on my parents for support. Of course, it gave me the greatest delight to inform the New York Symphony, the New York Philharmonic, and the Cleveland Symphony that I was no longer available.

We rehearsed daily except Sundays, from nine to one, at the Joseph Pulitzer town house. Ralph and Frederica Pulitzer lived next door in a much smaller house. Since the death of her

Our beloved Mr. and Mrs. Cyril H. Jones, circa 1925.

husband in 1911, the elder Mrs. Pulitzer had made her home elsewhere, and her house was deserted except for a small crew of servants. Therefore, we were allowed to use her husband's study for our practice room—ideal because it was soundproof. "Old J. P.," as he was affectionately called, was a crotchety person. As he became more blind he seemed to develop a more acute sense of hearing, and so the slightest extraneous noises annoyed him. Hence, his sections of their houses were soundproofed.

We were fortunate to have such a beautifully furnished and quiet room to rehearse in for some three years, although we never saw Mrs. J. P. in all that time. (Before her marriage she was Kate Davis, a daughter of Jefferson Davis, President of the Confederacy, and was reputed to have been the most beautiful belle of the South.)

Now I had to make a decision. It was thirty miles into New York from New Rochelle, and it took an hour and a half to get from door to door, if there were no delays. Balancing the pros and cons, I chose to sacrifice the three hours because I preferred my girl, my room, and the chance to see grass and trees to apartment living in New York City. Actually, the three hours spent in transit turned out to be an advantage, because I had time to read the New York *World* or the New York *Times* from cover to cover. I was able to catch up with what was happening in America, something I had missed for eight long years.

After about a week's rehearsing, it was clear that we fitted together like four peas in a pod. Of course, each of us had his own preferences in interpretation. Much time was consumed in discussion until we concluded that it would be best to let each player lead according to his feeling whenever he had the principal part. This gave our quartet the reputation, later on, of playing with more freedom and abandon than others, and proved to be one of the reasons for our success.

Now it was suggested by our violist and cellist that Cadek and I try exchanging first and second violin parts for a few months to see which combination sounded best. In a first-class quartet there is no such thing as who is the better player. If any player is inferior, he will do the combination no good and will not be acceptable. In an orchestra you might be able to conceal an inferior player, but in a quartet, where every man is a soloist and each part is totally exposed, any inferiority is evident, especially when there are three others with which to be compared. The problem thus resolves into fitting the playing to the part.

As an illustration, let us take a vocal quartet. It takes a completely different type of singing and singer when singing soprano and alto. The latter voice requires more robustness and so progressively down the scale to the bass, who must be heaviest and most virile.

We might equate the idea with baseball, where there are nine positions. Rarely do you find a man who can play more than one or two of them well. Ballplayers are chosen because their playing has certain qualities which fit the positions they are to play. So it is with players in a string quartet.

It is in the nature of acoustics that the two outside voices sound more prominently than the two inside voices. This is best explained by the fact that in a seventy-piece band only one piccolo and one tuba player are required along with the other sixty-eight. Indeed, in good music appreciation classes one is taught, when listening to a quartet, to concentrate on the two middle voices because the other two will be heard without effort.

We experimented by changing parts for about six months when we and others whose opinions we valued concluded that the total balance was much better when I played second violin. Having settled this, we stopped changing parts except on rare occasions.

Now came the problem of seating arrangements. You who are knowledgeable in this matter will have noticed that some quartets seat the second violinist opposite the first and some seat the violist there. Either way, you can be sure that of the two his tone is the more powerful, because he is the only one of the four whose instrument is facing with f-holes away from the audience and is therefore playing at a great disadvantage as far as audibility is concerned. Of course, the musicians could sit in a row facing the audience, but they would have the greater disadvantage of not being able to see each other. So, since they all recognize the handicap which the man seated in that position is under, they allow him to play a little louder.

After some experimentation, I was chosen for the spot opposite the first violinist. That settled the seating arrangement for the life of the quartet. Now we settled down to perfecting our ensemble and devoting more time to detail.

All that winter we rehearsed four hours a day, six days a week, and gave a Sunday evening performance for a group at the Pulitzers' house once a month. Early in May the Pulitzers moved to Kiluna Farms, their summer place at Manhasset, Long Island. We spent many a weekend there, playing tennis, cards, and swimming, as well as performing as a quartet. At least ten other guests were always there; so we came to know many interesting people.

During the second spring of the quartet, Mrs. Pulitzer surprised us with a proposal that we all spend the summer in a large house near Burlington, Vermont, on Lake Champlain. This was the first house her parents had built on coming to that state and was close to Shelburne Farms, the 5,000-acre estate on which they now lived. We all were enthusiastic about the idea, and we moved there in early June. It was a Shangri-la, nicely isolated, in which to prepare for our debut in New York, planned for the fall of 1922.

There were ten of us in our little colony: Mrs. Pulitzer and one son, two maids, a chauffeur, four of us musicians, and the cellist's wife. (The violist's wife chose to stay in New York. Cadek and I were still bachelors.) What with boating, swimming, hiking, and a Rolls Royce at our disposal, life was idyllic, to say the very least.

One day, however, we almost had a fatal catastrophe, which could have brought the whole dream to a tragic end. About six of us were having a swim in a bay which was bounded partly by the shore and partly by a dock which the Webbs had constructed for their yacht. This bay was about the width of two football fields measured lengthwise. I had just constructed a fifteen-foot-high diving board on the dock and was standing there getting set to take my first dive. Suddenly I heard cries of "Help!" coming from the middle of the bay.

Looking up, I saw Mrs. Pultizer struggling to keep afloat. Quick as a flash, I dived in and raced to her side. Fortunately, she hadn't swallowed much water and was not panicky. I said quietly, "Put your hand on my shoulder and go limp." This she did, and I towed her to shore without any trouble. She recovered quickly and explained that she had had a cramp in one leg. I felt grateful that I happened to be there at this particular time because all the others in our party were weak swimmers who could not have helped her. Thereafter, we were more cautious and had a rowboat handy at all times.

In September we returned to New York and resumed our regular practicing routine.

On November 4, 1921, Eunice Ball and I were married in a civil ceremony at the Marriage Bureau in New York City Hall. After a delicious wedding supper at Sherry's with Eunice's family, we returned to New Rochelle, Eunice and I to our new six-room house, which we had just purchased on a shoestring.

In retrospect, I can't think of a more foolish act than the purchase of that house, though we did get great pleasure in gradually furnishing it through the years. The small down payment was mostly borrowed money, the house was in a declining neighborhood and was much bigger than we needed, the mortgage payments were enormous in proportion to our income, and the future of the quartet was by no means assured.

Up to this time no American string quartet had been able to support itself from concerts alone. Being immature in chamber music and uncertain as to how the quartet would be received by the public, my wife and I were buried in a multiplicity of intangibles. (Fortunately, the quartet turned out to be a great success. With Eunice working as a schoolteacher and my doing any and all repairs around the house, we managed to keep the wolf from our door.)

At Christmastime Mrs. Pulitzer invited the quartet and their wives to spend the holidays at the 50,000 acre Webb estate at Nehasene, in the Adirondacks. The place was so secluded that the only way to get into it was by the railroad which Dr. Webb had had built from Utica to Montreal. There was a railroad station inside the confines of Nehasene, but no one was allowed to alight there without written permission from the Webbs. Although there were roads within the estate, there were none leading into it. Ten families lived there the year around, taking care of forestry chores.

Here we spent ten delightful days at the hunting lodge, which had an enormous fireplace into which were fed logs as thick as telephone poles and eight feet long. A hill behind the lodge gave us some good tobogganing and snowshoeing.

When the thermometer got down to forty-two below zero for four or five days, no one ventured out. Eunice and I thought the others were sissies; so we decided to show them. We weren't out more than two or three minutes before we rushed back in, the tips of our fingers and toes hurting intensely. This astounded me, because I had spent two winters in St. Petersburg without suffering.

All winter the quartet rehearsed daily and continued the monthly intimate recitals, by springtime we had covered the greater part of quartet and quintet literature.

Now Mrs. Pulitzer came up with another surprise. She first asked if we would like to spend the summer on Lake Champlain again. This query received a resounding yes. Then she offered to build each of us a cottage of his own on the property. Those who preferred to live in the big house as they had last year could do so.

I was the only one to accept the offer. Two months later Eunice and I moved into our own cottage right on the shore of Lake Champlain, with a view of the Adirondack mountains across the lake. Of course we had to work to make the place livable, but soon we were ready for the parade of relatives and friends who came to visit us.

Eunice and I loved the outdoors; it was most restful to lie in bed listening to the waves playing a lullaby on the rocks just below us.

The cottage was nearly a mile from the big house. Every day I walked there through the meadows, rain or shine. Rehearsals were now being directed toward our New York debut in Aeolian Hall on October 26, 1922.

Back in the city in mid-September, the quartet got right down to the regular routine, but it seemed as though the big night would never arrive. On October 25, something unexpected happened.

I was chopping wood in our cellar when a foot-long piece of kindling flew up and struck me across the right eye. It ruptured the iris, leaving it sightless, and the left eye with but little vision. What a pretty how-do-you-do, the day before the big concert! Eunice and I rushed to New York City to a specialist, who explained that the left eye was suffering from shock because of the accident to the right one, and there was nothing he could do but bandage the eyes. I was to go to bed for about two weeks to give them a chance to heal.

Home I went for the rest of that day and the next. With Eunice's help, I appeared at Aeolian Hall in time to play. Of course I had been in touch with the other members of the

My wife Eunice on the shore of Lake Champlain at Shelburne, Vermont, shortly after we were married, 1921.

quartet, and they were apprehensive—so was I, for that matter—as to whether I would be able to play my part more or less from memory. But at this late hour I could only give it a good try and hope that with the thorough rehearsing we had given the program, all would go well.

At Aeolian Hall, we all retired to separate dressing rooms to limber up our fingers. Promptly at 8:30 a knock and a man's voice sounded at the door, summoning us on stage. Removing the patch from my damaged eye, I proceeded, trembling, to the stagedoor, where my companions already stood waiting. The houselights were being dimmed, and slowly the chatter of the audience subsided. All four of us were in a state of high tension. This was the great moment that we had been aiming at for three years. Just when we were expecting to see that door open, the attendant whispered loudly, "Gentlemen, are your pants buttoned?" We smothered our bursts of laughter; and when he finally opened the door, we walked out in a much more composed state.

During the first fifteen minutes, there were some ragged moments due to our nervousness; but after that we played in our best form. I was able to see a little up to the middle of the program, which was a big help; then my good eye began to tire. By the end I could see nothing but large objects. Right from the beginning I had been testing out my memory, so that when the little sight I had began to fail, I was prepared for it. But let's be honest: my relief when the concert was over—and successful—was enormous.

Eunice and I went home as soon as we could tear ourselves away from a host of well-wishers. The rest of our party left for an after-concert supper given by the Pulitzers.

The next day I had a thorough examination. The ophthalmologist ordered me to go to bed and stay there, with both eyes bandaged, for two weeks, in order to give the ruptured iris a chance to heal. After the two weeks were up, I returned for another examination and got the good news that the sight in the undamaged eye had returned to normal and that, with the help of eye glasses the vision in both eyes would be restored to twenty-twenty. I don't need to elaborate on my joy at hearing this wonderful news.

Our concert proved to be such a success that we immediately

made plans for two more within three months. They turned out even more happily. This led to signing with Arthur Judson, manager of the New York Philharmonic and Philadelphia Orchestras and head of the most important concert bureau in the country. He wasn't sanguine about getting extensive bookings outside New York City, remarking that the American public was not yet educated to chamber music, but he was willing to give it a try.

Before we left for our summer home at Shelburne, early in June, we reserved three dates for concerts the following season, this time in Town Hall, because Aeolian Hall was being demolished.

Subsequently, we gave over a hundred concerts of our own in Town Hall, as well as many others under other auspices. I love the place dearly because of the thrills that ran up and down my spine when playing the music of the masters to the most appreciative audiences in the United States. The acoustics at Town Hall were quite good, although the interior decorating was uninspiring.

In retrospect, however, after playing in some fifteen hundred halls throughout the country, I still remember Carnegie Hall in New York and Carnegie Hall in Pittsburgh and the hall at Bryn Mawr College as the most beautiful and acoustically perfect.

We spent another happy summer on Lake Champlain with the usual mixture of work and sports.

In New York early in October, we were happy to learn that our manager had been able to book us for a few concerts in the East before the first of the year; another immediately thereafter—a joint concert with the great pianist Ossip Gabrilovitch, for the swank Palm Beach Musical Society; and then a two-month tour on the Pacific Coast with the brilliant pianist Percy Grainger.

About this time we were approached by the Western Electric Company, which is the manufacturing and experimental division of the Bell Telephone Company, to make some tests for a new apparatus which reproduced sound simultaneously with pictures. (Later this became television.) It had reached the stage in its development where it could be used for nonmoving objects. They were experimenting with a combination of sound and movement which seemed insoluble, but the prospects of using this medium for bringing great music and great artists to outlying districts

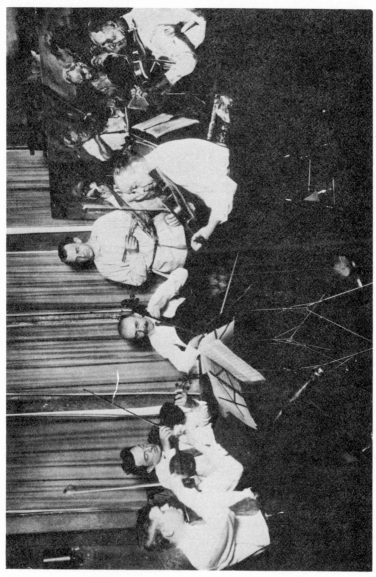

The New York String Quartet being painted by artist Walter Goldbeck. *Left to right:* Ottokar Cadek, violin; Jaroslav Siskovsky, violin; Bedrich Vaska, cello; Ludvik Schwab, viola. This photo appeared in the Sunday rotogravure section of the New York *Times*, August 2, 1925.

seemed feasible. Anticipating this as a source of great profit, we made arrangements to go to the company laboratories on the lower west side of Manhattan. At least a dozen technicians hovered around, positioning us in relation to klieg lights, cameras, and sound equipment. After many short tests which were played back and to which we listened, offering suggestions, it was decided that we should play a whole composition. We started, and within a few minutes were perspiring as if we were in a steam bath. Still we kept on playing; but when the varnish on our violins began to smell, we jumped up and got as far away as possible from the klieg lights. So ended our venture into television.

Before the Christmas holidays we gave about a dozen concerts within an area of 300 miles of New York City, including two of the three scheduled for Town Hall.

In January 1923 we took the train to Palm Beach, where we were welcomed by a Mr. Reiter. His palatial house had a beautiful music room seating about 300, where the concert for the Palm Beach Music Club was to take place. A rehearsal was arranged for that afternoon with the pianist, Gabrilovitch, who was to play the Schumann quintet with us.

We were invited to dinner with the Reiters before the concert. During cocktails it was my good fortune to meet Mrs. Gabrilovitch, who was Clara Clemens, daughter of Mark Twain. She seemed rather taciturn at first, but by the time we sat down to dinner next to each other, a couple of cocktails had limbered up our tongues considerably.

Here was a chance to learn about one of my favorite authors. Clara, seeing that the subject was dear to my heart, entertained me with stories about life with father. One thing she said that surprised me was that he hated writing. Although it was his only source of income, he would keep putting it off until his debts were so numerous that no one would sell him anything on credit. Then, and only then, would he isolate himself, writing all hours of the day or night, usually propped up in bed, until he had finished a book or enough magazine articles to pay the debts. Then he would resume his favorite pastime—playing billiards with the boys at the pool hall until the wee hours of the morning, then going home to sleep most of the day.

Clara was an accomplished singer with a very good alto voice; so at her suggestion, we gave about ten joint concerts in as many cities in the East a year later, during which we became very good friends.

The music room at the Reiters' was filled to capacity with a most select audience, almost every one of whom was known in the financial, industrial, business, or art world. The concert was a huge success. The soft applause had given us concern; but, we found out later, it was due to the fact that the ladies, who were in the majority, all wore gloves. Any doubts were dispelled when, after the concert, Paris Singer, son of the sewing machine magnate, came to us with congratulations and a request to discuss the possibility of our giving a daily concert for a month during the following winter. We assured him we would be available and would meet him next morning as requested.

Arriving punctually the next morning, we found Mr. Singer in an exuberant mood. He told us that he had studied the cello for about eight years, was a lover of chamber music, and had lain awake all night making plans for just such quartet evenings as he had proposed to us.

He was in the process of remodeling a hotel which the government had used to house convalescing officers during World War I. It was to be the Everglades Club. There he would have his personal apartment and a music room seating about a hundred people. He offered to pay us just what we received for concerts on the road. This appealed to us since it eliminated all traveling expenses except transportation to and from New York. It didn't take long to sign a contract to appear from January 15 to February 15 the following year. We returned to New York for our third Town Hall concert, four very happy men.

When we reached Washington station, a freshly fallen two inches of snow lay on the platform. This was the first sight of snow for most of those Floridians; and their gambols, feeling, tasting and smelling it, were very amusing, finally winding up with a snowball fight.

Immediately after this concert we left with Percy Grainger for a tour of about thirty cities on the West Coast. Grainger was a loner if there ever was one. Except for rehearsals, concerts, and interviews with reporters, we rarely saw him. We rode in

Pullman sleepers all the way; he rode in the day coach. I paid a few visits to him there; but, although polite enough, he made it quite clear that his mind was on other things.

One morning I went in rather early, to find him having breakfast out of that small carton usually handed out as one serving of Wheaties. He volunteered the information that dry cereal and a glass of water was all he ever had for breakfast.

Listen to him at an interview with reporters, though, and you would label him an extrovert. Once he got started, it was difficult to get a word in edgewise. Normally this tactic could be annoying, but he was so articulate, amusing, and interesting that we thoroughly enjoyed listening to him. Since none of us was as clever at repartee as he was, we were reluctant to break into the conversation except when asked a question point-blank. Of course, this meant that he got most of the publicity, but we couldn't do much about that.

We found the West Coast well developed musically. Our concerts, without exception, were enthusiastically received.

Let me turn to a few amusing incidents. It was our custom to arrive at a hall a half hour early for limbering up purposes. We invariably found Grainger there in his street clothes, seated at the piano, practicing away like an old trooper. He would continue until the hall was a quarter- to half-full, and would then vault off the stage, dart up the middle aisle, and out the entrance, through the incoming audience, to his hotel, where he would change into full dress and be back in time for his solo number, second on the program! This was possible because we opened with a string quartet which lasted forty minutes. He followed with the Grieg Piano Concerto, of about thirty minutes, after which we joined forces in a piano quintet.

It so happened that in one of the cities the piano furnished us lacked the short supporting stick for the lid which is used for chamber music and accompaniments. Without it, the piano, with lid fully open, would sound much too loud. Grainger did not discover this until we had seated ourselves for the third number and he had started to lower the lid. Finding the short stick missing, he quickly darted back stage to search for a substitute. Audience and quartet waited in silence for about three minutes. Suddenly he popped out of the wings, a broad smile on

129

his face, holding high an axe with half its handle broken off, which he proceeded to insert under the lid. The stillness was shattered by a paroxysm of laughter which could have been heard for blocks. This put the icing on the cake. After that we could have played anything and they would have enjoyed it.

A similar thing occurred which was even more bizarre in another city. We had just begun the piano quintet when Grainger put too much pressure on the pedals and the whole supporting lyre contraption fell to the floor. Taking a quick survey of what had happened, he darted back stage and luckily found the janitor, who supplied him with a monkey wrench. This he held on high as he proceeded to lie down on his back, in full dress, under the piano to reassemble the whole unit, within five minutes or so, while the audience giggled, and finally broke out in thunderous applause as he rose with the job completed.

This kind of unexpected mishap is loved by audiences everywhere and if you perform often enough you are bound to have them. Indeed, I know of a few artists who have contrived some of their own "mishaps" in order to assure the success of a concert.

The concert in Portland, Oregon, stands out as the highlight of that tour. It happened to fall on Armistice Day, only a few years after the end of World War I, when people celebrated by riding around in their cars backfiring their mufflers. As we rode in a taxi to the auditorium, the explosions all over town were deafening. We commented that we wouldn't be able to hear ourselves, nor would the audience hear us; but what a surprise when, two blocks from our destination, we were stopped by police who inquired if we were going to the concert—if not, we could not enter a two-block perimeter which had been cordoned off around the auditorium. Inside, the noise was very faint and not in the least disturbing.

What a thrill it was to step out before this enormous applauding audience, some 5,000 strong! Every seat was occupied, and standees were on the lower as well as the upper levels. When you first come out you don't see individuals, but rather a sea with waves of bobbing human heads. Later, after many bows, certain individuals in about the first ten rows will, for some reason or other, stand out and come to your attention.

Once you start playing (at least this is what happens to me) you become so absorbed in the music that the audience disappears as if by magic. Maybe it is because I have a one-track mind. But this audience couldn't be forgotten between numbers because the enthusiasm with which it applauded was so heart-warming. Huge crowds react to one another to intensify excitement.

In San Francisco we were entertained by a Sir X, who was court violinist to Queen Liliuokalani of Hawaii. At the luncheon we asked him how he came to be knighted, "Well, it was like this," he said. "One night I played exceptionally well for the queen. As I was leaving, she said, 'Good night,' and that did it."

We had had two months of being important people whose autographs were sought after, whose opinions were prized by reporters; whose playing was applauded by thousands; who had received rare praise from the critics, and who were wined, dined, and idolized by the musical gentry in the different cities.

With all the applause and adulation still ringing in our ears, we arrived home, where nobody knew a thing about it; so back we went to being treated like ordinary human beings. Such is life. Anyway, we were glad to get home after such a strenuous trip, ready to get started for summer camp early in June. When I say strenuous, I mean not only the concerts but the after-concert soirees and the travelling and the never-ending visits by well-meaning local individuals asking for favors and advice on how to become a great artist in six easy lessons, parents bringing their sons or daughters for us to confirm their opinion that they were nurturing a genius. Worst of all were the violin makers who had discovered the lost art of violin making, you find one or two in each city. Would we please try several of their violins? We would be surprised to hear how superior the tone was even to a Strad. Of course, we were never surprised, but did not want to hurt their feelings, since most of them were fanatics on the subject. It took some doing to think up enough innocuous platitudes to send the fellows home in a hopeful mood.

We started for our summer home early in June. All through the season we had a constant procession of Eunice's and my relatives which we enjoyed very much; but of course nothing was allowed to interfere with quartet practice, since we had been forewarned by our manager that the coming season would be a busy one.

That summer Mrs. Pulitzer told us that she had an opportunity

My mother, my sister Sylvia, and I when they visited us on the shore of Lake Champlain in Vermont in 1930.

to sell the 250-acre Oak Ledge property on which we were living; so we would not be returning to it next year. Instead, we were invited to move to the 5,000-acre Webb estate just across Shelburne Bay on Shelburne Point, where a large house was available for the other three members of the quartet and to which our cottage would be moved to a location of our choice.

Returning to New York early in October, we were happy to learn that our manager had already booked us for almost fifty concerts. These, added to the schedule at Palm Beach, would be considered a very big season for any artist.

For us it was a double satisfaction, not only because of the bookings, but also because now we could go to Mr. and Mrs. Pulitzer, thank them for the start they had given us, and say that now we would be able to carry on without further subsidy from them. This gesture endeared us to them while it deeply gratified us.

Now we were on our own, like young birds leaving their nest under the watchful eye of their proud mother. We were never in need of help for the remaining years of the quartet's existence.

During that time we gave three to five concerts every year at Town Hall, trying always to play a new work on each program, preferably by a modern composer. Thus, we introduced works by such musical giants as Sibelius, Hindemith, Bloch, and many others to New York audiences. They were little known in the United States in the early 1900s.

We also played many concerts for the Beethoven Association and the Bohemians, two musical clubs composed of concert artists from all over the world. The Beethoven Association was organized by concert pianist Harold Bauer for the purpose of giving five concerts yearly to benefit indigent musicians. The only way to join it was to be asked to participate in the concerts, which automatically made you a member. The programs were performed by top musicians in various combinations and became so popular that they were sold out a year in advance. I played in five concerts with different groups.

On the other hand, the Bohemians were practically the same musicians who met once a month at the Harvard Club for social purposes. They presented each member of our quartet with a silver cup. The inscription on my cup read, "With expression of highest esteem to their colleague, Jaroslav Siskovsky, from the Bohemians—New York."

On one evening, never to be forgotten, the Bohemians celebrated Kreisler's fiftieth birthday, and we were chosen to play his string quartet. After we had finished, Kreisler and other great violinists, such as Auer, Elman, and Zimbalist, took turns playing quartets on our instruments until four in the morning.

Then there were concerts at Carnegie Hall. On one occasion sixty harpists played at once. We played a harp quintet with Carlos Salzedo, probably the most famous harpist of all time.

At this time Carolyn Beebe organized the New York Chamber Music Society. Using our quartet as a nucleus, she added up to ten first-chair men from the New York Philharmonic Orchestra, according to instrumentation of the compositions played. Thus, we were able to present a rich repertoire of music seldom played for the public.

Six concerts a year were given in the ballroom of the Plaza Hotel to a select audience which paid $15 a person for a fine dinner and a concert. Since these were always on Sunday nights and only once a month, they did not interfere with our own quartet work; indeed, we were glad of the opportunity to become acquainted with this repertoire and to have that added variety. Then, too, we did quite a bit of playing in every one of the New York broadcasting studios—NBC, ABC, CBS, WOR. You can see that we were able to spend very little time at home.

Most of the time we were traveling. It was no easy job for our manager to arrange dates at a minimum cost and with a minimum amount of travel. All this had to be done a year in advance.

Since most of our concerts were without unusual incident, it would be tedious to quote many criticisms. Let me choose an account of just one.

The following criticism by Harvey Gaul, which appeared in the Pittsburgh *Post* on March 25, 1927, is typical of those we received all over the country.

You always may trust the Art Society to close well. One can't remember a season when this organization finished poorly, and last night at Carnegie Hall the Society closed its year, as it began, in a truly notable fashion. It was our finest evening of chamber music, chamber music that wasn't so formidable that it was disagreeable, but a list of compositions that was most attractive. The New York String Quartet we have heard before, but never to better advantage. What is it that makes a string quartet? Tone? Phrasing? Unanimity? If those are the attributes, then the New York String Quartet has them to a superlative degree.

Here one found *musique en camera* with the utmost minutiae, with the most polished phrasings, with a unanimity that knew not legato alone, but staccato and spiccato, and all timed like a single voice. It was a remarkable exposition, and, for those who enjoy ensemble playing, it was a sheer delight.

Then, going into a detailed description of each composition and the way it was played, Gaul ended his article with the following comment, "It was as perfect an evening of chamber music as we ever expect to hear, and the only regret is that it had to end."

On the road we were slaves to the timetables of the railroads. At that time there was little or no travel by bus, and we often had to travel several hundred miles in order to get to a town a relatively short distance away. This was especially true around Chicago and St. Louis, which were like the hubs of a wheel, where in order to get from one spoke to another you had to go into the hub and out again. Most of the time we took the sleeper, which got us to our next destination at odd hours the next day, sometimes inconveniently at 3:00 or 4:00 in the morning.

I always preferred an upper berth, because the air and the bed were better. Of course, one had to do a contortion act in dressing and undressing; but practice makes perfect. I even learned to climb up without bothering the porter for the ladder. Unfortunately, due to the high tension of my nerves after a concert and the irregularity of our hours, I never was able to sleep well on a train. My violin was the first thing that went into the hammock beside me, and then my clothes on top of that.

Vaska, our cellist, always took a lower berth, suspending his cello in his hammock above himself. Schwab, being a 200-pounder, always preferred a lower. And Cadek, our first violinist, took either berth with no preference.

Speaking of clothes reminds me of the fact that in our first few years we wore the conventional full dress when we appeared on the podium, namely, coat with tails, stiff bosom shirt front, high stiff collar, and white tie. It was like a strait jacket, an instrument of torture, and was most uncomfortable to play in. Being of an iconoclastic nature, I proposed one day that we play in tuxedos with soft silk shirts and low, soft collars. At first the others were horrified at the thought. It would be breaking with tradition. Still, I had the clinching argument on my side; that was that all agreed the outfits prevented freedom of movement. Let's give it a try and see what happens, I pleaded. We did, and from that time on we never wore full dress again. Actually, I think very few people noticed the difference.

We tried not to give more than four concerts a week, but there were frequently compelling circumstances which altered this resolve and made us add one or two more.

Because of differing train schedules, there is no such thing as a typical day, but I will attempt to give you a composite.

After having breakfast and going to our hotel rooms, we would be welcomed by the concert manager and any number of reporters, depending on the size of the town. After this interview, we would be driven around and shown "the best town in the United States." Then, most likely, there would be an invitation to attend a chamber of commerce, Rotary, or Kiwanis Club luncheon, which we did our best to avoid, but occasionally, for diplomatic reasons, had to attend. Usually they requested us to bring our instruments along and play a few tunes for them; but since they didn't mention payment for our services, we usually left our instruments behind.

After lunch we would separate, each going his own way. I would usually go walking into the central, older sections of the cities which were more representative and which our guide of the morning carefully avoided. No wonder; there wasn't much to be proud of there. Snce I wasn't able to sleep on trains, I always tried to nap from 4:00 to 6:00, which relaxed my nerves in preparation for the concert.

Vaska, our cellist, was a gregarious person. He seemed to have friends in almost every city and spent his afternoons either visiting them or writing and telephoning. The other two would go about their own business, mostly walking or napping.

The evening meal we had together; then we would taxi to the concert hall or theater early enough to have at least a half-hour to exercise our fingers and bow arms. During this period one always experiences a certain amount of nervous tension, but once seated before the audience and playing, this changes into great exhilaration.

After the concert there was the usual influx of enthusiasts into the dressing rooms; many music students among them, each wanting his program autographed or some advice pertaining to the art of violin playing.

Then there was usually a reception at the home of one of the principal devotees of music in the city. This was in Prohibition days, and when I think of the homemade or home-concocted hooch from dubious alcohol that we drank all over the country, I wonder how we ever survived such punishment. In the northern part of the country it was bathtub gin, which tasted horrible and didn't sit well. Around New Jersey it was applejack, which tasted a little better. On the West Coast it was a type of cognac made from grapes, which wasn't bad, but the only lift from it was a headache. Best of all was a corn liquor called white mule, common all over the South. Going down, it had an unpleasant, raw taste; but once down, the mule spread a warm glow all over you. I can't remember a single instance, no matter in what part of the country, where this kind of drinking didn't take place, which goes to show what hypocrisy Prohibition was.

On days when we had no concert we would spend mornings rehearsing, mostly on new works which composers kept sending in. There was no such thing as a boss, either when we were playing or other wise. You couldn't imagine a more democratic setup. Everything was decided by common consent. Our profits were remarkably small at the end of the year, after we paid hotel, railroad, managerial, and advertising expenses. We did stay in the best hotels on the road, but at home we had to live modestly.

Would that it were possible to convey to the layman the depth of feeling, the heavenly exultation that pervade one when performing a work by one of the great masters before a knowledgeable audience. As for me, I never had a richer reward.

We worked in complete harmony. In some music great liberties were taken, but after three or four years of rehearsing we could anticipate each other's action no matter how much it deviated from the conventional interpretation. Thus, all four of us were leaders at different times, depending on the construction of the music.

Cadek and I divided the chore of contact with our manager, Arthur Judson. Ordinarily, the manager lays out the railroad schedules. But, having worked for the railroads, I preferred to do it myself. That gave us much more freedom.

The social life on the road was not my cup of tea. I enjoyed it grudgingly, since the talk was mostly trivial. Occasionally, as in Burlington, Vermont, someone like Robert Frost, the poet, would come back stage to compliment us. It was a joy to hear him speak.

Always, alluring thoughts of getting home, where there would be peace and quiet, were on my mind; but this seldom came to pass. So many important and interesting events that we were anxious to attend were constantly taking place in New York that we could not bear to miss them. Being with the biggest manager in the business, we could get complimentary tickets for any of his concerts that weren't sold out, including the New York Philharmonic and Philadelphia orchestras.

We had become so friendly that for many years Mrs. Webb sent Eunice and me the tickets for her opera box for every Saturday night of the season. Eunice had no difficulty in filling the box with friends. When the opera was one she didn't care for, she would pass the tickets on.

Then there were the receptions, where we rubbed elbows with world-famous people in the arts and in business. All this made for a full and exciting life amongst people who could talk about something besides good food, baseball, and the weather. By June we were pretty frazzled; so the quartet stopped rehearsing and separated for a holiday of at least a month.

In the beginning, Eunice and I had tried renting our home for the summer, but we had had such bad luck with tenants leaving the place in a mess that we gave that up and left it closed. This had the added advantage that we could go when we pleased. Some years we were able to slip away as early as the middle of May. This advantage had one disadvantage in that Vermont was usually cold and rainy at this time of the year. In its new location on Shelburne Point, our cottage was facing the Green Mountains on a rocky elevation about fifteen feet above the shore of Lake Champlain and three-quarters of a mile from the closest habitation. In mid-May the ice in the lake would have just melted.

Our usual plan was to get there about 2:00 p.m., take the shutters off the porch and windows, unload the baggage from the car, and then take a quick hop into the lake and a quicker one out. When I say quick, I mean quick, for those icy waters can really put zip into your carburetor. The first dip seems to feel the coldest. A brisk rubdown, and we would feel as though we could lick the devil with one hand tied behind our backs. But wait a minute—then we would have a couple stiff drinks, and we would feel as though we could lick a hundred devils. After that we would sit down to supper, at which I would say the only grace of the year, "Blessed be peace," and we would go to bed early.

The blessed peace lasted until early June, when our guests and relatives started arriving for their vacations. This procession continued until well after Labor Day—one group leaving in the morning and another group arriving in the afternoon.

Our facilities were primitive. Cooking was done on a three-burner kerosene stove. At first a neighboring farmer supplied our icebox with ice cut from the lake, but later on we bought a kerosene-burning icebox, considered a luxury. On cold days—and there were many—heat was supplied by a brick fireplace, which a local bricklayer and I built. Water for cooking and washing was pumped from the lake by hand into a small tank. I dug a well about ten feet deep, and this supplied delicious drinking water.

The cottage was a wooden structure with two small bedrooms, a living room, a small kitchen, and a porch around two sides ten by twenty feet. On this porch Eunice and I ate our meals and slept on convertible couches. In fact, this is where we and our guests spent much of our time, going indoors only in the most inclement weather.

The cottage nestled in a white pine grove at the foot of thickly wooded Allen's Hill. (In the American Revolution Ethan Allen's Green Mountain boys had a cannon on its top to protect that section from the British in Canada.) I once found a tomahawk head on the hill. About 150 feet from our cottage we had a shack with four bunks for our visitors, and 100 feet in the other direction was a deluxe two-holer.

At first, a few Vermonters were unfriendly to us. One of the farmers, noticing the New York license on our car, stepped up to me in the general store and said, "Why don't you fellows stay down where you come from instead of coming up here and wearing out the roads for which we spend our hard-earned money?"

The store carried everything from licorice straps to men's celluloid collars and cuffs to horse collars. At the butcher shop all cuts of meat were twenty-five cents a pound—hamburger, stew meat, or filet mignon—because the butcher said it was so much easier to figure. When we asked if he had any kidneys, he said, "There is no sale for them. I usually give them away to my customers for their cats, but I happen to have a few on hand at the moment and I will gladly give them to you." From then on, he saved all his kidneys for Eunice and never charged for them.

Many were the mornings in early autumn when we sat on our porch having breakfast and heard the hunting horn and the barking of hounds approaching. It was the Webbs and their guests on a fox hunt. Soon we saw the fox running through our pine grove at a comfortable pace, followed by a pack of foxhounds barking their heads off and running with throttles wide open, the hunters close on their heels on horseback. Most of the ladies still rode sidesaddle. On one such occasion we had a niece visiting us. She, wanting to get a better look at the show, quickly ran out our back door and almost bumped into the fox. It is a debatable question which of the two was more scared.

We became friends with a farmer who seemed to be particularly successful at producing good crops. Once I asked him about the proper time to prune apple trees, of which there were several in the meadow behind the cottage. Scratching his head, he said, "W-e-ll, I'll tell you, the proper time is when your saw is sharp." He had been ailing for some time, and his local doctor had urged him to go to the hospital for a checkup. "But," he said, "them fellers never fail to find something wrong. I'd rather go to a feller I know who is the seventh son of a seventh son. When he lays hands on me I feel better right away."

This man's farm had been in his family for generations, but

when the Rutland Railroad was built, it became necessary to lay the tracks right through the middle of it and split the property in half, leaving the barns on one side and most of the grazing land on the other. This meant that the farmer had to drive his herd over the tracks to graze in the morning and return them to the barns via the same route in the evening.

With the advent of the automobile, this crossing became a dangerous one; and the local population raised a rumpus about it. After the usual procrastination, the railroad decided to hold a public hearing at which all complaints would be aired. Some thirty witnesses appeared at the hearing, of whom twenty claimed the crossing to be dangerous and demanded an underpass. Finally, it came down to our farmer, on whom the company official wasn't even going to call, feeling sure that he would have a just complaint. The citizens were sure that he would be on their side and that his testimony would clinch their case, and insisted on his being heard. After some scratching of his pate, he rose slowly and drawled, "All I know is that I been drivin' my cows back and forth over that crossing every day for well nigh onto fifty years and I han't lost a single head yet."

One summer when we returned we noticed that he looked about ten years younger. It developed that he had been elected to the legislature and, before going to Montpelier, he had decided his appearance would be enhanced by a new set of teeth. In answer to my question, "Do you feel that you represented your district well?" he said, "To tell you the real truth, every one of those damned bills they brought up was written in such legal language I didn't know what the hell they were talking about. There was only one bill where it said they would raise the taxes in my district 10 percent. That I understood and stamped my foot hard as I could and said, 'By gum, over my dead body you will.'" To another query as to how he knew how to vote, his reply was, "Oh, that was easy; I and most of the other fellers followed instructions from our political boss."

We became very close friends of a well-to-do couple living about two miles away. For many years he was Republican State Committee Chairman, and his wife was chairman of the women's branch. For some reason or other, they enjoyed our company and would inveigle us to accompany them on some of their travels around the state to various committee meetings. We enjoyed these outings because it gave us a chance to see out-of-the-way places and learn something about the chicanery that goes on in politics that the public knows nothing about, even in as small a state as Vermont. At one meeting in the state capitol, my friend came to me and whispered, pointing to a certain man, "You see that fellow over there? He is the political boss and the most powerful man in the state—even more powerful than the governor. He keeps himself in the background; that's why so few people know about him." On another occasion my friend was lamenting the fact that his choice for governor had just been defeated by a man with slightly liberal tendencies. Then after a slight pause, he consoled himself with the remark, "Oh well, he can't do anything; we have his hands tied." You may have three guesses as to who the powers were that he meant by "we."

One night this couple gave a big dinner for three governors and their wives, representing Maine, New Hampshire, and Vermont, to which Eunice and I were, for some reason, invited. For us it was a memorable occasion.

We frequently played golf with friends on the beautiful nine-hole course of the Webb estate. This course was originally built with eighteen holes, but as Dr. and Mrs. Webb grew older it was reduced to nine.

The terrain was hilly, with a magnificent view of the Adirondacks to the west and the Green Mountains to the east. The quartet was invited to use it whenever we chose, but Eunice and I and our guests were the only ones to make use of it.

In the thirty years that Eunice and I played we never had to buy a golf ball, because whenever we knocked a ball into the rough and went looking for it we found at least one other. Members of the family wouldn't spend more than thirty seconds looking for one they had lost. On Watson Webb's fiftieth birthday, some hundred guests were invited for a celebration. Most of them came from New York City and vicinity by special train. The party lasted two days. Many of the guests played golf and, to sharpen their eyesight, a bar was placed near every green. Suffice it to say, we played the course after the party and found enough golf balls to last us for years!

142

One couple we often played with suggested an oddball foursome. This means that each team plays only one ball, rotating turns at each shot. We had exchanged wives as partners. At one point in the game I hit our ball into a sand trap and it came to rest against the bottom of a bunker about three feet high. To get the ball out required a shot with quite some loft. After surveying the situation, my partner picked the niblick from her bag and took one mighty swing. The ball lofted nicely but, incredibly, dropped straight down inside the v-neck of her blouse. Quick as a flash her husband shouted at me, "You've got to play it as it lies."

Besides golf, we enjoyed mountain climbing. I think we climbed every peak between Rutland and the Canadian border. Camel's Hump, over 4,000 feet, was our favorite (we climbed it at least thirty times) because its summit came to a rocky peak from which you could see a goodly portion of Lake Champlain as well as the Adirondacks to the west, the White Mountains to the east, and the Green Mountains to the north and south. One week we climbed Camel's Hump three times because we had three different groups of visitors who were anxious to climb it.

14

RETURN TO PALM BEACH

Now let us leave our secluded paradise in Vermont and turn to the quartet's second visit to Palm Beach, this time under the sponsorship of Paris Singer, a benevolent dictator of the colony, at that time. He was one, if not the only, instigator of the Florida boom of that period. Singer had been educated in England and was more cultivated than the average rich American who wintered in Palm Beach in those days; therefore he was respected in his efforts to make the city a showplace the whole world would admire. When we arrived, Palm Beach was so crowded with real estate salesmen and buyers that the hotels were jammed.

Land was selling in such a speculative fever and so fast that prices were zooming to fantastic, unrealistic heights. Many buyers were so eager to get in on the profits that they didn't bother to have the titles searched or even to look at the property. For that matter, if they had tried to see the acreage, they might not have been able to find it, for a large portion was under water and the rest had no markings except on some dealer's map. Swindlers were having a ball, especially those who were selling by mail to suckers up north.

Having learned about these conditions from passengers on the trip to Florida, we were apprehensive about our sleeping accommodations. This worry was quickly dispelled on arrival, for Mr. Singer's chauffeur met us in a Rolls Royce, drove us to a little cottage adjacent to the Everglades Club, and told us to make ourselves at home. Mr. Singer would be in to see us shortly.

Our cottage had four nicely furnished rooms, each with a double bed in it. We settled in and waited for Mr. Singer. Soon he came in, all smiles with the query "Have you had breakfast?" Reassured, he said that the cottage would be at our disposal for the duration of our stay and handed us four tickets for meals at Topolino's, a very good restaurant across the street.

"I just can't wait to see how you are going to like the acoustics of the music room," he said. "I built it especially for these concerts, next to my apartment in the Everglades Club. When will you have time to try it out?" "Right now," one of us answered, and so he took us over.

On entering, we stood dumbfounded at the beauty of the room. It was about a hundred feet long, seventy feet wide, and possibly sixty feet high. Up the back wall an ornamental staircase led to the Singer apartment. The whole decor was early Spanish. Tables and chairs, candelabra, and even the four music stands we were to use were antiques.

We uncased our instruments and started to play, smiling and nodding our heads in agreement as to how well we sounded in the room. All the while we were playing Mr. Singer walked about, stopping to listen in different locations.

When we stopped at the end of the first number, he asked, "Well, what do you think of it?" We told him we thought it magnificent. "Stay and rehearse if you like," he said. We did, and rehearsed for another three hours. Seating himself on a comfortable chair in the back of the room, Mr. Singer did not speak once until we had finished. Then he said, in a heart-throbbing voice, "How beautiful!" That evening as we entered the room, a sense of well-being overtook me; and the thought came to my mind that this charming setting must be very like the courts of Europe in the eighteenth and nineteenth centuries.

Casually and comfortably seated were some fifty of the most prominent people in America. Light came from real candles in the candelabra; only our music stands had electric bulbs cleverly concealed. We played our best for an hour, but the applause was light and hesitant due to the fact, we later learned, that nobody was sure of what Mr. Singer's wishes would be in this regard. Before the month was over, they were applauding heartily; and we got to know some of them so well that they were inviting us to their homes for dinner.

In all, we played twenty-five concerts, without repeating a

single composition. A completely new program every day was quite a feat in itself, especially since Mr. Singer insisted that we stick to the standard classical repertoire and not interject popular numbers. He requested that we submit a copy of the program for the day to him every morning. We took turns doing this, and always found his office a madhouse.

Here is a sample of what happened one morning when it was my turn. Mr. Singer's secretary informed me that he was at the barber's across the street and he'd left word that important callers should be sent there. I found him in a barber's chair surrounded by at least a dozen people. A bootblack was shining his shoes, a manicurist was polishing his nails, the barber was trimming his hair, and a doctor was winding a tourniquet around his arm to take his blood pressure. About eight other men were standing around awaiting their turn for some service or other.

It was about five minutes before he spotted me standing at the edge of the group. Immediately he motioned for me to step forward and stuck out his hand for the program. One quick look and a nod of his head in agreement and that took care of me. How much he actually knew about the programs we never found out because he never requested any changes. We did know that he was deeply moved at every concert and never missed one.

Almost everything Mr. Singer did was in the grand manner. One year he imported from London a whole musical comedy company of over a hundred people to perform at the Palm Beach Theatre. We were highly flattered when he invited us to sit with him and his wife in their loge. In a few years we became the status symbol of Palm Beach. Those whom Paris Singer did not invite to the chamber concerts got the idea that their prestige was suffering.

Soon we were getting requests to give concerts at people's homes. At first we said no, feeling sure that Mr. Singer would object. But when we mentioned it to him, he asked, "Why don't you do it?" We replied that we thought he might not like it. "To the contrary, I would feel flattered to have started something that others would want to emulate," he said. And so we accepted a few engagements after finishing Mr. Singer's series.

On the whole, these concerts were unrewarding since most of the people invited to them weren't familiar with classical music, let alone chamber music, and we ran into experiences such as this one. At the house of a dime store heiress we were greeted at the door by her husband. His face was wreathed in smiles; but, after looking us over, his expression quickly turned to anguish, and he burst out with, "What, are there only four of you?" Naturally, this was an awkward moment, which took some of the wind out of our sails. Recovering, one of us inquired if there were anything special he would like us to play. "Yes," he said, "'Roses of Picardy.'" Needless to say, we did not enjoy that concert.

Another similar event was at the home of a J. P. Morgan partner whose mansion was one of the most lavish in the colony. He also greeted us at the door with smiles; but, after looking us over, his smile vanished and he exclaimed, "Where'd you leave your drummer?" This concert wasn't very successful either! Had we known, we wouldn't have accepted either one. Mr. Singer never invited anyone who did not appreciate good music.

All this was taking place during Prohibition days. As far as Palm Beach was concerned, there was no such thing as Prohibition. The British island of Bimini lay only a short distance offshore, and an army of bootleggers plied their trade unmolested. All the time I was there I never heard of anyone's being arrested by a government agent.

There was no difficulty in procuring the best liquor at reasonable prices. I would go down from New York with a suitcase filled with my wardrobe, and on the day of departure would ship the wardrobe home in a carton and return with a suitcase loaded with liquor. It was astonishing how friends would welcome home the wandering boy.

Eventually we played in most of the mansions there and came to know the people well with cordiality similar to that which they showed each other. Then came the real estate bust in 1927-28. Values of all property dropped drastically; and almost everybody involved went broke, including our Mr. Singer.

There was a paradox in this. Listening to these multimillionaire friends in earlier years, I had heard many complaints that the government was interfering too much in their affairs. Now the cry "Why doesn't the government do something?" was on all lips. Many of the big mansions stood vacant for years, and Florida was almost deserted.

147

Of course, we suffered some financial loss; but what we missed most was playing in the atmosphere of Mr. Singer's music room. But by this time we were well established; and since our work load was increasing, with the addition of radio work and making records for Brunswick, the loss of Palm Beach was easily overcome.

15

AN UNEXPECTED GIFT

Let us not forget about my dear friend Gilfillan (Gil). He had fled Berlin as World War I broke out and had gone back to work for the Weyerhauser Timber Company in Tacoma. I had gone to Russia, and thus we lost track of each other. I figured that he would stay in Europe, possibly Spain, and there wasn't much chance of finding him.

It wasn't until I was in the army that he surprised me with a letter. Knowing that I was from Cleveland, he had contacted my parents via the city directory and got my address. And so we were in touch again.

After the war he returned to Europe, divorced his first wife, married one of the nicest Swiss girls, and built a beautiful villa on the slopes of the Alps overlooking Cannes. Every two years or so he would pass through New York on his way to Tacoma on business and would advise me in advance. If I happened not to be on the road, I would meet his ship and we would have dinner together, retire to his hotel room and, over a bottle of Scotch, discuss the world's problems as well as our own. Time seemed to fly so fast that, on rather unsteady legs, I would depart for Grand Central Station to catch the 2:00 a.m. train for New Rochelle; where Eunice would be waiting with that quizzical look on her face.

On one occasion he came over on the first trip the Graf Zeppelin made to this country. I met him at Lakehurst Naval Station where the balloon landed. As he came toward me, I became frightened; he was pale, distraught, and shivering from head to foot; a nervous wreck. All he said was, "My God, never again!" I took him in tow and we taxied to his favorite hotel.

Not until he had had a bath and a couple of drinks of Scotch did he tell me about his journey. It was a harrowing tale of how for the past two days they had traveled through a vicious storm which tossed the airship around like a tumbleweed. Several times it took nose dives to within feet of the ocean. Some of the baggage, as well as the piano in the drawing room, came loose, and the interior was battered into a shambles. It was a miracle that the ship came through.

After a good dinner, a few more Scotches, and much talk in the hotel room, I again barely caught the last train for New Rochelle. To sum up our relationship: aside from our eight months in Prague, when we were together two or three times a week, and the three-week auto trip to Italy, we saw each other once every three or four years and then only for a few hours. I tried hard to get him to New Rochelle to meet Eunice, but he was always in a hurry and couldn't make it. The only words I can think of to describe this friendship are "a haphazard relationship, but a very close one." Nevertheless, I was floored when in 1931 I received a letter from Gil, the gist of which follows: "Dear Sis: For some years my will has contained the proviso that my Guarnerius is to go to you. Noting what a success you have made of yourself, I have come to the conclusion that you can get more use and pleasure out of it than I, letting it lie in a bank vault. Therefore, I am making you a present of it and am shipping same to my bank in New York, which will notify you when to come for delivery. Have your lawyer draw up papers to this effect and mail to me for my signature."

Needless to say, this was news of the greatest magnitude. I lived with mounting impatience for a month until a notice arrived from the bank asking me to call for the violin. I lost no time in going for it. As for the episode of the actual delivery, I can do no better than to copy an article entitled "Guaranty Acts as Agent in Delivery of Rare Guarnerius Violin to Siskovsky," which appeared in the *Guaranty News*, June 1931, a monthly magazine published by the Guaranty Trust Company, New York.

The mundane procession of wills, reviews and wordy documents which occupies a large measure of the day's activities in the Personal Trust Department was broken recently by a pleasant interlude. It involved the proper care and transfer of a valuable Guarnerius violin said to be worth about $50,000, and the Trust Department, accustomed to unusual requests, handled the matter in a way satisfactory to the aesthetic and business sense of all concerned. A rare violin, its music mellowed by more than two hundred years of preservation, and even its appearance savoring of the romance of early Italian craftsmanship, the generosity of a businessman who was giving the instrument to a musician most capable of transmitting its tonal fragrance to a music-loving audience, and the anecdotes of the violin related by the musician, were aspects of the transaction that lifted it out of the commonplace. Gift of F. J. Gilfillan. The party of the first part was the bank's customer and friend, who will be remembered by readers as one of the passengers on the Graf Zeppelin on its transatlantic flight to New York two years ago. A musician of accomplishment himself and a one-time concertmaster in a leading orchestra in Prague, Mr. Gilfillan nevertheless felt that the violin, to be of the greatest human benefit, should be placed in the hands of a concert performer.

He remembered Jaroslav Siskovsky, with whom he studied in Prague in 1912 and who had held, played and loved the instrument as only a musician can. Mr. Gilfillan is in Europe and Mr. Siskovsky is in New York, where he is playing in the well-known New York String Quartet.

So Mr. Gilfillan, combining his culture with sound business sense, had the instrument sent to the Guaranty Trust Company with instructions to present it to Mr. Siskovsky. For safekeeping the violin was entrusted to R. F. Allen, Vice President of Guaranty Trust Company.

As soon as he was notified of the instrument's arrival, Mr. Siskovsky came to receive the gift. His emotions were not easily concealed. An instrument of immortals, ranking with Stradivarius, and handed down from one great musician to another for more than two hundred years, was now about to become his. The case was brought out. The keys sent by Mr. Gilfillan were tried on the lock. The case couldn't be opened.

With nerves considerably on edge, Mr. Siskovsky stood by while our Ben Hepworth secured some tools and proceeded gently but firmly to open the case backwards. Fearfully expectant that something might have gone wrong, Mr. Siskovsky lifted the violin from its case and fondled it like a long-lost child. He had only to draw the bow once to know by its melodious tone that it could be no other than the one he had never forgotten.

He related to Ben Wittschen something of the history of the instrument and of its maker, a fellow citizen of Stradivarius in Cremona; indeed, they were contemporaries. The fact that Stradivari is generally better known than Guarneri is attributable to the fact that the former died in 1737 at the age of ninety-three while Guarneri died at age forty-six. This accounts for the fact that there are about 550 examples of Stradivari's work and only 160 violins extant made by Guarneri. Among artists it is a matter of taste which instrument performs the better. Certainly, it is one of the mysteries of aesthetic history that none of the present-day violin makers has been able to approach the work of the medieval artisans.

In days of necromancy, alchemists looking for the preternatural elixir of life, in dark low-ceilinged shops where craftsmen were willing to give a lifetime to a piece of work—in that environment were violins made that were to carry an immortal music down through the centuries. Painstaking craftsmanship was there and some other ingredients that the modern day has not been able to duplicate. Some believe that the secret lies in the varnish, the formula for which was never divulged.

Mr. Gilfillan attempted to duplicate the famous violin by having two reproductions made as close to the original as was humanly possible. He took the instrument to the most famous violin maker in Germany, who searched for one year for wood whose grain and texture would match the original. Even though he followed the shape and measurements to the finest degree, the reproductions could not come up to the original either in tone or appearance.

Mr. Siskovsky closed the interview by saying that he once saw a violin made by Guarneri which he believes was made from the same log as the one he now owns. The New York firm of Wurlitzer now has the violin and for about $50,000 could be induced to part with it.

I hastened home up in the clouds, on a flying carpet, hugging my prized possession all the way. After showing it to my wife, I spent the afternoon playing and admiring it. The gut in the strings was quite dry after lying in storage for a number of years, and the strings lacked resonance. But that was to be expected. A set of new ones would remedy that. I thought the varnish looked dull, so I brought out my special polish and tenderly polished it. Oh, how beautiful it looked! Otherwise it seemed to be in perfect condition. How could anyone ever stop being grateful to such a friend as Gil?

Well do I remember when he bought this violin. It was about three months after I arrived in Prague. He and I were studying at the Prague Conservatory, where we had become friends. About Christmastime Gil told me that he was going to London for a couple of weeks.

On his return he proudly produced two fine violins that he had purchased in London. One was the Guarnerius and the other a lovely Guadagnini. The Guarneri was the more valuable. He would let me play on it at quartet sessions; but, since it was his favorite, he preferred to use it for practice. I didn't have the nerve to ask to borrow it. I was still using the violin my father bought at the pawnshop for three dollars. You can imagine the comedown it was—almost the difference between night and day. An excellent description with a full-page spread of three different views of the violin appeared in the London magazine *The Strad* in January 1913. This magazine was considered tops in matters pertaining to violin making and playing. Since there are some fascinating bits of history, I will insert the article, omitting items of technical interest only.

The splendid specimen figured this month, and known to connoisseurs as the "La Font," ranks high amongst the more finished productions of Guarnerius. There seems to be no doubt that it was at one time the property of the great fiddler after whom it is named and who, it is said, possessed two instruments made by the great Guarneri. Perhaps it was on this very fiddle that La Font performed in the famous contest which took place between him and Paganini in Milan in 1816. On that memorable occasion the Frenchman was worsted, but even Paganini himself is said to have admitted that La Font surpassed him in tone.

The tone of this violin is characteristic of its maker and possesses the usual reedy quality which one looks for in a Guarneri in anything like good condition. It is in excellent preservation and still retains a good deal of the glorious varnish of its maker. The belly exhibits the well-known sap stain which is to be seen on the great majority of the maker's violins. The label is original. Messrs. Hill, most respected experts in London, who guarantee it, assign the violin to the year 1733 as stated on the label, and the style and finish of it are certainly in accordance with that met with in Guarneri's violins in that year. Of the head of the violin it is unnecessary to say more than that it is a fine specimen of its class.

A word of thanks must be accorded to Mr. Gilfillan, the fortunate owner, for the fine photographs and for kind permission to publish them.

Soon after I acquired the violin, I took it to Mr. Sacconi, universally acknowledged to be one of the top repair experts in the world, who was associated with the Wurlitzer Company in New York. He examined it carefully and recommended installing a new bass bar, a common practice in adjusting the violin to our climate. Soon I was having the thrill of playing on it in concert halls all over the country. However, the Guarnerius had been lying unplayed for many years, and it took about a year of playing for the tone to return to the richness and fullness of which it was capable.

16

TRIALS AND TRIBULATIONS

The life of the artist on the road is a strenuous one, especially with the irregular hours. But the scenery and people keep changing, and so one simply doesn't have time to feel tired. A bit of humor comes as a relief when something unusual happens, especially at a performance when the audience has fun. Recently I read about two top-notch quartets whose members avoided each other like the plague when not playing together—one group even tried to travel separately. To me it is inconceivable that any group can make music together if they find each other obnoxious. Yet they seem to be doing it. As for not traveling together, that would seem risky because of the uncertainty of time schedules, whether by train, air, or bus, especially in the wintertime. The chances of one musician not arriving on time are multiplied by four, and no quartet is worth a hoot with one member missing.

The New York Quartet always traveled together. There were disagreements, some very heated, but they were always settled amicably, and no one bore a grudge. We played a good many joint concerts with most of the top pianists of the time as well as stars from the Metropolitan Opera. Rehearsals and concerts with them created a diversion which was always a welcome change from the usual.

Now to the unusual. At Bennington College in Vermont, just as we sat down to play, the lights went out. There we and the audience sat for at least a half-hour in the dark. Finally, the chairman of the Music Department came up to us. "Could you proceed under the light of candles?" "Yes," we replied. Shortly, four beautiful girls marched up the aisle, each bearing a lighted

155

candle. Seating themselves next to each one of us, they held the flames close to the music. Thus the concert was performed, with many encores, for as long as the candles lasted. The lights never did come on, and we all departed through the semidarkness in a jolly mood.

After a concert in Houston, we were entertained by a gracious lady who was a staunch patron of the arts in that city. Her father was ex-governor Hogg of Texas, and he had conceived the brilliant idea of naming his three children (two girls and a boy) Ima Hogg, Yura Hogg, and Will B. Our hostess was Ima.

In one city our program had closed with the beautiful Schumann quintet assisted by the world-famous pianist, Wilhelm Backhaus. Continuous applause called for an encore, but having none at hand, we repeated the final movement of the quintet. Imagine our surprise when the local music critic appeared back stage and requested the name of the encore!

In Peoria, Illinois, we were in the middle of a concert, playing a number which required some fancy bowing on my part at the frog of the bow. Since the passages were rapid, it was necessary to hold the bow very lightly. I went at it with gusto and was having a fine time, when suddenly the bow slipped out of my fingers and went sailing off into the audience, landing in the lap of a woman in the front row. The sudden roar from the audience was deafening and lasted for some time. Presently the woman got up and returned the bow to me amidst great hilarity. When things had settled down, we played the composition from the beginning.

In one prominent educational institution the quartet played under an unusual handicap. The two young sons of the school's president were seated in one of the front rows and occupied themselves by surreptitiously shooting wads of paper at the artists, who presented convenient targets. Every now and then an unusually sharp accent from one of the players announced that a missile had found its mark. The sport lasted only through the first number, fortunately, as the boys found themselves suddenly removed from the hall.

The prize for the most frustrating concert in our career is easily won by a performance in St. Joseph, Missouri, where the auditorium was constructed over a bowling alley. Imagine our consternation when we arrived and heard a frightful noise from below. We speculated that St. Joe must have had some crack keglers because every roll sounded like a strike. It didn't seem possible that this noise would be allowed to continue, but when we spoke to the manager he replied in the most casual manner, "Oh, pay no attention to that; our audiences are used to it."

Now, what to do about it? We had come a long way, and the auditorium was already filled. So we decided to put up with it and play *forte* all the way through. We were nervous wrecks at the finish. The only consolation being that the manager was right: the audience was used to it, for they applauded vociferously and demanded encores just as if nothing unusual had happened.

Considerably more flattering to the artistic ego was the tale told by a fond mother in Iowa who had brought her six-year-old son to the concert. After the first few notes, he turned to her and said. "Mother, they ought to pay those men a whole lot of money because they play such beautiful music."

It took us eight hours to inch our way for almost fifty miles from Little Rock to Hot Springs, Arkansas—a trip that ordinarily lasted about one and one half hours—over rails that were flooded to at least the depth of a foot by the Arkansas River.

Another year the Ohio River was so badly flooded we could not reach Ashland, Kentucky, from Cincinnati in time for the concert. Fortunately, we were able to postpone it to a week later. This was the only date we ever missed in all our travels. The following was perilously close, however.

We had played at Purdue University in Lafayette, Indiana. The next morning at eight we left by train for Grand Rapids, Michigan, where we were to play that night. (Practically all our traveling was done by train because bus and air travel was not as organized as it is now.) Having snowed all the day before, there was about one and a half feet of fresh snow on the ground; and the temperature was somewhere around twenty below zero. It was evident right from the start that the poor engine was having a hard job bucking the snow drifts, for we were proceeding with hesitation and were making frequent stops to allow it to build up steam so as to be able to move at all. In order to accomplish this, the engineers even had to cut off the steam in the coaches, which became so cold that we froze all the way into Chicago, where we finally arrived six hours late, at 5:00 p.m. instead of 11:00 a.m.

The station was in a state of near riot, jammed with people hurrying in all directions. The first thing we did was to find when the next train was to leave for Grand Rapids. The information desk said it was due to leave at 7:00 p.m., but under existing conditions there was no certainty. Ordinarily, the trip took several hours; so we assumed that we would arrive too late for a concert and that we might as well spend the night in Chicago. We called the manager at Grand Rapids to inform him of developments. He begged us to come on the first train and promised to keep the audience waiting.

To make a long story short, our seven o'clock train departed at eight o'clock, and at eleven o'clock, several stations before Grand Rapids, we received a telegram which said, "Audience still waiting; please come quickly as possible." With this we got busy cleaning up and putting on our dress suits.

At the station in Grand Rapids, a Cadillac was waiting. It whisked us at high speed to the auditorium, where we were greeted with thunderous applause by a packed house exactly as a clock in some belfry struck midnight. Of course, we were cold and fatigued; but soon, due to the enthusiasm of the audience, we were playing at our best.

When the program was finished at about 1:30, the audience kept applauding in great excitement; and we kept playing encores until 2:00 a.m. As the manager drove us to a hotel, he remarked with a sigh, "This evening will be talked about and remembered in Grand Rapids for many, many years."

One year we played sixty concerts in sixty days, each one in a different city. That meant travel after each concert, mostly by sleeper. I got very little rest; so, if possible, I would climb into bed for an hour's nap before a concert. After about six weeks we were so exhausted that even the thought of going out to face an audience seemed revolting. But once started, we became so absorbed in the music that all feeling of fatigue vanished and we were again operating full steam ahead. Fortunately, this happened at the end of the season, when we could be thinking about a nice long rest at our summer camp in Shelburne, Vermont.

That reminds me of an incident which happened at one of our annual concerts at the University of Vermont, in Burlington, close to Shelburne. My four-year-old niece, Frances Swain, was visiting us; and we took her to the concert. To let her have a good view, my wife placed her on an end seat in the middle aisle. Just as the quartet had seated itself, little Frances jumped up and started up the middle aisle toward the stage, shouting, "That's my Uncle Jaro up there!" The audience exploded with laughter while Eunice did a quick five-yard sprint to haul the child back to her seat. I can't think of a better way to start off a concert and put an audience into a genial mood.

At one of our concerts in the ballroom of the Bellevue Stratford Hotel in Philadelphia the stage was in the center like a prizefight ring. The walk to reach it through the seated audience seemed interminable. We hadn't been playing more than five minutes when suddenly the gut loop on the tailpiece of our viola snapped with a bang, and the whole string assembly flew into the air. The music stopped; and we sat there wondering what to do, for none of us ever carried more than one instrument on trips.

You could have heard a pin drop in the audience, for they too were wondering, when, lo and behold, like a lighthouse in a storm, there came salvation up one of the aisles in the form of our colleague, Samuel Lifshey (first-chair viola of the Philadephia Orchestra), who by great good fortune was attending the concert. He offered to get his viola and be back in twenty minutes. We announced our good fortune to the audience, which didn't seem to mind the wait. Lifshey performed even better than his word, for he was back in fifteen minutes; and we finished the concert as though nothing had happened. How about that for good luck?

In Washington, D.C., we played at the Czechoslovakian embassy twice and the French embassy once. This was during Prohibition days. Of course, all the embassies were free from Prohibition; so they served the best imported liquors at will. Oh, how popular events at embassies were with our legislators; and oh, how many of them there were voting dry in the daytime and getting liquored up at these events at night. After the concerts we always had a few ourselves.

The ambassador had chosen an all-Czech program so as to acquaint our senators and representatives with his country's music. The concert was supposed to start promptly at 10:00

p.m., but vice-president Dawes, the highest-ranking legislator to be invited, did not arrive until shortly after eleven. This necessitated delaying everything until his arrival—everything that is, except the drinks. So by the time we got started, so many of the guests were plastered that, even though drinks were to have been served only between numbers, there were a certain number of unruly ones who couldn't keep quiet. It was a most disconcerting concert for those who wanted to listen, as well as for us performers. As we were leaving, the ambassador profusely apologized; but we sympathized with him, realizing that he hadn't liked it any better than we did.

One of the most pleasant memories is of our visit to Rochester, Minnesota. The son of Mr. Verbruggen, conductor of the Minneapolis Symphony, took us in tow. He was an intern at the Mayo Clinic and spent half a day showing us around through the clinic complex. There were some gruesome cancer specimens, but it was a rewarding experience.

A luncheon was held in our honor that was attended mostly by doctors, including the Mayo brothers, Will and Charles. Somehow or other, musicians and doctors have a special affinity for one another. It was one of the few luncheons on the road that I thoroughly enjoyed. Indeed, in our travels we learned that there are so many doctors who play musical instruments that they have their own orchestras and chamber music groups all over the country.

After the concert, Dr. and Mrs. Judd (Mrs. Judd was a sister of the Mayos) held a reception at their house at which there were fifty guests, mostly doctors. There was much talk, with food and drink, during which someone shouted, "Please play us another encore," and we played for them until two in the morning. We had to catch a train at 7:00 the next morning, but we loved every minute of our stay.

In Nashville, Tennessee, the concert was held in an ancient relic of Civil War days; I think it was called Memorial Hall. We were obliged to sit on folding chairs. We had started to play the second movement of the Debussy Quartet, which opens with a short pianissimo solo by the muted second violin. I had just finished playing this delicate little motif, and our viola was supposed to reply with an echo of the same. Ludvik Schwab was in the habit of keeping his mute on the music stand when not in use. Just as I finished, it dawned on him that his mute was not on his viola. Leaning forward, he made a quick grab for it, the folding chair collapsed under him, and he fell sprawling into our four stands. He was a husky 200 pounds! His bow went flying across the stage, stands fell in all directions, and we scrambled out of their way to protect ourselves and our instruments. When all the hubbub subsided, there was Schwab lying on his back in the middle of this mess of music, chairs, and stands, holding his viola high in the air, instinctively trying to protect it.

The audience looked on in shocked silence; but when they saw him get up, they burst out laughing. Of course, we laughed right with them. No one was hurt, and those precious instruments didn't receive a single scratch, but it did take us some time to find the bow that had gone flying off into the wings. Luckily, it, too, was undamaged. Then two stands that were badly bent had to be straightened. After that concert we resolved never to play on folding chairs again.

Returning to New York from a concert in Montreal, we chose the sleeper, which departed at 9:00 p.m. Since Canada didn't have prohibition, the temptation to smuggle in a few bottles of liquor was great; and we gave in to it. I tried to get to our train early in order to hide three quarts of gin under the mattress of my berth before many passengers arrived. And so it was that not a soul was there but the porter. When I thought he wasn't looking, I carefully secreted my treasure under the mattress of my berth. When the train reached the border, the customs officers came in. One of them entered our sleeper and, although my berth was in the center, walked right up to it, rolled up the mattress, and confiscated my three bottles. After examining the contents of my suitcase, he turned his attention to a man sitting in a seat across the aisle. "Have you anything to declare?" he asked. "No," was the answer. "Any liquor?" "No." "Please open your suitcase," the officer requested, and there on top in plain view lay a bottle of whiskey. Now, a bit irked, the officer said, "I thought you told me you didn't have liquor." "I haven't," was the quick reply. "Well—what do you call that?" said the officer, pointing to the bottle. "Oh, that—that's my nightcap," said the man with a smile. This produced a broad grin on the officer's face. He slammed the lid shut and walked away, leaving the bottle.

From the way the customs officer walked right up to my hidden cache, it was evident that someone must have tipped him off. Who did it puzzled me until I learned later that a regular racket existed between the customs officers, who would confiscate the liquor, and the conductors and porters, who would take it right on the same train to New York City and sell it at a fancy price, and later distribute the proceeds among themselves.

While we are on this subject, it might be fitting to tell about several Prohibition escapades out of a great many trips which we made over the Canadian border from Shelburne, only sixty miles distant.

It was customary whenever we had guests to take them across the border for lunch and return, every member of the party having several bottles strapped to his body. Occasionally we got caught, but all they could do was confiscate the liquor. Since we were successful about 90 percent of the time, we considered the chances worthwhile. We were returning from one of these trips with two of Eunice's sisters as guests. When we got to St. Albans, one of them happened to remember that one of their college classmates was a prominent businessman in the town; and nothing would dissuade them from stopping to say hello.

We found him at his place of business, and he was delighted to see the girls after so many years. After some small talk, he said, "Gosh, I wish we could celebrate this reunion somehow, but my wife is having a bridge party at the house this afternoon. So that's out. But you follow me in your car. You'll never guess where we are going."

We followed him onto a maze of islands in northern Lake Champlain, finally stopping in front of a building marked "Headquarters, U.S. Customs." Our friend, preceding us, had already arrived and was being welcomed by three or four customs agents to whom we were introduced and told to make ourselves at home.

Soon we were seated at a table and were asked what we wanted to drink. "What have you got?" we asked.

"You name it, we've got it," replied the customs officer. He pointed to hundreds of cases stacked up all over the place. We each named our choice and soon he returned with the order. He even produced potato chips. After an hour, and about three refills, we decided that with some forty miles to go, we had better get going or we might never make it.

As we parted with our friend at St. Albans, he explained where we had been. It was headquarters for the naval unit of Prohibition agents who cruised the lake in an effort to apprehend smugglers.

One of the tricks these smugglers used was to tow a boat which, when loaded with cargo, water pumped into tanks, would sink to a depth of some four feet, where it would ride along unseen. If a customs boat approached, they would cut the towline and proceed as innocent fishermen. Later, when the coast was clear, they picked up their craft, towed it to an isolated dock, and pumped the water out of the tanks. Then the boat would rise to the surface ready for unloading. We made it back to camp without incident, amused to have experienced such an unusual episode.

Another safer way we had of supplying ourselves with liquor was through a very good Shelburne friend who had a friend employed as customs officer at one of the stations on the border. My friend, knowing which hours his friend would be on duty, would notify him of the exact time we would be coming through from Canada, and there he would be waiting for us. We pretended not to know him while he went through the motions of making an examination and then waved us on. In this way we brought back many a case.

Leaving Vermont, we will again return to the adventures of the quartet.

On one occasion we had a booking in Brownsville, Texas, where the local manager had long been interested in finding out whether a concert in Matamoros, Mexico, would prove to be a successful venture. Were we willing to try this experiment at a reduced rate if it were a matinee on the same day as the Brownsville concert? We agreed to this.

As was our custom, we arrived a half-hour early, and found that we were to perform in a charming little theatre dating back to Maximilian's time. After admiring it, we retired into separate dressing rooms to do our warm-up chores.

At starting time, the manager called us and, with a disappointed look on his face, announced that there wasn't a single soul in the audience except for a man in overalls sitting in a box. The decision to cancel the concert was made quickly, and the curtain was raised so that the manager could express our regrets. The man in the box rose and said, "Oh, that's all right. I am the janitor." Thus ended our first and last appearance in Mexico.

A red-letter day in the life of the quartet was December 15, 1927, during the Coolidge administration. We, two other quartets, two string basses from the Philadelphia Orchestra, Olga Samaroff, pianist, and Charles Courboin, organist, were chosen by Thaddeus Rich, concertmaster of the Philadelphia Orchestra, to give a concert in the East Room of the White House following the diplomatic corps dinner, by tradition the top social event of the year. Mr. Rodman Wanamaker sponsored the concert. He told Mr. Rich to spare no expense in preparing it and to engage the services of the best chamber musicians available.

Mr. Wanamaker owned an unusually fine collection of stringed instruments; he sent these down from Philadelphia for the occasion in specially constructed strongboxes in care of a guard.

A rehearsal had been planned for four o'clock, and at 3:00 we entered the outside gates of the White House, only to be stopped for interrogation by several guards who had been informed to expect us; so they made no fuss and allowed us to proceed. At the front steps other guards did more questioning; and as we reached the top step, the double doors were flung open by two handsome blacks in full livery, who looked like twins.

At such a moment one feels very important, wondering if entering the gates of heaven is anything like this. Then, stepping over the threshold, the aroma of chicken stewing in the kitchen came wafting toward us, and suddenly we dropped from the clouds in full realization that people live here just as we do in our own homes. What an anticlimax!

A doorman escorted us to a room in the basement, where some thirty of Mr. Wanamaker's fine instruments had been deposited; and the guard told us that we were free to make a choice. This was a violinist's dream, the chance to try out so many fine instruments. All of us walked around playing, absorbed in deciding which instrument we preferred.

We were called to the East Room at four for rehearsal, our only one, and played for two hours without incident. Mrs. Coolidge, in the next room, listened, and occasionally peeked around the corner to smile at us.

After the rehearsal we were asked to return the violins (mine was a beautiful Strad) to their cases. We were told to be back in full dress at nine. Most of us had a light supper and a short rest in bed in our hotel rooms. Appearing at the White House promptly, we were disturbed to discover that the room where our instruments were was locked and the guard nowhere in sight. There was nothing to do but stand around in the corridors until he came. We could hear talk from the banquet room upstairs where ambassadors from about ninety nations were dining. An army of waiters kept passing back and forth in front of us.

At 9:30 the guard still had not arrived. Apprehension ran rampant through our group. To be late for such an august event would be a major catastrophe. A courier was dispatched to try to find the missing guard. Lo and behold, he was found in bed, snoring his head off. Rushing back to the White House, he arrived just in time for us to unpack our instruments and appear upstairs at one minute to 10:00.

The East Room was packed with a colorful and distinguished audience comprising the ambassadors and about 400 of their secretaries, who were invited only for the concert, all in full-dress native costumes.

We had only a few minutes to wait before the assemblage stood up while President and Mrs. Coolidge were escorted in: she, smiling graciously, on the arm of a marine officer; he, dour as usual, on the arm of a navy officer, looking as though he had just stepped into something that smelled bad. They were seated in the center of the front row. Now it was our turn. Protocol demanded that women performers be escorted onto the stage by a military officer. Olga Samaroff, the only woman among the performers, led the parade with her escort at her side.

I was seated so that I could see President and Mrs. Coolidge out of the corner of my eye. She beamed all evening, and there could be no doubt that she thoroughly enjoyed the concert. In contrast, the president looked dejected. Indeed, if she had not given him a poke in the ribs occasionally he would have undoubtedly fallen asleep.

The audience was generous with its applause. The concert

ended with everyone standing as we were led, one by one, to shake hands with the Coolidges, who then left the room. Many of the ambassadors and secretaries came up to us, asking about our instruments and wanting to look at them. I enjoyed an opportunity of speaking with some of them in their own languages.

We deposited the instruments with the guard and went to the diningroom for a light supper and then a tour of the lower floor of the White House.

The next incident is, in my opinion, the funniest of all. It happened in Greenville, Mississippi. While we were there, Old Man River flooded the countryside inland for about forty miles. We were booked to play in Chicago the next night! The railroad running through Greenville was out of commission. What could we do? With the help of the railroad office, we discovered that another railroad, about sixty miles inland in unflooded territory, had a train making a stop at a certain station at four in the morning. If we could catch it, we would reach Chicago the next afternoon at five o'clock.

This seemed to be our solution. The problem was how to get to that station through about forty miles of flooded territory. Our local manager recommended an old taxi driver who had confronted similar problems. "If anybody can make it, he can," he said.

We found the driver and explained our situation. He replied in his slow southern way, "This is a pretty bad flood, and I reckon the ordinary taxi would never make it. But a friend of mine has a Model T Ford which I could borrow, and I am reasonably certain that the old jitney will get us there on time if we allow four hours for the trip."

Since we had no alternative, we agreed on the price and the time to leave, which was midnight.

Because of the flood, the concert hall that evening was only three-quarters full. People from the outlying districts couldn't get in. Most of Greenville proper, on higher ground, was not flooded. Those enthusiasts who came made up for the absent by demanding so many encores that the concert didn't end until 10:45. Then we were asked to come to a reception at one of the larger houses in the city. When we explained our dilemma, they promised to get us back to our hotel by midnight.

166

Nearly everybody from the audience was at the mansion, and we soon mingled with the crowd. At short intervals a Negro in livery appeared with what was called white mule, but actually was just plain corn liquor. Compared with the concoctions we had been served up North, this was super-fine. What with the jolly talk and the liquor, tempus fugited too fast, and our host gathered us up with the news that it was 12:15 and we would have to hurry.

He drove us at high speed to the hotel, where the taxi driver and his Model T were waiting. To save time, we did not change from full dress into our street clothes, but hurriedly grabbed our instruments and baggage and ran to the street, where precious time was spent tying four suitcases to the front mudguards and figuring out how best to fit five fairly stocky men and two violins, a viola, and a cello into the interior. At last we were off, worrying that we wouldn't be able to make it by four. The first mile was easy, all on dry land. Then we began traveling in mud and water, sometimes hub deep. But the good old Ford kept moving along, although at times hesitantly. Our confidence rose with each inch we progressed until, about ten miles out, we struck dirt roads. The wheels started churning, and we were stuck. We were miles from habitation, and there was nothing to do but get out and push.

I took off my dress coat, white vest, shoes and socks, rolled my trousers up to my knees, and stepped off into the muck; which came almost to my rolled-up trousers. The car did its best, and I pushed with all my might; but it still wouldn't budge. Another man had to get out and help. Cadek undressed as I had; and with his help, we got out of that rut and proceeded. The two of us had to repeat this performance at least five times until at one point we struck a rut so deep that Schwab, too, had to come to our aid; but this was the last of the mud.

Soon after, we reached dry ground and arrived at the station fifteen minutes before train time. Fortunately, we had telephoned ahead to the stationmaster that we expected to board that train and would he please have the waiting room open. From afar we could see it all lighted up. The place was deserted, but the waiting room and washrooms were open, and we made haste to wash up.

Vaska, sitting in the front seat with the driver and not having had to get out, was in pretty good shape. The other three of us were a mess. Imagine how we must have looked after pushing the car in knee-deep mud with the churning rear wheels splashing filth all over us. It took some time to stop laughing over how awful we looked. Someone said, "Oh, if our audience could only see us now!" But there was no time to lose. We removed most of the mess and changed into our street clothes. Fortunately, the train was late, so by the time it arrived we were fairly clean.

We got berths, in which we slept until noon, and arrived in Chicago on time, about 5:00 p.m. After booking rooms at a hotel, one of us reported our muddy clothes predicament to the manager. He immediately put his tailoring establishment on the job, and freshly cleaned and pressed outfits were delivered to us at 7:00. At 8:15 we stepped onto the stage ready for another concert, just as though nothing had happened.

One concert that gave us the greatest satisfaction was played for the benefit of just one person. This was in Tucson, Arizona. A reporter was on hand and wrote an account of it for the Arizona *Daily Star*, April 13, 1927. The headline read:

QUARTET CUTS DATES TO BE PART OF DREAM

New Yorkers Stay Over in Tucson to Play at Bedside of Violinist Who Could not Attend Concert

In truth this is not a story, but a tribute to four gallant gentlemen, Ottokar Cadek, Jaroslav Siskovsky, Ludvik Schwab and Bedrich Vaska—the New York String Quartet. It is the tale of a moment in which they gave of their art freely to bring joy to the soul of a brother artist, carrying their music to his bedside while he, for the first time in several years, drank to his heart's content from the brimming bowl of melody.

Josef Morrison, student of the violin, was a friend of Ottokar Cadek. They were not only closely associated, but found a common ground in their love of the instrument they played. That was a number of years ago, but, since, they had not met.

Morrison, however, followed the work of his friend through the periodicals of the musical world and near his bedside in his home a phonograph played the records made by the quartet.

Then the quartet came to play a concert sponsored by the Morning Musical Club. Morrison had waited for the date, each day planning with his mother on attending the concert, each day assuring her that he would be strong enough for that night. But it was not to be. The quartet came but Morrison was not of the audience.

Cadek, hearing of his friend in the city, sought him out; and, on discovering that his illness had prevented his attendance at the concert, at once conferred with his fellow artists. To them he told the story of the sick youth, of his love for the violin which he could no longer play, of his desire to hear again the melodies of the strings touched by the hands of artists and not as recorded on discs of the phonograph. It didn't take long for them to agree. It was decided that Morrison was to have his concert.

Train schedules interfered, but they were changed. Arrangements were made; and yesterday morning, without warning to their impromptu audience, the Quartet went to the little house on Euclid Avenue. Morrison, from his bed, answered the ring at the door, calling out "Come in," then stared almost speechless with surprise as the Quartet, with its cased instruments, crowded into the little room. Slowly he realized what was happening; then in his tear-wet eyes and his smile, the artists received their accolade. His deep-set eye [were] alight . . . and a soft brown beard all but hid the sensitive lips beaming with happiness. Morrison attempted to thank his visitors, but they would have none of it.

Jokingly they talked with the sick youth, comparing notes of the musical world in which all find their interests. Unpacking their instruments, they prepared for their unscheduled concert to an audience of one.

. . . "Here, Joe," said Cadek. "Would you like to hold a good fiddle again?" and he handed across to the sick man the mellow-toned reddish brown Stradivarius. The thin wasted hands of the stricken friend clasped the instrument lovingly. . . .

Schwab, also at the bedside, held over his viola for inspection as did Siskovsky and Vaska their own instruments.

Continuing their laughing conversation, the members of the quartet seated themselves, Cadek close to the door of his friend's room, perched on the edge of a small rocking chair,

Siskovsky opposite him. Schwab occupied a divan in a corner while Vaska, with bristling black mustachios belying his greying hair and benign eyes, arranged his cello in front of the little fireplace. Then the concert began.

Morrison, score in hand, lay quietly as the quartet slipped into the first movement of Smetana's *From My Life*. They were painting with their music the early years of the composer, of his love of music, his romanticism, and toned the sweep of their playing to the confines of the small room in which they played. . . .

Next, the second movement in the life story of the composer painted the joys of youth as written by Smetana, a quasi-polka, breathing the love of dance. The third movement was a picture of happiness, of love fulfilled. The fourth was one of pathos as the composer realized he was becoming deaf because of the sound of a high piping E continually ringing in his ears.

No thundering applause filled a crowd-jammed hall as the artists finished. There was nothing but the words of the sick man and the praise of his mother, who had slipped into the room during the opening number. But the artists seemed satisfied.

Then they played Haydn's Quartet in G Minor, with its charm and melody and its fiery brilliant finish. This was followed by a little Spanish Dance, lilting, sleepily provocative, by Albeniz. Morrison, from his bed, smiled at the group. "It is like living in a dream," he said; then, in answer to the query "What would you like to hear now?" he answered, "Anything by anybody. It is all so wonderful."

Siskovsky, sorting through his music, brought forth the next number, which was *By the Tarn* by Eugene Goosens. . . .

A glance at a watch and a comparison of bus schedules and Cadek announced that one more number, a happy jolly one, would of necessity complete the program. Then he picked from the portfolio at his feet Percy Grainger's *Molly on the Shore*. The laughing, lilting Celtic dance filled with the unbounded optimism of the Gael, made a fitting ending for the little concert, clearing the air of any touch of pathos and leaving in its place happiness for all concerned.

Goodbyes were said, wishes of best of luck and bon voyage exchanged, and the artists hurried away to catch the bus for the long ride to Phoenix. Joe Morrison hugs to his heart the memory of a joy-filled morning, while four gallant gentlemen, Ottokar Cadek, Jaroslav Siskovsky, Ludvik Schwab and Bedrich Vaska, resume their tour to play again to larger audiences in larger halls but for much smaller pay.

As an epilogue to the above episode, let me add that at the time Joe Morrison was in the last stages of tuberculosis; and no more than a month later we received the sad news from his mother that Joe was dead.

At Red Lodge, Montana, a small mining town, we experienced the only flop of our career. For the miners, our type of music was a little too sophisticated. We should never have been booked there in the first place. (Later, we found out that a well-meaning local benefactor was trying to bring some culture to the place.)

Our first number was Smetana's Quartet, which lasted about forty minutes. This was well received wherever we played it. All during this number we kept hearing a ping-pang-pong sound near the stage which was not in tune with us. We suffered through it and rose to take our bows. Applause was negligible. We realized that something would have to be done to try to save the evening for those who weren't enjoying it.

First we tried to locate and stop that infernal noise. We discovered that it was coming from three washtubs placed at strategic locations to catch the drip from a leaky roof on which snow was melting. It was a choice between being flooded or hearing sour notes; so we chose the latter. As for the program, we announced that because of a mishap to some of our music we were obliged to substitute other numbers which we hoped the listeners would like as well. From then on we played nothing but our encores, which they seemed to like better, although they were hardly enthusiastic. It is good to report that we left town next day unsung but unmolested.

When in New York, we went to many parties at private homes and clubs. One evening stands out in my memory above all the rest. It was a party given by Cobina Wright, a famous New York hostess. A hundred or more guests were present. To name a few, there were Mr. and Mrs. Walter Damrosch (she was the daughter of James G. Blaine), Mr. and Mrs. Clarence Mackay (she was

Grace Moore of the Metropolitan Opera), Mr. and Mrs. Felix Warburg, Mr. and Mrs. Oliver Harriman, Ethel Barrymore, Gloria Swanson, Jascha Heifetz, Rubinstein, Joe Davidson, and Mario Korbel (both sculptors).

Our quartet gave a short concert and then Cobina sang. Her voice was a beautiful lyric soprano which showed good training and put her in a class with professionals. Later, we were all asked to come to the bars for refreshments. One of these bars was for oysters; one was a long table loaded with Swedish smorgasbord; and a third was the liquor bar. In addition, several waiters passed champagne among the guests. The large living room was cleared, a five-piece orchestra started playing, guests began to dance, and soon the party was in full swing.

About midnight people began to wonder why Mr. Wright was not at the party. Cobina herself was in a state of apprehension. All she knew was that he had called early in the evening to say he would be late because of urgent business. His firm had a seat on the New York Stock Exchange.

The party continued with mounting gaiety until close to two o'clock. Then the door opened and Mr. Wright, looking haggard and disheveled, appeared with news of the stock market crash and his firm's bankruptcy.

This, of course, put an end to the festivities. Though the orchestra kept on playing, those of us still sober said good night as gracefully as we could. Eunice and I caught the last local for New Rochelle.

It was a free day for the quartet, and we were able to sleep late; we awakened about noon to learn that the country was shaken to its foundations. We were about to witness what proved to be the worst panic and the longest depression in our history. Stock prices plummeted, banks went broke and closed. Businesses began to shut down and unemployment reached staggering proportions.

Now we had the very situation that kindly President Hoover had been warning Wall Street would happen if it didn't cease the malpractices which had gradually built up after World War I during the Harding and Coolidge administrations, only to be told by Wall Street to go to hell and mind his own business in Washington. Such was the power of money. To be sure, he was a weak and inarticulate president, his speeches were uninspiring, but I doubt there was a person living who could have done better to control the madly insane speculation taking place on the exchanges at that particular time.

It was a pathetic sight to travel around the country and observe the factories which usually hummed with activity now standing silent and deserted. Unemployed were standing on street corners trying to sell chestnuts, apples, almost anything, just to make a few pennies to buy something to eat.

Soldiers from World War I who still hadn't been able to find jobs organized a march on Washington, where thousands of them built a shanty town from which they appealed to the government for help. Delegations were sent to present their case to various officials, including the president; but as far as I know, nothing came of their efforts. They were allowed to stay at their campsite for probably close to a month when President Hoover served notice that the premises must be vacated by a certain date. Well, the premises weren't vacated on that date; so the president sent General McArthur in with a detachment from the regular army which cleaned out shacks and men in a hurry. There must be a difference of opinion on whether such a high-handed method should or should not have been used, but it certainly was no display of appreciation to men who risked their lives for their country at $18 a month.

Conditions gradually became more chaotic, with hunger rampant and a loss of faith in government, people, and institutions; but worst of all was the loss of hope. This was a condition ripe for a communist takeover. Indeed, they made a good try by infiltrating the unions as they had in Russia. There the unions were the backbone of the revolution and made it a success. Here our unions created a strong middle class which resisted infiltration and thereby saved our country from going communist.

The chaotic financial situation created serious problems for everyone in the country, including the New York String Quartet. A few years back the advent of talking pictures had dealt a punishing blow to the record business. Now the sale of records was so negligible that our company, Brunswick, went out of business; and for a time even Victor was threatened. Somehow or other it managed to survive. Because of improvements in long-playing records and sound reproduction, the phonograph experienced a revival.

Attendance at concerts was falling off. We had been accustomed to playing to full houses; now we noticed more and more empty seats. Music on an empty stomach doesn't sound very beautiful.

However, the biggest problem we had to face at the beginning of the 1930 season was a series of about thirty engagements for the Community Concerts Organization. These concerts were designed to bring fine music to communities all over the country. The system works as follows. An association of music-loving people is formed to sponsor a series of concerts. Season tickets are bought at the end of a season for the following one, and purchasers automatically become members. According to the amount taken in, the local elected officers select the next year's programs without risk to anyone. This money is deposited in a local bank and dispensed to the artists the following season.

I said "without risk to anyone," but it was just this factor which now became a risk to us and other artists filling Community Concerts engagements. All over the country banks were failing and not paying depositors. No one knew just how serious the situation really was or how long it would last.

We had conferences with our manager, Arthur Judson. Should we cancel the concerts or should we take the risk of receiving only partial payment or none at all? The decision was a vital one because traveling and hotel expenses ate up much of our pay left from the relatively small fees we were getting for four people.

We hesitated for at least a week. Then we decided to take our manager's optimistic advice that the depression would probably not last very long, that even if we weren't paid at once, we would be paid eventually. With the knowledge that these concert bookings were dovetailed with some thirty other concerts in cities under private managers whose ticket sales were made just prior to the event, we decided to take our chances and play the dates.

At this point it might be well to skip ahead in the narrative and tell what actually happened. The depression lasted over ten years. We received our pay for all concerts under private managers plus five of the Community Concerts, but for the remainder of the latter we received 10 percent to 20 percent on the dollar for about half and nothing for the rest. Hence, when we disbanded I was in a state of nervous exhaustion. This was in itself a major calamity in my life. And soon thereafter my dear mother died.

This was followed by the death of Mrs. Webb (Lila Vanderbilt). Mrs. Webb's funeral services were held at the Episcopal church in Shelburne, where every nook and cranny of the church was filled with masses of white lilies, her favorite flower. My whole being was vibrating with utmost emotion when I played Handel's Largo as I had never played it before or since. So deeply did it overwhelm me that my face and the top of my precious Guarneri violin were covered with a flood of tears at the conclusion. Most of Shelburne and the environs were present to pay their last respects to one they adored.

These two, happening in close succession, didn't give me much time to recuperate, but the peace and quiet at our cottage proved to be a balm.

All this time the problem and uncertainty of our next move was on my mind. We owned our home in New Rochelle, which was a problem. Percy Grainger once told me something which still remains in my memory: "Whenever you buy property, you automatically become a slave to it." This I have found to be true. With the depression on, houses were being foreclosed in great numbers. There were so many of them on the market that prices were ridiculously low; even then they stood vacant for years. This was a very bad time to sell.

Simultaneously, New York City was glutted with fine unemployed musicians from all over the world. To start teaching independently would take years building up a class; so the most feasible solution was to try for a teaching job in some college or music school.

We both hated the cold winters in the north; so the one thing we were agreed on was that if we did leave the environs of New York City we would go to a warm climate.

One day a letter from my good friend, Gilfillan, arrived which broke the impasse. In reply to a letter I had written him about the demise of the New York String Quartet, he answered, "Before you settle down to a new job, why don't you and Eunice come and visit us in France for as long as you can? We would like nothing better." Eunice and I looked at each other and said, "Why not?"

We were at our cottage in Vermont at the time, and it took several weeks to come to a definite decision. We would return to New Rochelle, we would leave New York, we would sell our house at a sacrifice, put our furniture into storage, spend nine months in different parts of Europe, and leave the decision of where in the southern United States we would settle until we returned after we had had a good rest. Coming to this decision, I immediately wrote Gil of our plans, that we were thrilled to accept their kind invitation and that we hoped to sail as soon as we could sell our house.

It was already late in August, so we hurried back to New Rochelle. We advertised in the New York *Times* and, for half what we paid for it, the house was sold in about a month. What a relief to be rid of it. More time was consumed completing details, but we finally sailed from New York on the U.S. freighter *Exermont* on October 30, 1936, bound via Genoa to Magagnosc, France, a small town three miles east of Grasse, the perfume capital of the world, situated halfway up the southern slopes of the Alps, with a gorgeous view of the Mediterranean Sea and the city of Cannes straight ahead some five miles.

Two of our New Rochelle friends offered to drive us to the pier in Hoboken, New Jersey, from which our ship would sail. There we received a double surprise. First, there was a bevy of our New Jersey friends waiting to see us off, and, the dock was barren of any ship that looked capable of undertaking a European voyage. Enquiring at the pier office, we were assured that we were in the right place, but that owing to the imminence of a seamen's strike, which might be proclaimed at any moment, as a matter of precaution the ship had left the pier the previous night and anchored out in the harbor some two miles away. It was further explained that according to the rules, as long as the ship was at the pier the seamen were privileged to strike at will; but once the ship is away from the dock, a strike is classed as mutiny and punishable by law. Furthermore, he requested that we wait about an hour, when we and our baggage would be taken out to the ship.

17

GILFILLAN VISIT

True to his word, in about an hour we ignominiously, and to the delight of our hilarious friends, boarded a tugboat on our journey to Europe. About fifteen minutes later we were transferred to the *Exermont* and on our way in a ship rated at 8,000 tons.

It was a cold, dark, and dreary day; so after we passed the Ambrose Channel lightship and out into the open ocean, it was quite rough. It was around 9:00 p.m.; so after a quite hectic day, we retired early.

Our cabin, with upper and lower bunks, was a good-sized one with the bathroom so situated that the cabin on the other side also had use of it. Then there was a fair-sized reading and sitting room, adjoining which was a small dining room with three tables in it. Since we had no intention of spending much time indoors except to eat and sleep, we found the facilities to our liking, because they were comfortable and clean even though unpretentious. In charge of this menage was a young Filipino steward who couldn't have been nicer or more willing to please. The food was delicious and varied.

There was only one other couple aboard as passengers, of whom we saw very little except at mealtimes, when we ate together at one table. She was a nice person and interesting to talk to. He was the son of some big businessman and could talk of nothing but business the few times we spoke together. I still remember his repetition of his father's admonition, "Never mix charity with business; they are like oil and water—they don't mix." He was a bore; but, worse yet, he was the type of confirmed alcoholic who kept himself soused from the time he awakened until the time he went to sleep. Hence, they spent most of their time in their cabin, while we spent most of ours sitting in comfortable deck chairs or roaming the ship at will.

The second day out the weather became warm and balmy and stayed that way all during the trip across. My two previous crossings were made to north European cities; so when we reached the Rock of Gibraltar, I was surprised that it didn't look anything like the picture of it shown on Prudential Insurance calendars. It wasn't till we were a good piece eastward of the strait that the outline of the Prudential picture showed up in the back of the rock pointing to the Spanish mainland.

As we turned our course northward along the Spanish east coast, our luck ran out; and on entering the Gulf de Lyon, we struck the worst storm of my whole life. Because of our hasty departure from New York, our ship was loaded to only one-fourth of her capacity; hence, we were tossed about in all directions. Every so often we were lying on one side or the other. I thought surely she was going to tip over. Then the bow went almost straight up into the air and returned with a big splash deep into the oncoming wave, bringing the stern high out of the water with its racing propeller shaking the ship like a cat shakes a mouse. Of course we were scared, but it had to be endured for about sixteen hours, with nothing to eat but cold sandwiches, it being impossible to do any cooking. Much damage was done to the ship and its furnishings. We were doubly thankful to arrive safely in Genoa a few days later. It was just after dark; so we and our two fellow passengers decided to go into the city for a real Italian dinner. The stairs which hugged the side of the ship were not lighted as the four of us descended to go ashore, and at the bottom of these stairs there was a small platform from which it was necessary to make a sharp left turn to step onto the pier. Eunice, the other lady and I negotiated this turn nicely, but our alcoholic friend, being last in line, walked straight ahead into the chasm between ship and dock and into the water. The ship's crew came running and pulled him out badly cut by barnacles. This ended our night out in the city.

Arriving in Genoa, we wired the Gilfillans that, as long as our ship was laying over in the harbor for three days and we were allowed to stay aboard at our discretion, we had decided to take advantage of this opportunity to sight-see for two days and then depart by train, arriving at Nice at a certain time—would they please meet us?

I had read stories about the great violinist Paganini willing his very fine Guarneri to his native city of Genoa and that it was on display in the city museum; so, naturally, I couldn't get there fast enough the first thing next morning. There a guide led us to a nook where it was beautifully displayed in a domed glass container especially constructed for this display. Of course, it was under lock and key and well guarded, but when I told a genial guard that I was a violinist and would like to examine the violin more closely (with the help of a generous tip), I was allowed to enter a roped area which prevented the ordinary visitor from getting any closer than about five feet to the glass case in which the violin was mounted in an upright position. Now I had an opportunity to examine the violin closely from all sides. This I did for about a half-hour while Eunice roamed about seeing other exhibits. I noted that the violin had a varnish which was a deeper red than mine and that its condition was not as good, owing to the fact that in Paganini's days cases were not built with brackets that firmly anchored bows to the upper lid of the case as in present times, but rather were merely laid loosely on top of the violin, which eventually wore a long streak in the varnish next to and as long as the fingerboard. The guard informed me that an expert examines the violin periodically and keeps it in repair; otherwise, except on very rare occasions when some great violinist with enough of the proper influence gets permission to play on it briefly, its voice is stilled forever. For me this half-hour was an experience of devotional reverence.

So after two exciting days we took the train which traveled along a route famous for its beautiful scenery, feasting our eyes on the Italian and French Rivieras. At Nice, on the platform we spotted Gil and Jeanne approaching us, all smiles, with open arms. After much exciting talk, we clambered into "Lizette," their Model T Ford, and drove over narrow winding roads along

179

the famed Cote d'Azur to their home in Magagnosc. This road is situated half-way up the Alps, which descend here and drown their feet in the Mediterranean a few miles distant.

As we were leaving Nice, the sun was already setting. So by the time we reached the upper heights, we could see the lights popping on all over the hills below us all the way to the lighted necklaces along the shore of the Mediterranean. It was a beautiful sight, but we were so excited and had so much to gab about that most of it passed by without our observation.

Our hosts had only been married a couple of years, so this was our first meeting with Jeanne. Little did we realize at the time that we were meeting one of the most kind and thoughtful human beings in our lives and that soon she would become one of our most cherished and devoted friends.

It was dark when we arrived in Magagnosc; so we could not see what the outside of the villa looked like. But I do remember that because of the narrow road and the sharp turns Gil had to do much forward and backward zigzagging in order to get into his garage.

Entering the villa, we were shown eight large rooms all tastefully furnished with nothing but antiques. Two bathrooms and kitchen had all modern equipment. I daresay the antique furniture along with the paintings were more valuable than the property. In short, it was evident that people of some means with good taste and love for antiques lived here.

We were shown to our room; and after freshening up a bit, we went downstairs, where Jeanne was already setting dinner on the table. After such a hectic day, I was sharpening up my whistle for a cocktail or two or three; but none seemed to be forthcoming. A little later Gil appeared at the door with two bottles of champagne in his hand. This being my favorite drink, thoughts of cocktails immediately disappeared. Dinner was a gourmet's delight; so we sat talking and drinking champagne until quite late.

During the evening they broke the news to us that a few days previously Gil had received a telegram from the Weyerhauser Timber Company, of which he was an official, that his presence was required in the States to settle some business. With profuse apologies they expressed regret at having to leave us in about two weeks but not to be too discouraged because they would be away at least six months and wished we would stay on until their return or as long as we could.

Then Gil went on to explain that he had already made some twenty round trips across the Atlantic but not a one across the Pacific. So since Jeanne also hadn't had the pleasure of this experience, a prolonged trip to the Far East had been on their minds for some time. Now with this business meeting taking place in Tacoma, Washington, if ever they were going to do it, this would be an appropriate time.

They said we would be left with a full-time handyman-gardener and a part-time maid, who would do all the housework except the cooking, but that neither of them slept on the premises. They said that if we stayed on, their minds would be more at ease with the knowledge that there was less likelihood of the house being broken into with someone living there.

Of course, this came as a big surprise to us, but since our intentions were to spend eight or nine months in Europe anyway, this was the chance of a lifetime. So it didn't take us long to accept their kind invitation and inform them that a stay of about five months would be a godsend to us which could be fitted into our plans nicely.

We slept late the next day. The first thing we did after breakfast on that warm sunny morning was to take a stroll into their garden, which sloped down steeply in terraces no more than eight feet wide on a plot about the size of a football field. Lying on the southern slopes of the Alps, this whole Riviera territory is sheltered from the cold north winds sweeping over the tops of the mountains, which make the northern shore of the Mediterranean much warmer than the southern, which is Africa. My guess is that the climate is very similar to that of northern Florida. Occasionally, they will have an inch or two of snowfall, but that usually lasts only a very short time. Weatherwise, what the natives loathe most of all is a wind called the mistral which blows from the east and is cold, damp, clammy, and disagreeable. The elevation of our villa was 1,200 feet, which in itself made it a bit cooler than the lower levels; but the view was magnificent.

Arriving as we did in the middle of November and what was

supposed to be their usual rainy season, we struck a spell of good weather; and the Gils informed us that so far they hadn't had to use heat in the house. Tramping through the garden, we noticed that there were very few signs of fall as yet. Everything was lusciously green and well kept. The vegetable garden had every seasonable vegetable in it you can imagine, and the gardener kept us supplied from it all winter, coming to ask Eunice daily what her preference was that day.

Flowers of many varieties were scattered about in great profusion all over the terraces with emphasis on the large Parma violets and jasmine. Incidentally, Grasse, the perfume capital of the world, was only three and one-half miles distant; so the whole territory for miles around was planted in flowers by residents who sold their product to the perfumery. Since there were no smokestacks belching smoke anywhere for miles around, our neighborhood breathed air which was loaded with the sweet smelling aroma of flowers twenty-four hours a day.

There was a regular forest of trees on the place. Eunice, being interested in horticulture, made the following list: eucalyptus, pepper, mimosa, apple, pear, plum, peach, persimmon, medlar, orange, lemon, fig, date palms, palms, oaks, cork oaks, cypress, umbrella pines, long-needle pines, willow, and plane trees. Now to cap this list, there were fifty-one olive trees mixed in with all the above. Later we took frequent strolls along the paths of this garden, always finding something we hadn't noticed before.

The Gils were inveterate hikers like ourselves, so the four of us spent the two weeks before their departure taking long walks over the hills of that beautiful area regardless of the weather. All of it is mountainous; so until we got acclimated, our leg muscles were quite sore.

Wherever inhabited, the mountainside was terraced by stone walls averaging anywhere from six to fifteen feet in height and often only two feet in width, depending on the lay of the land. This, of course, made gardening an expensive proposition, not only because of the original cost, but also for upkeep, because these walls were forever needing attention to keep them from sliding downhill.

With all the walking and auto trips we took with the Gils before they left, we got a pretty good idea of the surroundings for many miles around and met many of their friends. Away from the seashore, which was lined with modern hotels and apartments catering to the tourist trade, the hinterland was dotted with ancient villages and deserted castles dating back to medieval times, a joy for historians and antiquarians to visit.

With all the gallivanting the four of us did, the two weeks passed all too quickly and the day arrived when we and Andre, with a wheelbarrow loaded with their luggage, escorted them about a quarter mile up the hill to the main road, where they boarded a bus for Nice enroute to Marseilles, where they had passage on one of the large French ships sailing for Singapore. Dejectedly, we walked back to the villa with Andre, the gardener, and his wheelbarrow; and there we sat down with expressions of praise for the Gils which must have burned their ears.

We thanked our lucky stars for the opportunity to be masters of such a lovely establishment in such a superbly beautiful location. Also, being a quarter of a mile from the main road, which at that time carried very little traffic, plus the fact that there was an eight-foot-high stone wall which surrounded the place, it was so peaceful that one heard only the songs of the multitude of birds in the garden.

At last we began to relax, realizing that we were nervously exhausted. What with the sale of our house, the demise of the quartet, the uncertainty of our future, and a very small cash balance, we had plenty to worry about. Fortunately, we had one pretty solid fortress to lean on, the Guarneri; but I wouldn't have sold that come hell or high water. So it was an early supper and early bed that night; and for several weeks thereafter we did nothing but eat, sleep, read, and take short walks. Gradually our walks were lengthened; and often we would be out all day stopping for lunch at some rustic inn or farmhouse, where we would get delicious homemade cheese, milk, and really fresh eggs.

Realizing that this idyllic existence wasn't going to last forever and I soon would be forced to show my wares in order to make a living, I resumed practice on the violin about three hours a day. Eunice would take a book and lie happily in the sun reading for hours on end. I preferred to do my reading at night in bed.

Incidentally, the only thing I missed all the time we were there was the New York *Times*, of which I have been an avid reader all my adult life. In the bigger cities of Europe, the New York *Herald Tribune* or London *Times* were procurable; so these sufficed for the time.

I have never acquired calluses on my posterior from sitting; so it wasn't long before I went looking for something to do, preferably something useful. It didn't take long to find an almost inexhaustible source in all that antique furniture. There was hardly a piece that didn't need regluing, patching, or staining somewhere. For weeks this kept me busy when I wasn't practicing or walking.

I had noticed that the shutters, windows, door trim, and screen frames needed painting; so into Grasse we went to buy paint, putty, and brushes. This kept me busy for several months.

Eunice, of course, did the cooking, which also entailed doing all the shopping except for vegetables. Here is where her knowledge of French came in very handy. She had taken a course in the language in high school and at Vassar but with disuse had forgotten much. It tickled me to notice how much more fluent she got day by day.

I, on the other hand, learned to say, "Bon soleil, Andre. Beaucoup travail," which was my standard greeting to our gardener when he appeared each morning. He was a kindly soul, and we both took it as a joke as time went by. Occasionally we would lend him a helping hand, for instance, when the fifty-one olive trees were harvested and the olives taken to the mill to be transformed into oil.

Of course, our vegetables were fresh from the garden; but so were our baked goods fresh from the bakery. I still can taste those delicious croissants (crescents), brioches, and that superb French bread. We wondered how we could ever go back to eating that stuff called bread in the States. Then there was a brand of spaghetti, along with a Parmesan cheese, which was freshly ground before our eyes, the combination of which tasted superior to any we have eaten anywhere either before or since.

In a neighboring valley we would walk to an apiary, where we bought a mixture of thyme and lavender honey, which, in our opinion, was as delicious as the famous Hymettus honey of Greece.

All in all, we led a peaceful, contented life—just what we wanted—but at the end of two months, if we wished to stay any longer in France, we would have had to go through a lot of red tape. So, since we wanted to tour Italy anyway, we decided to go there for about a month and then return for another two months, which was allowable.

Combining a minimum amount of our belongings into one suitcase, we set off by train from Nice to Milan. Here it might be well to mention that to go into detail on this trip as well as on future ones would entail the writing of several more books, and then they would be travelogues. My intention is to write the story of a life. Besides, Eunice has kept a diary on all our travels and written far better than I could; so it behooves me to give just the highlights.

It must be remembered that by this time I had done a fabulous amount of traveling in Europe and America; so with my being able to speak four languages, plus Eunice's French, there was never a time that we had to go very far to be understood in one of them.

This idea of being herded around in droves, in buses, with guides explaining points of interest is fine for novices; and I recommend it highly. But it is confusing with the crowd's chattering, the getting in and out of buses, the difficulty of hearing and understanding what the guide is saying. So we chose to do it another way. But this can only be done by those with time unlimited and strong legs.

We would take our Baedeker, which gave us a synopsis of all the points of interest in all Europe, select those that interested us most, and go visit them that day. This way we could stay in any place as long as we wanted to and also put our minds on the subject without the confusion of a crowd. So the night before, we would make a list of the things we wished to see, start out after breakfast, and do the town by foot, bus, or taxi in leisurely fashion.

At this time American dollars were at a premium and were exchanged for two to three times as much in local currency all over Europe. Even then we chose to stay at pensions because they were much less expensive yet much more homey than hotels. You met people from all over the world who spoke to each other, whereas in a hotel everyone was indifferent to other guests.

Besides, you avoided that awful custom in Europe where everybody who served you in any way lined up at the exit as you were departing, expecting a handout.

Milan is the most industrialized city in Italy; therefore, most of the buildings are of modern architecture, so not of much interest to us. We did spend all morning doing the famous "Il Duomo" (cathedral) from top to bottom. Part of the afternoon we spent visiting other points of interest of which Leonardo da Vinci's fresco of Christ's Last Supper on the wall of a convent was the most important. We almost cried seeing how it was deteriorating.

We tried to get tickets for the La Scala for that night with no luck; so, as we had exhausted our choices in Milan, on the spur of the moment we decided to move on to Venice.

As it turned out, our express didn't arrive until shortly after midnight. A pension was recommended to us which was only two blocks from the railroad station. Two inches of freshly fallen snow lay on the ground, and the air was so thick with dampness that we could almost swim in it. Sloshing through wet snow, we arrived at the pension to find the place dark. Our feet were wet, the street was practically deserted, and we were in no mood to start looking further. So I took courage in hand and rang the doorbell. After two or three minutes a little half-sleepy old lady appeared at the door; and, having been forewarned that she was Swiss German, I, in her native tongue, apologized for awakening her and inquired if she had a vacant room for the night. She replied in the affirmative but that, unfortunately, the furnace was out of order and the rooms were without heat. Any place seemed better than that awful weather outside, so we gladly took one of her rooms. We were already chilled to the bones, but up in that room it seemed colder than ever; so we hastily popped into the double bed and cuddled up under an enormous feather bed, but even then we didn't thaw out for several hours and it was not until early morning before either of us was warm enough to fall asleep. Next day we both agreed that that was the coldest experience of our lives—and I'm not forgetting the two winters I spent in Petrograd, where the winters are dark and long and the thermometer frequently dips to 40 degrees below.

We were awake by 8:00; and after a continental breakfast of a bun and hot coffee and learning that it was uncertain when the place would have heat, we set out to look for a room elsewhere. It being the off season, with tourists as scarce as hen's teeth, we had no difficulty finding comfortable quarters in a small, modest hotel at reduced winter rates. Of course, as was the custom all over Europe, the heat was on low all day, say about 50 degrees; and then around 5:00 p.m. it would be increased to about 65 degrees. It isn't only a question of economy; that is the way they like it.

After transferring our luggage, we set out to explore Venice on foot since the only other means of transportation was by gondola. The latter we made good use of when the weather improved in a day or two.

It would be presumptuous on my part to sing the praises of Venice in this account, for poets and authors have been doing just that for generations; and they are still doing it today, for the subject is inexhaustible. The whole city is like one big museum of precious objects.

Suffice it to say that we were out daily from morn till night wth our constant companion, the Baedeker, exploring and generally winding up at St. Mark's Cathedral, because it was so beautiful inside as well as outside and because there always seemed to be some kind of pageantry going on there.

Our hotel was only about three blocks away. The room was nicely furnished and comfortable. The meals were excellent. So what with all the wonders we were seeing, we lingered in paradise for a whole week, departing early one morning for the railroad station by gondola via the Grand Canal, passing open markets along its banks busily selling mostly fish and farm products, which created a picturesque contrast with the palaces which lined the banks.

At the station we boarded a train for Florence. The first half of the journey we traveled through Lombardy farming country with its quaint thatch-roofed farmhouses and its super abundance of those famous stately and shapely Lombardy poplars. Later on we entered a mountainous region which seemed like one tunnel after another with short stretches in between of farming country which propagated olive trees.

In Florence we stopped at another pension for four days, tramping the streets from early morn till night with our trust-

187

worthy Baedeker, absorbing the treasure trove that lay all about us. Here Savonarola ruled with an iron hand trying to make people be good even if he had to kill them. Here also lie entombed in the Church of Santa Croce such all-time greats as Michelangelo, Galileo, Machiavelli, Rossini, Cherubini, and many more to whom we bowed with great reverence as we strode by.

Unique and very picturesque is the Ponte Vecchio with silversmith shops and little homes looking like pigeon coops hanging from all sides of it. Otherwise, there are famous sculptures and paintings everywhere plus more Della Robbia bas reliefs than can be seen elsewhere. Again, we lived in a blissful trance, seeing and living amongst these masterpieces of art of which we had read.

With apologies for abruptness, we must go on to Rome. Here again we shacked up in a good pension in the Eternal City. I give up. It took Gibbon volumes to write about the rise and fall of the Roman Empire; so since most people with any kind of an education know more about Rome than any other foreign city, I will be very brief, saying that we spent four glorious and exciting days seeing all the interesting sights which suited our fancy. There was an inexhaustible plethora of these; but since there were more places we wished to visit, we had to adhere to a planned time schedule. As it happened, we almost didn't adhere to it anyway.

While we were there a pope lay dying in his chambers in Vatican City. On our tour of St. Peter's basilica we climbed to the cupola atop the dome, from which we got a fine view of Rome and Vatican City directly below us. Our guide pointed out what he said were doctors rushing in and out of a door leading to the pope's chambers; but as it happened, he lingered on. We certainly would have stayed for the funeral if he had died while we were there, but Pope Pius XI survived for another two years.

Our next stop by train was Naples. We had no recommendation for a pension; so we chose the Hotel Britannique recommended by the American Express. It was situated on a hill; and as we drove higher and higher in our taxi, we noticed what a stupendous view we would have and so resolved to try for a room fronting on this panorama. We were successful. Not only that, but when we reached our room expecting to have two windows from which to look out at such a gorgeous sight, to our delight we found in addition a door leading onto a private balcony.

As soon as we got rid of our bellboy, the first thing we did, it being a warm sunny day, was to go out there and sit looking at Vesuvius to the left, puffing away at his cigar. Directly in front of us was the Bay of Naples and the Tyrrhenean Sea, the harbor of which was a beehive of activity with the loading and unloading of ships from all nations. In the distance the islands of Capri and Ischia could be seen.

I'm trying very hard not to make this a travelogue, so will sum up an exciting four days' stay by saying that we took the funicular to the top of Mount Vesuvius, visited the buried but partially excavated cities of Pompeii and Herculaneum, from which artifacts had been taken and placed in the Naples Museum, and finally made the boat trip to the beautiful Isle of Capri. This island is a focal point for newlyweds from all over Europe on their honeymoons just as Niagara Falls is in the United States.

When we arrived at the dock from which a boat about fifty feet in length (built something like a scow, with railings around the deck against which were placed benches) was about to depart, there were already thirty of these couples cavorting around, smooching and having a gay old time. Dressed up in their best bibs and tuckers, they were a heart-warming sight to behold. All aboard and off we started.

While in the harbor things stayed pretty gay; but when we struck open water, it was very rough. And slowly but surely 90 percent of our party started to turn greener and greener, and one by one they started dashing for the railing. Some made it in time; some didn't. It is a four-hour trip; so when we arrived at Capri, the boat was a mess. As for our happy couples, most were a forlorn sight with disheveled clothes, tousled hair and a deathly pallor on their faces with many lying on benches, not able to stand up. We spent all day on the island and coming back on the same boat in the evening it was a repeat performance. "Ah, love is a many splendored thing."

On to Pisa to see the famous leaning tower. We stopped at a hotel where the clerk told us that Charles Lindbergh and family were staying. Sure enough, we saw them at dinner that night.

First thing in the morning we went to climb the leaning tower. Looking at it from the outside you could easily see that it really leaned, but it was when you climbed up the stairs inside and then walked around balconies at each story on the outside that you realized how much. Going up one side of the balcony gives one a peculiar sensation. It requires vigorous uphill pushing. Going downhill on the other side you really have to put on the brakes for fear you will get going too fast and plunge down over the railing to the ground below.

Our next stop was San Remo, on the Italian Riviera, noted as a gambling town with a casino rivaling that at Monte Carlo. We only stopped here overnight because the train we were on would have gotten us into Nice at midnight; so we stopped over for a train the next morning, which got us into Nice at noon. We took a bus which brought us back to Magagnosc by 2:00 p.m.

Eunice had written the gardener as to when we would arrive, and the villa was freshly cleaned, with flowers in every room. It felt good to be back and be able to relax for a change. It didn't take long to get back into the pattern of life which we had enjoyed so much previously. I would practice mornings, and afternoons were devoted to excursions which this time we extended further afield, namely, Monte Carlo and Vence, to mention two of the most famous. In between, I painted the shutters on the villa, which I was determined to get finished before our departure.

So another two months at the villa passed like the wind. I was pretty well run-down when we first arrived, but this did me a world of good. I was feeling more like my old self again.

Our predetermined destination was Vienna, but dear Venice seemed to be on our minds. So one of us came up with the idea of stopping there for a week on the way. Alas, the day of departure arrived; and, bidding our friends a fond farewell, we departed.

In Venice we spent another glorious week revisiting some of the sights previously seen, as well as new ones, but often returning to our favored St. Mark's Cathedral and Square.

Now, a parting thought. As we were leaving Italy, I heard many people complaining about the trains being late and the gypping of the tourists, etc., etc. But they should have seen it in pre-Mussolini days as I did. Let me give the devil his due; he *did* much to bring order out of chaos, cleaned up the country, and reduced corruption.

18

RETURN TO VIENNA, PISEK, AND PRAGUE

Now to Vienna, through and over the Alps, all the way by train, arriving about 9:00 p.m., and putting up at the Hammerand Hotel, where I had stopped several times in my student days. By the time we checked in it was 10:00 p.m.; but since we were only a few blocks from the big Rathskeller in the City Hall, I suggested we go there for a beer before going to bed. And so we did. It being Good Friday, the place was almost deserted. Still, they were serving; so we ordered Oster Brau, a kind of bock beer sold only at Easter time. This tasted so good we drank two big steins apiece.

Next morning, as we roamed about the city, it struck me forcibly how shabby and run-down things looked in comparison to my student days, when it was the head of the Austro-Hungarian Empire ruled by Franz Josef. No wonder, since now it was only the Austrian Republic, having been obliged to sever its connections with vassal states such as Hungary, Czechoslovakia, part of Poland, and several of the Balkan states by treaty after World War I. Although Austrians speak the German language, they are temperamentally more like the Bavarians—more happy-go-lucky than Germans.

Of course, losing all the tax money that poured into Vienna from all those vassal states must have meant a terrific readjustment in the whole economy; but I couldn't help but notice that, in spite of lowered standards in almost everything else, musical standards were just as high, with even more musical activity than in my day. Many of the abandoned palaces were used as concert halls, and it was quite usual to see twenty or more concerts advertised to take place in one night.

191

I had six cousins living here in various stages of affluence; so we paid them all several visits and were entertained by them in various ways. This gave Eunice an opportunity to meet Viennese people and see how they lived.

In between we tramped the beautiful Vienna woods as I did almost every Sunday of yore with other students. We hiked from Heiligenstadt to the top of Kahlenberg along the same path that Beethoven frequented, which is purported to have been the inspiration for his *Pastoral* Symphony.

On Easter Sunday we went to the service at Stefans Kirche, where the choral singing was magnificent. And so two busy and exciting weeks passed by all too quickly; and we were on our way to Písek, Czechoslovakia, with my cousin Hedda seeing us off at the train, holding a bouquet of flowers for Eunice.

Písek was a very small town located in among hills similar to the Berkshires, where my teacher, Professor Sevcik, lived and lies buried, and where I had spent a year and three summers. We arrived there at 11:00 p.m. The town was deserted, almost everybody having gone to bed except at the hotel, where the proprietor was just in the act of closing up. As we entered, he looked up and almost turned to stone as he immediately recognized me. Then we had a good laugh and good chat before retiring for the night.

It must be remembered that twenty-three years had elapsed since I departed as a student. World War I had taken place, after which Czechoslovakia was liberated from the yoke of the Austro-Hungarian Empire and made a free republic. I was most anxious to see how much better conditions would be. The next day I took Eunice around to meet many of my old friends, who, of course, were all dumbfounded to see us, since I hadn't written anyone that we would be coming. One of the first innovations that came to my attention was that most of the men were not wearing hats. Twenty-three years prior to this I was the only one in town who had the temerity to commit such a horrible sin.

Just from observation, I couldn't see that economically people were much better off than they were under the Kaiser. There were still too many people walking around looking ill-fed, in shabby clothes, with awful-looking teeth. Actually, when I was there as a student, my colleagues and I, as well as the citizenry, had just as much freedom under the kaiser as we had in the States, except for the privilege of denigrating the monarchy. One of my young smart-aleck colleagues from Chicago tested this out at a concert which opened with the playing of the Austrian National Anthem, at which everyone stood up except he. After the finish of the anthem, a gendarme tapped our friend on the shoulder and led him off to jail, where he was held for two months, then tried and expelled from the country. Incidentally, all the time I was there in my student days I never heard of a robbery or other crime being committed except when roving gypsies were in the neighborhood, when a chicken or goose would mysteriously disappear. There had been only one gendarme for the whole town, and he had been on duty only at night.

It was good to be back and again hear the bugler sounding off from the high belfry tower of the local church with a call after each hour of the night just after the clock struck. This is a colorful custom that has survived from the middle ages, akin to the "All's well" by the night watchman; only here the man's principal duty is to watch out for fires.

At the end of each day revisiting friends and old haunts, we made it a custom after dinner to visit a wine shop which was run by one of my best friends; and there we would spend most of our evenings drinking excellent wine and talking to other friends and customers who would drop in. Everybody knew everybody else; so it was always like one happy family.

After about two weeks of this, we decided to make a walking trip of about forty miles to visit two peasant cousins who lived back in the hinterland, many miles from the railroad or any form of public transportation. The spring weather all over central Europe is much like that of New England, cold and rainy. So it had been ever since we left the Riviera; and so it was that morning we started out on our hike, me with a knapsack on my back containing the barest of our necessities.

We tramped all day in the mud along the beautiful gorge of the Otava River, inhaling the pungent smell of wet pine needles all the way. After about twenty miles, we came to a small country inn; and, since daylight was already ebbing, we decided to stop. We had a choice of two unheated rooms, after which the proprietor kindly invited us to join him and his family in the kitchen, where it was warm. On entering it, and since it takes up almost a quarter of the room, the first thing that came to our notice was the enormous six-by-ten-foot combination ceramic stove, bake oven and bed, which is common in country towns all over Europe. One small portion of it is used for cooking. The interior is a large bake oven in which they bake that delicious rye bread than which I never tasted any better; and in winter the whole family sleeps on its flat warm top, provided they don't exceed four or five in number. We were greeted warmly by the lady of the house, who was in the process of doing some chores, with a hen sitting on eggs in one basket and a duck doing the same in another. In a corner sat a young son having his hair cut by an itinerant barber.

After asking if we wouldn't like to remove our wet shoes, which we did, curiosity got the better of them. Since they could plainly tell we were foreigners, they began to ply me with questions such as "Where are you from?" and "Where are you bound for?" I told them we were Americans and that we were on our way to visit my two cousins in neighboring villages about twenty miles distant. With that they all shouted in unison, "We know them well!" From that moment on it was like old home week. We all had supper together and, after a continuous talking spree, we retired to our warmed room for a restful sleep.

The next morning we hiked in the mud to the small farmhouse of one of my cousins, some ten miles distant. Since I hadn't written him, my expectations were that this would be a big surprise; but the itinerant barber had preceded us by several hours. So by the time we got there, the whole village knew about it; and there stood my two cousins at the door, waiting to welcome us. The second cousin who lived another ten miles in a village further on just happened to be on a visit to his brother that day. So we three cousins had a grand reunion, babbling on in Czech for several hours, of which poor Eunice didn't understand a word; but she bore it stoically, because this being her first experience in a peasant cottage, there was so much novelty in the surroundings that time didn't hang heavy.

After a lunch of cabbage soup and the ever-present delicious rye bread, since this cousin had only one room for living purposes and the visiting cousin had two, it was decided that we would put up with the second cousin. Shortly after lunch the three of us set off on foot to tramp another ten miles to his home. Even though it was muddy, cold, and damp, the trip was through beautiful, well-kept, aromatic white pine forests and hilly country; so we enjoyed the whole trip in spite of the weather. Arriving at my cousin's abode shortly after dark, our entry almost floored my cousin's wife and son and his wife, who stared at us bug-eyed. Nothing unusual except births, marriages, and deaths ever happens in these villages; so the unexpected arrival of a cousin and his wife from America was a momentous event.

After things settled down a bit, we were served a supper of pea soup, cheese, and milk. Then we all sat down beside the large bake oven stove into which every so often my cousin would throw a handful of little broken twigs no bigger than match sticks, which the family had gleaned from amongst pine needles used as bedding for the cow, and this kept us tolerably warm while we talked. I told them about America and their relatives there and they told me about relatives in that neighborhood where my father was born.

It was late before we all went to bed. The four of them slept atop the bake oven, while Eunice and I shared a double bed in an unheated room with a temperature close to the freezing point; but with a mountainous feather bed for cover, cuddling up, and the excitement and walking of the day, we soon were warm and fast asleep. We both slept like logs and didn't awake until we heard stirrings in the kitchen around daybreak.

In the cold room we moved with great speed so fast that I did not notice that my body was covered from neck to toes with flea bites. This prompted Eunice to examine herself; but, lo and behold, she was untouched. To this day I am trying to figure out how come they considered me such a choice morsel. At breakfast, consisting of roasted rye "coffee" with butter-smeared rye bread, I mentioned this enigma to my cousin, whose reply was, "Oh, those fleas, pay no attention to them; they won't hurt you. You'll get used to them and they'll get used to you."

After breakfast we were shown the premises, which consisted of a building with thatched roof containing the following. There was the one fairly large room in which we sleep (about twenty feet square), containing a double bed, a bureau, a dresser, a table and an assortment of chairs constructed of wood in a simple design. We later learned that this room was usually rented out to visitors from Prague who spent their vacations here. Adjoining this was the kitchen, about fifteen feet square, containing the big bake oven mentioned before, which took up about a half the space. The rest was taken up by a table, chairs, and a cupboard for dishes. It really should be called a living room, because this was where the family cooked and ate their meals and spent most of their time, especially in the winter, because it was the only heated room in the house. Adjoining this on the rear of the house was the son's small bedroom, just large enough to contain a double bed, a dresser, and a chair, squeezed fairly close together. Adjoining on the front side was a fairly large barn (actually a part of the house), about twenty feet by thirty feet, which contained a stall for the cow, one for a pig, and one for a few geese and chickens, along with a wagon and some farm implements. The cow was used for dray purposes as well as for milk supply. Above all this was the hayloft. In front of the barn and running almost all the way across the front of the house was a pit about ten feet deep and equally wide in which they stored all their manure, which for them was very precious because it was their only source of fertilizer. Indeed, when stepping out of the front door, one had to be very careful not to stumble over the wooden shoes that were always parked there; otherwise one might go catapulting head-long into the manure pit. These shoes were always taken off on entering the house, where one then walked in padded stockings. Water was drawn from a well no more than ten feet from the manure pit, which must have been frightfully contaminated, to which contamination they no doubt had become immune. This we avoided unless it was boiled. This was no hardship for us because the beer in Czechoslovakia was so delicious that I made many trips to the local pub to keep all of us amply supplied the whole time we were there, which was about two weeks. We helped with the chores as much as possible, and at night we would sit next to the bake oven and drink beer during our talks.

One Sunday they took us to the small country church where my father was christened. It was about a one-mile walk. Just before reaching the church, the men and ladies separated onto two different paths into the woods to do what comes naturally, reuniting at the door of the church.

Another day Eunice and I spent floating and shooting the rapids down the river Moldau on a long raft the size of a football field. The scenery was very beautiful, similar to our Berkshires, and the constant interchange of peaceful floating with shooting of rapids was thrilling. The raft was on its way to distant parts, possibly Prague; but we debarked at a point where we would have a five-mile walk back, just in time to reach my cousin's home in time for supper.

Another day was spent accompanying my cousin's son and his wife, who was eight months' pregnant, on a trip to their small scattered fields to plant sugar beets, from which they make molasses or grind up to feed the cow. The nearest field was a twenty-mile walk away and had already been plowed. Down the center of the ridges the girl was walking, bent over, half doubled up, making an indentation with a spoon with one hand, while sprinkling the seed and covering it over with the other. Her husband followed her, leveling off the tops of the ridges with a rake. They had rye, clover for their rabbits, and poppy seed for baking in other parts of this field. There wasn't much we could do to assist them in this operation; so we stood on the sidelines feeling sorry for the fetus. On the way home, she carried a hamper filled with clover on her back while he carried the rake.

On another day we made the most memorable trip of our whole stay. Its objective was to buy and bring home a young pregnant cow from a larger town some five miles distant in which the Jahrmark (akin to our country fair) was being held. We were called at 5:00, just full daylight and brilliantly clear. After a quick breakfast, we started on a hike that has remained indelibly imprinted on our memories as one of the most enchanting experiences of our lives.

The sun was just rising over the horizon. The sky was deep blue and cloudless. The woods through which we trudged were pine-scented and still. To crown this delectable treat, the cuckoos began calling back and forth to each other from all directions. It was the first time Eunice had heard such a symphony of cuckoos, and time and again she stopped walking, absolutely entranced.

As we got well on our way, we fell into a scattered parade of

197

other peasants, many leading cows or bulls to the sale, followed by a wife with a stick urging the animals on. From the high spots we could see the same processions converging into the small town of Mylevsko—lying snugly in a valley—via all roads and trails in all directions. It was a good two-hour walk.

Having thoroughly surveyed the fair, it was lunchtime, so we ambled over to the local hotel for a bite to eat after making arrangements with cousin Joseph to meet us there when he had finished his business activities. After several hours he came, dragging a reluctant cow up the street. We went to meet him, whereupon he handed me the rope and said. "Here, you lead her while I coax from behind with this stick." It immediately became evident that this pregnant cow had made up her mind she wasn't going anywhere. So my leading soon degenerated into a pulling match of the front portion, while cousin Joseph hit her legs with a stick and pushed the hind portion. This was strenuous work; so we changed places frequently, while the cow remained adamant, and Eunice never stopped laughing in all the four hours it took us to get home. This was twice as long as it took us to get there. Even the cuckoos laughed at us, but we finally got her home. So it was early to bed for all of us that night.

After this event and making a trip to the cousin we had first visited, we bade sad farewells all around and hiked back to Písek via a different route from the one on which we had come. It felt good to get back to Písek from the backwoods and once again hear the bugler blow "All's well" from the church tower every hour of the night and, more importantly, to be able to take a bath—something we hadn't done in over two weeks.

Our original plans had been to leave Písek a few days earlier, but when we learned that President Benes and his wife were honoring the city with a visit, we changed our minds, especially since we were invited by the president of the biggest bank in town (who was an old friend) to come and sit on his second-floor balcony, which overlooked the square where all the welcoming ceremonies would be held. The event had been looked forward to for a long time, resulting in the repainting of most of the buildings, which were several hundred years old.

We couldn't have had better seats from which to view a thrilling affair. There were the usual speeches, military parades, bands playing, excellent choral singing, etc.; but best of all, we liked the colorful national costumes worn by peasants who had come to town from the outlying country, mostly on foot. Many of these also performed their native dances, to our great delight. In short, something was happening from 10:00 a.m. until 10:00 p.m., and we stuck it out to the bitter end.

We then went to my good friend Franta Kolar's for a glass of wine and then to bed, two very tired people. In a few days we departed for Prague, taking Marenka with us, (the sister of Franta,) in whose wine establishment we spent so many pleasant evenings. She had a cousin who was chief of police in Prague. My heart was heavy, for I dearly loved the people who had been so hospitable to me, for at that time I never dreamed of being able to pay another visit.

Arriving at the station in Prague, I got my first pleasant surprise when I noticed that instead of being called the Franz Joseph Station, the station had been renamed the Woodrow Wilson Station. The panorama one beholds is as beautiful as can be found in any city anywhere. Since great pains have been taken by previous generations to preserve its beauty and antiquity, Prague is a delight to the inquisitive individual who cares to read up on what he or she is seeing, especially the old town, where every stone and building has a place in history. Steering clear of making this account into a travelogue, let me conclude by saying that we spent at least three-quarters of our ten-day stay sight-seeing. Having lived here almost a year twenty-five years previously, it gave me great joy and satisfaction to act as guide for Eunice and to reappraise with my greater knowledge and experience the value and charm of things seen and studied on my first visit. I can assure you that now my opinions were much more humble.

Otherwise, we spent quite a bit of time with my stepsister, Josephine, who accompanied us on many expeditions. She was born in Vienna and was brought to the States by mother, who was her aunt as well as stepmother. She was educated through college and became a public school teacher in Cleveland, but at about age twenty-five she took to religion too seriously and had a nervous breakdown. After a couple of years in an insane asylum, she was released with the advice that a change to a more peaceful environment might be the answer to her problem. And so it was that my father sent her to Prague, where she established herself as a teacher of English. At the time of our visit, after living there some thirty years, she seemed perfectly happy.

We saw Marenka on several occasions, but I think the most memorable was when we took her to the opera to hear *The Bartered Bride*. This opera is so distinctly nationalistic, I can't conceive of it being done elsewhere nearly as well; so the three of us got a big kick out of it.

Another memorable occasion was when the chief of police and his wife invited us to sit with them on their barge on the Moldau to witness the celebration of St. John's Day, one of the major holidays in Czechoslovakia. In return, we invited him and his wife and Marenka to have dinner with us at one of the best restaurants just before the ceremonies. When we reached the banks of the river in the police chief's auto, we saw it jammed with innumerable rowboats, canoes, and barges gliding about slowly and silently, all brilliantly lighted up with Japanese lanterns. We were escorted to the chief's barge, which was anchored to the bank and on which a few of his friends had already congregated and to whom we were forthwith introduced. He had work to do; so he left us while we sat talking to his wife and others. As soon as darkness became absolute, numerous buildings along the banks were floodlighted and the fireworks began, set off from an island in the middle of the river. The sky was filled with brightly shining stars and a small sliver of the moon. The air was soft and warm; and with all the slowly moving lights, it seemed like fairyland. There we sat entranced for at least an hour, watching the most extravagantly lavish display of fireworks either of us had ever seen. Now in our old age, we still talk about it.

Czechoslovakia is famous for its skill in smoked meats, especially Prague ham, which is in great demand all over Europe. Its sausages and frankfurters are most delectable, especially with that equally delectable beer, either dark or light. In fact, our whole stay was delectable; but since we wanted to spend the summer at Shelburne, Vermont, and wanted to stop in a number of other places, it was time to get going.

Our next stop was Nuremberg, the city made famous by

Wagner with his *Meistersinger*. It was a city of medieval times with many of those ancient buildings still standing, well preserved; so we spent three days there finding much of interest that was rewarding. Now we were in Germany; and although Hindenburg was still president, the Hitler movement had already gained so much strength (especially here) where it started that the people were already greeting each other with the raised arm sign and the "Heil Hitler" slogan. Twenty-five years earlier, everything looked neat and well groomed under the kaiser; now it looked run-down. Signs were painted on store windows reading "This is a Jew".

Our next stop was Rothenburg, a town so enchanting and so well preserved that it looked as though not a change had been made in it from the Middle Ages on. A photo of it would look as though it had been cut out of a book of fairy tales. Here we lingered and explored for three days as if in a dream. This is one of the outstanding sights of Germany.

Moving on to Mainz, we took the boat trip on the most picturesque part of the Rhine to Cologne. Here we spent a day of exploration, mostly in the glorious cathedral, and took the train to Amsterdam.

Stopping at the Hotel Victoria, we soon discovered that it was crowded with wealthy East Indians making a stopover from the English coronation of George VI. They were very picturesque, with their dark skins, the men in their white turbans and the women in conventional long evening dresses over which they had saris draped over one shoulder and caste marks pasted in the middle of their foreheads.

The streets of Amsterdam were choked with armadas of bicycle riders constantly dodging in and out amongst the plentiful numbers of autos and streetcars. It is also a city of canals filled with barges and floating trash, through which our launch threaded its way.

We also visited the picturesque islands of Vollendam and Maarken. In the group on the canal trip were several Bavarian youths clad in their native costumes, with light short leather breeches with broad gaily embroidered cloth suspenders, short green jackets, knee-length white hand-knit socks, and heavy hiking boots. Their hats were small and round, flat on top, with narrow brims and what looked like our shaving brushes stuck upright into their hat bands. At Vollendam and Maarken the girls wore ankle-length, very full dark skirts, colored aprons, printed blouses, sleeveless, short, bright jackets, and tight white caps. The young boys were dressed just like the girls, there was a circle of coloured cloth on the flat tops of their caps. Everyone, young and old, wore wooden shoes. The confrontation of these two groups was an amusing commentary on human nature. There they stood laughing at each other, each group thinking that the other was comprised of the funniest dressed people imaginable. These islands have now ceased to be islands since the Zuider Zee has been dyked and drained. We found the diamond-cutting establishments especially interesting.

Then by train we went on to The Hague, passing through miles of tulip beds; but, unfortunately, we were several weeks too late to see them in full bloom. A day of sight-seeing was spent here and then a twenty-five minute train trip landed us in Rotterdam, where we spent the day sight-seeing and then at 9:00 p.m. boarded the Holland American Line steamer, the *Veendam*, due to leave for New York at midnight, thus terminating our European hegira of over seven months' duration.

The trip of ten days was peaceful, comfortable and uneventful. But when we entered New York harbor and that grand old lady holding the torch came into view, our pulse rates increased considerably.

We lost no time in getting to our camp at Shelburne as quickly as was convenient. Here we spent a delightful summer, mostly at the big mansion with our very dear friends, Seward and Gertrude Webb, as we had done many summers previously. But this summer, the elder Mrs. Webb, having died the past year, was missed very much.

We faced the future with nebulous plans. We had nothing definite in mind, except that we wanted to get away from the cold winters up north. So, from my vast travel experience, I had chosen San Antonio, Texas, as a most appealing place. In the autumn of 1937 we piled a few of our belongings in the rear of our car and headed for that city. Having seen over 1,500 other cities, it seemed to me that, with the exception of four or five, the rest looked the same, hastily built, drab and dirty. It was the

Mexican influence that appealed to me (as it did in El Paso), that gave the city a distinct and different personality. Then, too, along with the climate, I was fond of Mexican food. We chose the southern route purposely so we could explore New Orleans for three days and eat oysters Rockefeller at Antoines.

19

SAN ANTONIO, TEXAS

Arriving in San Antonio, we headed straight for the house of a couple who were friends of mine in El Paso. They urged us to stay with them until we found a small furnished house of our own, which took about a week. These were the only people we knew in a city of some 75,000; but he was a fairly good pianist and had only been in the city a few years, working up a class of pupils. So we teamed up, playing concerts at women's and musical clubs, churches, etc., where we hoped to make ourselves known. Our quartet had given a very successful concert there some ten years previously, but memories are short. Very few people remembered me.

At the end of three months, I had one pupil, when the violin teacher at the University of San Antonio (now Trinity College) passed away. I lost no time in applying for the job. In fact, I played at his funeral. The president of the university welcomed me cordially and said that he would be glad to have me on the faculty, but first I ought to know what the situation was. Then, with utter frankness, which endeared him to me, he explained that the university was in financial straits and that the job could pay no salary, but that I could set my own price for lessons and keep all of it. They would furnish me a studio with a piano all my own at no cost and there were six students taking violin lessons who would probably come to me, especially if I gave a concert at the school at the earliest convenient time. Of course, I was disappointed that there would be no salary, but what was there to lose? Compared to what I had, it was a windfall. It gave me the prestige of the university, a studio with piano from which to operate, even for private pupils; and it gave free access to a very great number of students, any one of whom could become a violin pupil at any time.

The studio was fairly large—about thirty by forty feet—and the only thing needed to enhance its attractiveness was to furnish it with curtains. This we did at once. Soon thereafter I gave a concert for the whole school, after which within a week all six pupils of the previous teacher applied for lessons.

College students at this age are just beginning to make some sense out of life; and I took a great liking to them, which they in turn reciprocated. And it wasn't long before I was on friendly terms with several hundred of them. Freshmen were the most difficult to befriend. After being held under strict discipline during grade and high schools, the change to a much freer and more independent way of life is at first very perplexing. The extrovert will tend to abuse this freedom, while the introvert will tend to clam up and appear to be dazed and confused. It is a period of trial and error which usually fades after the first year, when a new and more earnest personality develops in the sophomore year and thereafter. It was with a never-ending sense of interest and joy that I watched these changes taking place.

So it was with me that within three months I was a well-established participant in the life of the school. This applied to my wife, too, who did much accompanying for me as well as all the accompanying for my pupils. Needless to say, we made many new friends. The faculty were especially to our liking because they were intelligent, broad-minded, and dedicated.

Six months later we were fairly happy and contented but apprehensive because my class wasn't growing fast enough. I had only nine pupils, and these weren't nearly enough to cover our expenses; so we were living on what remained of our meager savings after the big depression. These were diminishing at an alarming rate. The San Antonio Symphony was making me offers to join but even though I needed the money, the thought of participating in such an inferior organization seemed repulsive to me. It was now evident that, with the depression still on, the possibility of getting any more pupils from the student body was slim; so some new measures would have to be tried to enlist private pupils.

By this time I was pretty well known in local circles, so there was nowhere else to go but the environs to solicit pupils. After giving the matter much thought, I approached President Jackson with a plan whereby we would travel to key cities within a radius of 300 miles in which Eunice and I would give a one-hour concert and he a fifteen-minute talk with the idea of promoting attendance at the university. His eyes brightened at once; and he smilingly replied, "This is just what I have had in the back of my mind for some time, but the difficulty has been in finding a side attraction which would make the evening more interesting than my talk." From there on he offered to do all the preliminary preparations such as selecting the cities, dates, halls, advertising, etc. This took some time to prepare, but by the end of the school year we had appeared in about fifteen cities. The results of these peregrinations were not evident until the opening of the next school year when student enrollment showed a sizeable gain and my class increased by four out-of-town pupils, two of whom came every two weeks from Del Rio, a distance of about 150 miles.

That year Jascha Heifetz played with the Symphony Orchestra, and it was a most exciting renewal of our friendship. I had written him beforehand, inviting him and his accompanist to come to our house after the concert; and he accepted. We also invited all my pupils.

The day of the concert was unusually cold. When we awoke we discovered that our water pipes were frozen. I had an appointment with newspaper photographers to have Heifetz and myself photographed with our sister Guarnerius violins at the concert hall. At the same time I stayed to listen to the rehearsal.

Arriving home at noon, Eunice broke the news that after numerous tries all morning she had been unsuccessful in getting a plumber. By this time the frozen portion of the pipe had already burst; so by borrowing a Stillson wrench and a hacksaw from a neighbor, I spent most of the afternoon putting our water pipes back in order.

After the concert, Eunice went directly home with friends to open our house and receive our guests while I and a favorite pupil of mine, eight-year-old Lee Cunningham, waited for Heifetz and his accompanist to drive them to our home in our car. Heifetz

Heifetz and I comparing our sister Guarneri violins before the concert Heifetz played in San Antonio in 1939.

immediately took a shine to Lee; so he let him carry his double violin case, containing two of the most famous violins in the world, one a Strad and one a Guarneri, together worth about $150,000 at that time. Lee was in seventh heaven and felt like the most important person in San Antonio.

Arriving home, we found an assembly of about twenty persons, mostly pupils and parents, awaiting us, to whom we quickly introduced Jascha and his accompanist, shortly after which Eunice and I excused ourselves and took our two honored guests out into the kitchen, where Eunice cooked two enormous hamburger steaks for each of them while I concocted scotch highballs and talked with Jascha about many things, for we hadn't seen each other in quite a few years. They were both ravenously hungry, which goes to prove how strenuous a concert is physically, even for Heifetz, who appears to be doing it with the greatest of ease.

During the course of our discussions, I asked him if he still had trouble with his practice. He replied, "Some days one feels more like it than others; but on the whole, I am now practicing more than before." Then I said to him, "I see that you are the proud owner of two of the most famous violins in the world, one a Guarneri and one a Strad. Naturally, every violinist is partial to the one that he owns and has gotten used to. You can afford to be impartial; so tell me which you prefer and why." His reply was, "I prefer the Guarneri, because in fortissimo passages its quantity of tone seems inexhaustible no matter how much I bear down on the strings. With the Strad, I have to be more careful, because it has a limit which, if I exceed, the tone caves in and becomes a dud. In good condition they are pretty well equal in other respects." It wasn't long after that he sold his Strad and now uses his Guarneri exclusively. The preference he mentioned is a most desirable asset in the modern big halls.

A little later on we left the kitchen to mingle with the other guests. Jascha autographed their programs and chatted until about 1:00 a.m., when I drove the two artists back to their hotel. The party was the talk of the town for some time, especially since the Symphony Society had taken it for granted that he would attend an after-concert party which they had organized without letting him know beforehand. The fact that he came to our house created a furor of monumental proportions, and several of the directors let me know in no uncertain terms how they felt about it. But I couldn't have cared less. My answer was that he made the decision to come to our house of his own free will and that I had been in no position to make him come if he hadn't wished to.

Lee Cunningham was one of my first pupils and an unusual case. His father was an officer in the army stationed at Fort Sam Houston. The boy was physically underdeveloped and had a low immunity to germs; therefore, the army doctor prescribed horseback riding as a mild form of exercise. One day he fell off the horse, and the hoof of the animal mangled his left thumb so badly that it had to be amputated.

It so happens that the left thumb is very necessary to support the violin when playing in the higher positions. He had already had a few lessons and loved the violin dearly. His teacher and several others had told the parents that it would be impossible for Lee to play the violin without that thumb; so it would be advisable to shift to some other instrument. When Lee was told this news, he was brokenhearted and became morose.

This happened about three months after my arrival in San Antonio. In despair, the parents came to me for an opinion. During the interview they mentioned the names of three or four of the most prominent violin teachers in town who advised them that it was absolutely impossible to play the violin without that left thumb. All my life it has been like waving a red cape in front of a bull to have anyone tell me, "This thing is impossible; it can't be done." It triggers off a reaction within me which sets up a dogged determination to prove that it can be done. So it was in this case. Therefore, without committing myself one way or another, I asked the parents to bring the boy in and told them I would give them my opinion after watching and hearing him play.

A few days later they brought him, and it soon became apparent that he was musically inclined from the way he interpreted the music and from his clean intonation. His pieces were easy ones, all in the first position, and where the lack of that thumb would be missed the least. The difficulty would be most apparent when he reached the high positions (the higher, the more difficult). Therefore, it would be folly for me to make any

209

predictions until we could see what happened when we got there. I judged that it would be about a year before we got to that point; so I offered to take Lee on as a trial pupil for a year if the parents were willing to take that chance. They consented immediately.

Of course, I had to teach him differently from all the rest, but this made it all the more interesting. By close observation, I was able to help him do what comes naturally, so that by the end of the first year we got along so well that I felt confident enough to tell the parents, "I doubt he will ever play well enough to make a career as solo violinist, but if he continues at the present rate, he will play quite well." At the end of two years he was playing in the San Antonio Symphony. More about Lee later in these memoirs.

The following year we had an unusual experience with one of my more advanced pupils, a girl about sixteen years of age. Crystal City, a town of about 1,000 in population, about 150 miles west of San Antonio, was the center of a farming area which specialized in growing spinach. Every year they would ship innumerable carloads of this delicacy to markets all over the United States and after completion of the harvest would celebrate by holding a spinach festival and choosing a spinach queen. My aforementioned pupil, Wanda by name, was chosen lady in waiting to the queen, having as one of her duties to play a violin solo. She had diligently practiced her piece with an accompanist for weeks, but at 7:00 a.m. the day of the event she phoned us in panic saying that her accompanist had suddenly become ill and couldn't attend; what could she do about it?

After a short conference with Eunice, we decided that the easiest way to solve the problem was to go ourselves and Eunice would accompany her. You should have heard the sigh of relief that came back from the other end of the line when Wanda heard this news. We lost no time in getting started. So that with monotonously straight roads, well paved, and little traffic, we arrived at Crystal City about noon to find a twenty-foot statue of Popeye flexing his muscles staring us in the face right in the middle of the square. After taking a little ride around town, we entered a crowded restaurant in which every man within view was dressed in cowboy attire, wearing a six-shooter on his hip.

When we eventually were seated at a table, we found out from the waitress that they actually were cowboys who had come to town for the festivities, and I was the only male in the place not wearing a six-shooter. At 2:00 p.m. a sort of Mardi Gras parade took place. Then at 4:00 p.m. the crowning of the queen took place in the open air, with Popeye as a background in the square.

Wanda and Eunice did their stint rather well. Then after supper, Eunice and I decided to take it easy going home to try to relax after such an exciting day; so we chose less-traveled routes, making frequent stops to admire the beauty of the stars, which in the dry atmosphere of the desert appear brighter and closer. Then, too, the quietude was absolutely eerie, being devoid of any sound. We got home about midnight needing no lullabies to induce sleep after such a hectic day.

The following year Heifetz was booked to play in Austin; so we couldn't resist the temptation of traveling the seventy-five miles to see and hear him play. At the ticket window, we tried to buy two tickets but were told that everything including standing room had been sold out for weeks. Quickly I wrote Jascha a note telling of our plight and handed it to an usher, who delivered it and promptly returned, directing us to follow him to the stage, where we found two comfortable seats awaiting us in the wings. Of course, the resonance wasn't quite as good from this vantage point as from the auditorium. Still, we were thrilled with the performance and with the short visit we had with him afterward.

One of the winters we were there, there was a two-inch snowfall, something that hadn't occurred in twenty years. So the schools were closed to give the children an opportunity to play in it. Two days later there wasn't a trace of it left.

Another year there was a six-month drought with bright cloudless sunny weather day in and day out. The monotony of beautiful weather got so boring that whenever a small cloud appeared on the horizon, we would shout for joy. At the end of this spell, however, the powers that be wreaked vengeance on us by blackening the sky with darkness, pelting us with hailstones the size of golf balls and a lightning barrage the likes of which I had seldom seen. After it was over it was found that almost every roof in town had sustained different degrees of damage.

We liked the Mexican atmosphere so much that one year we

spent the Christmas holidays in Monterey and frequently crossed the border at different points of entry for short visits.

The following article appeared in the *Brand Iron* 1938, a San Antonio University student publication.

Siskovsky Specializing in Setting Strong Pendulums Swinging Startles School

If you have been amazed at his skill with the violin and sat enthralled with the melodious tones he has created and been captivated with his genial personality, you will probably be equally astounded to know that his skill extends to the art of clock and watch repair. In short, Mr. J. Siskovsky is the gentleman who is responsible for some of the unemployment in the watchmakers' union, for it is his hobby to repair timepieces of all types. However, as Mr. Siskovsky specializes in clocks and watches which have been given up by professional repairmen, it might be that he is the cause of unemployment in the watch factories. Regardless of any unemployment he may be the cause of, students of this university are more than ready to forgive him because it is due to his valiant work that the time-honored grandfather clock in the library is now swinging its mighty pendulum.

Toward the end of our third year, through the instrumentality of Cyril Jones, I received a flattering offer to teach violin at Milton Academy in Milton, Massachusetts. Cy and his wife, Frederica (the ex-Mrs. Pulitzer who had organized and backed the New York String Quartet for its first five years), had become our dearest friends. Thus the offer from Milton Academy struck us like manna from heaven. We would have given up the most favorable of situations just to be near them wherever they might be.

After almost three years in San Antonio I was able to build up a class of only twelve pupils, the income from which just barely paid our expenses. It can readily be seen that it didn't take but a moment to make up our minds to accept the Milton offer even though we shuddered at the thought of going back to those miserable winters up north which we had hoped never to experience again.

Certainly there was much that we liked at San Antonio, especially our contacts with the students and professors at the university. Several of my pupils displayed so much talent that I had high hopes of their turning professional. They did later on. Once you got away from the university, the mentality and atmosphere of the place was still very provincial. Whenever playing concerts outside the university, I always felt the audiences hadn't the slightest idea whether my performance was of a high order or just passable.

Every artist needs inspiration to bring out the best in him. It doesn't take very long for an experienced soloist to instinctively feel whether or not a particular audience is knowledgeable enough to appreciate his best efforts. Outside the university I rarely felt inspired, but no wonder—this was 1940 and only a short time after oil had been discovered in Texas. Conditions today are a far cry from what they were then. By the same token, these conditions were far advanced from what they had been on my first sojourn of five years in New Mexico and Texas. Then it was called the Wild West, cowboy country.

Probably the best way to describe our feelings at this point is to say we hated to leave our friends and the delightful climate, but not San Antonio. Soon I broke the news of our departure to President Jackson, who understood the situation and seemed very sorry that we were leaving. He expressed great appreciation for our wholehearted efforts in behalf of the university and regretted that he couldn't offer us a better financial inducement so we could stay. I didn't mention that there was no financial offer big enough to have kept us away from our dearest friends, Freddie and Cy Jones.

Hardest of all to part with were the students and pupils, whom I dearly loved, who kept breaking my heart with expressions of regret. This painful situation was getting on my nerves; so we decided to leave several weeks before graduation exercises took place. Thoughts of San Antonio remained with us for several hundred miles. But soon our thoughts turned to the future because of its rosy, challenging, and exciting outlook.

So we left behind a host of good friends which we made over a period of three years—all except Lee Cunningham and his family. They had decided that they wanted to follow us to Milton. So it was arranged that I would look into the matter of having him admitted as a student into Milton Academy. Subsequently, this was arranged.

We arrived at our camp about June 1 and as always, felt supremely happy. As soon as the chores were completed, we would start our daily eighteen holes of golf on the private course of the estate, and I would resume my two to four hours of daily violin practice. It was such a grand and glorious feeling looking forward to a whole summer in this heavenly spot.

This was early June 1940. Ever since 1922 we had had a continuous procession of family, relatives, and friends visiting us every summer. One group would move out of our guest cottage in the morning and another would move in in the afternoon. This hospitality had had to be curtailed sharply in the last few years due to the low ebb of our financial resources. This we regretted very much, because as our guests were scattered all over the country, it gave us the chance to keep our relationships burning plus the enormous satisfaction of giving them the chance to spend their vacations in such an unusual and beautiful place.

On the other hand, we finally had the chance to spend our time according to our notions and not have to worry about pleasing others. Freddie's brother, Seward, and his wife, Gertrude, were living in the big mansion summers; and we had become such fast friends that most of our time was spent with them, having fun in one way or another. In a place like that there is always something useful to do.

We spent one whole summer putting all the carriages that the family had used into shape to be presented to sister-in-law, Electra Webb, for her Shelburne Museum which was then in the final stages of planning. Along with these, Electra Webb had accumulated an enormous number of American artifacts such as a calliope, music boxes, clocks, butter churns, mechanical figures of every description, etc., which were to be placed in the museum and which I spent many pleasurable hours and many summers repairing in my spare time.

Seward, Gertrude, Eunice, and I frequently made trips to Canada and other parts of New England with Seward at the wheel. He was an excellent driver, but it was always a harrowing experience because he wasn't happy driving below ninety; so we had many a close shave on the narrow, bumpy, two-lane roads of that day.

As usual, the summer flew by all too quickly, even though we lived in eager anticipation of what the future had in store for us at Milton Academy. But before we left Shelburne, we received some very good news from the Joneses.

They had just decided to build a home on the half of the estate which Mrs. Webb had willed to them, about a mile from where our cottage stood and where they expected to spend their summers. With no other couple did we even come close to reaching the mutual compatibility that we did with the Joneses; but wait, on top of that was added the fact that they were taking their sabbatical and would be in Tucson, Arizona, the nine months of the school year, leaving the two maids and their German shepherd dog behind to take care of their house—and us, if we would condescend to live there.

We had to pinch ourselves to realize that all this could be true after some eight years of uncertainty in our lives. Even though we were anxious to get to Milton as soon as possible and the Joneses had invited us to come stay with them, since nothing could be accomplished by our getting there earlier than the opening day of school, we decided to stay in our cottage until the last minute and keep out of the Joneses' hair.

20

MILTON, MASSACHUSETTS

Arriving at the Joneses' house the afternoon before school opened, the maids informed us that we were expected to make ourselves at home in two guest rooms on the third floor. This we did; and by the time the Joneses got home, about 6:00 p.m., we were all unpacked and settled in for a long stay. It was an exhausting day for the Joneses; so after a few drinks and a delicious supper, it was early to bed for all four of us.

Next morning as we left for school, Cy said, "Nothing will be expected of you for three or four days; so the best thing you can do is to browse around and get acquainted with the campus and its buildings. Nobody is going to have much time to pay any attention to you, and that includes me." When we arrived on the campus, his parting words were, "So long. Go for lunch into the school dining room, meet me in the library at 5:00 p.m., and we'll go home together." He left me stranded but undismayed.

The campus was a melee of men and boys, resembling the scene at New York's Times Square at the after-theatre rush hour. I am sure that at that moment the lowliest freshman knew more about what he was doing than I did. They were running in all directions. So, nothing daunted, I dove right into their midst and started running like a chicken with its head cut off.

This lasted for about an hour, when I found myself practically alone on the campus. All the others apparently had found what they were looking for. But not I. I had nothing to look for. So, weary afoot by this time, I spied a rather ornate building close at hand, which turned out to be the library, with not a soul in it. Here peace and quiet reigned, contrasting sharply with what took place outside. I picked up a book and read for about an hour, after which I explored every nook and cranny on the place. At five o'clock I met Cy and we drove home.

I remarked that I hadn't accomplished a thing all day. Laughingly he replied, "You'll be in the thick of it before you know it."

It was three days before the head of the music department, Howard Abell explained what was expected of me. The orchestra was a joke. He hoped we could improve that. He hoped we could organize a series of four concerts a year amongst the music faculty. I would have charge of one forty-minute daytime and one one-hour evening study hall period per week. For this work I would receive my salary already agreed upon. Any and all violin lessons, for which I could set my own price, would be collected by the office and paid in full to me. There were many practice rooms in various buildings; so I arranged to teach the five pupils who had signed up for violin lessons at rooms and times convenient to them.

At this point it might be well to explain that Milton Academy is located at Milton, Massachusetts, a suburb of Boston, and is one of the more prominent prep schools in the New England area. Although governed by one headmaster, it is divided into three separate schools run by three separate heads. These are a boys' school serving grades seven through twelve, a girls' school serving the same grades, and a lower coeducational school for grades one through six. The boys' school enrollment averaged about 300, the girls' school about 200; and in both these cases about half were boarders from all parts of the United States and the world. The lower school averaged about 160 pupils, all from the surrounding area. All three schools contained potential prospects for violin lessons.

Aside from the two study hall periods, I was my own boss and therefore free to contribute what expertise I had to the general good. In this respect, as an extracurricular bonus, I had all the academy clocks, some 100 in number (of which many needed repair) back in running order in no time. It wasn't long, as Cy had prophesied, before I was engulfed in the swing of it.

At the end of the first week the Joneses threw a big party, to which the whole faculty was invited, for the purpose of our

217

getting acquainted. I played a number of violin solos with Howard Abell at the piano. The enthusiasm of our audience was hilarious (maybe it was the liquor), but at the time no one could foresee that this combination would bring joy and erudition to a whole generation of students, with innumerable concerts in the future. After the guests went home both Eunice and I told the Joneses that we had never met a more delightful, wholehearted group of people. And, praises be, in our whole thirteen years of tenure at the school, we never had occasion for one moment to change this evaluation.

Shortly thereafter the Joneses departed for Tucson, and we were left with two of the nicest Finnish girls and the German shepherd to take care of us and the establishment. We immediately told the girls that, except on very rare occasions, we had no intention of using any but the living room, which harbored a fine Steinway parlor grand, the breakfast nook, in which we would have all our meals, and, of course, the two guest rooms in which we slept. Therefore, if they approved of it, wouldn't it be a good idea to close off the other rooms to save themselves much work? Of course, the answer was in a very smiling affirmative. Eunice asked them to use their own judgment in planning the meals; but even then, every so often, they would ask if there was anything special we would like for dinner. Helen Jalonen was an expert cook; so by the end of the school year, we two were badly spoiled human beings in the culinary department.

After about a month's residency we decided to throw a chili party for the whole faculty. In our three years' stay in San Antonio Eunice had learned to cook chili the true Mexican way—plenty hot. This was to be a real treat for staid New Englanders. Everybody had plenty to drink, everybody had plenty of chili, and everybody had a hilarious time. Next day we learned that about a quarter of our guests suffered from nausea after reaching home. Apparently, the chili was too hot for them. Fortunately they didn't accuse us of any ulterior motives, but did give us credit for good intentions. Still, it was the talk of the community for some time.

By now my work had been organized into a regular schedule; and soon I gave the first of many concerts, to which the whole school and general public were invited. It immediately became apparent that here was an audience far more musically erudite than the Texas audiences I had been playing to, the result being a much more inspired performance on my part.

With this successful beginning, we planned and executed a series of four concerts yearly, which covered the whole gamut of musical literature, especially chamber music. Mostly with the help of Boston Symphony men, we put on concerts of such a high standard that Milton was the envy of other New England prep schools.

Eunice, too, had become deeply involved in the life of the school. What with many useful chores that faculty wives performed, her piano playing came in handy at dance classes and on many other occasions.

Our relations at the school, without exception, couldn't have been more cordial; the number of my pupils had increased to ten; and I was promised a raise in salary to double the amount I was getting. When the Joneses returned about two weeks before closing of school for the summer, they couldn't have found a happier couple anywhere. The thing most gratifying of all to us was that they heard nothing but songs of praise about their introduction of us into the community. Loudest praise came from the two maids, who became fast friends ever after.

The four of us now lived in the house until school closed, and we left for our cottage in Vermont, to be followed by them shortly thereafter. Things up there had changed considerably this year. The Vanderbilt Webbs (Freddie's youngest brother), who had inherited that half of the big estate on which the mansion stood, had now decided to spend their summers there.

Now that the Joneses had built a new home about a mile from our cottage, we spent almost every day of our vacation together, our favorite occupations being playing golf in the mornings, cutting down superfluous trees in the afternoons, and playing bridge in the evenings. Freddie and Eunice got almost as proficient pulling a two-handled saw as Cy and I were. We liked nothing better than doing this kind of work, raising a sweat, then jumping into the cool waters of Lake Champlain, then seating ourselves in lounge chairs, looking at the waters of the lake with the beautiful Green Mountains in the background while sipping a couple of highballs, then—the custom of farmers—turning in early for a good night's sleep. What with the lulling sound of the waves on the beach, the healthy outdoor exercise of the day, and the pure fresh air, none of us ever complained of insomnia.

After some three months of this happy life, the four of us returned to Milton fit to tackle any and all problems that arise at any school. Little did we realize how strenuous life would be, because no one had the slightest inkling that within a few months the Japanese would bomb Pearl Harbor.

Arriving in Milton, we found a six-room house to rent only a few blocks from the academy. All our house furnishings had been in storage at a warehouse in New Rochelle, New York, all during the four years since we left there; so we promptly had them delivered and got settled in no time. Of course, it was a far cry from conditions we had become accustomed to with two maids waiting on us; still, it was our own and we could do in it as we pleased. Of course, during all the maneuvers of getting settled, I had my chores at school to perform, when on December 7, 1941, the Japanese bombed Pearl Harbor, which overnight transformed Milton Academy from a beehive of activity into dynamic action.

The town of Milton comprised a population of about 20,000, mostly middle income, with a goodly number of wealthy, the majority of whom commuted to work in Boston. There was no industry in town except the Baker Chocolate Company plant just over the border in the Dorchester section of Boston, which wafted a sweet aroma of chocolate all over the area according to the direction of the wind.

War was declared on the Japanese almost immediately, and the nation prepared itself accordingly. Because of its concentration of buildings and intelligent minds, Milton Academy was chosen as the logical center from which to direct all civilian defense activities in the local area. Without delay, in case of air raids, volunteers were organized into groups to perform special duties. Eunice chose the group called wardens, whose duty it was to patrol the streets in our neighborhood to see that the new regulation to have windows shaded so tightly that no light could be seen from the outside was being obeyed and also to tell everybody not in civil defense work to get off the streets and seek shelter.

Volunteers, driving station wagons, joined the Red Cross unit. Another unit did four-hour stints atop our chapel tower day and night, watching for suspicious-looking aircraft.

I chose the rescue squad, which was supposed to rescue people from bombed-out buildings. Everyone in all the above groups now had to undergo a six-week course in first aid. As for training in rescue work, there was none. I suppose they depended on our ingenuity. It wasn't long before I had an opportunity to display mine.

After all the groups had finished their first aid training, a final meeting was called for all to assemble in the hall of one of the Milton public schools at 7:00 p.m. on a certain night to receive final instructions. Eunice and I got there promptly on time to find a crowd of about 300 people standing around unable to enter the building; so we stood there along with the rest for at least a half-hour. Getting restless by this time and wondering what the trouble was, I worked my way to the entrance, where one of my colleagues, in charge of the affair, informed me that the place was locked because the two men (the janitor and the principal) who had the only keys hadn't been informed of the event and that there were several men out searching for them.

I took one look at the lock on the door and turned to my colleague with the query, "Do you think it would be permissible for me to open it?" "Heavens, yes," was his reply. So I pulled out my trusty penknife, and within one minute the door was opened and the crowd streamed in.

We listened to instructions for some time. When those in charge were ready to distribute some leaflets printed especially for this occasion, it was discovered that they were locked up in the principal's office. There we were, stuck again. But soon my colleague came hastening toward me to explain the dilemma. So we marched to the office, and again my trusty penknife saved the day.

This ingenuity came in handy on many an occasion, but none more appreciated than the following. With tears in her eyes, one of the faculty wives stopped me one day to relate that her icebox had not been running for two days and that she had called every repairman in our area as well as a few in Boston, but to no avail. She was in despair because the box was loaded with food and said, "If repairs aren't made soon, everything in it will spoil." Would I please try to solve the predicament? We trudged to her home; and after checking that the current was on, I took off the plate covering the machinery at the bottom of the box. Lo and behold, there was their black cat, which had been missing for two days, dead as a doornail, squeezed to death, caught in between a belt and pulley. By shutting off the current, the cat was pulled out easily. Switching on the current again, the motor started and so did a big broad smile on the lady's face. Then I took the cat and buried it in the back yard.

After the civil defense activities were in full swing, I found myself doing a regular twice-a-week chapel four-hour turn at watching for strange aircraft from the tower, and another turn of equal duration manning the main switchboard in the basement of one of our buildings, to which all disaster calls were reported and disseminated.

Irregularly, I would assist the school doctor by tying tourniquets on the arms of inductees for blood tests. One boy was so fat that the doctor pushed the needle into different parts of his body twenty-two times to no avail. Finally, by pricking his earlobe, the doctor was able to squeeze out three measly drops.

It took me two months working single-handedly on Saturdays to build an obstacle course, such as fences to hurdle, high walls to clamber over, narrow tunnels to crawl through, etc., to give the boys training in guerrilla warfare. When they saw that I could do carpenter work, they asked me to build them a stand for hockey players on the lake where they played hockey. This I did, but it was the straw that broke the camel's back, for it convinced me that I couldn't do such rough jobs and delicate work on the violin at the same time.

It must be remembered that all the activity in civil defense enumerated above had to be done outside my regular schedule, which took up about eight hours daily, except Saturdays and Sundays. Most punishing were those hours spent all alone from midnight to daybreak up in the chapel tower, freezing, and the same number of hours spent manning the switchboard. On the other hand, I would have enjoyed them for their peace and quiet if I hadn't lived in constant fear that I would botch things up if a real disaster ever occurred. This fear was a good thing, because it made me doubly careful to review instructions every time I took over the watch.

It can be imagined that the pace of life was terrific. So by vacation time, everybody was pooped, especially the Joneses. He had been promoted to headmaster, so had to spend some time after school closed being indoctrinated into his new job; so they couldn't leave for Vermont until several weeks after we did.

Gasoline for auto driving had been rationed soon after the start of the war, but by hoarding our coupons all winter, we had saved enough to get us to Vermont and back with some to spare.

By the time the Joneses arrived, we had rested up enough to feel like being active again. But they were in no mood for anything but loafing. So we helped them loaf until they felt like getting back into our usual activities.

In the fall the four of us went back to Milton a little earlier than necessary, they, because Cy wanted to get an early start as headmaster, and we, because we liked Milton so well that we had decided to buy a house instead of renting.

We found just what we wanted in a few days only about eight blocks from the school within easy walking distance. It was a six-room New England colonial design with an eight-foot brook running on the back line. The cellar was finished off into two rooms, one of which I appropriated as a general workshop and the other especially for clock repair. We had lived in many houses in our time, but none did we like as well as this one, and we were comfortably settled before school began.

By this time the civil defense activities had become better organized and divided up into more helping hands; so chores had become routine. Most importantly, since no air raids had materialized, that panicky feeling had subsided and everybody's nerves were more relaxed. Just to give one example, the aircraft watch in the chapel tower was divided amongst volunteers from the two top classes. In order to be eligible, they had to familiarize themselves with designs of all United States planes. They would be up there all alone all hours of the day or night; so they got the feeling of urgency and importance. Competition for this post was very keen, and there never was a dearth of volunteers. Of course, their hours were fitted in so it would not interfere with regular studies.

Aside from an occasional meeting of the rescue squad, my regular civil defense work simmered down to two four-hour stints at night per week at the disaster switchboard. Hence, I could devote my efforts almost exclusively to music, which was my job. Let the reader not forget that we musicians, in order to play well, must, unfortunately, practice many hours a day. I never heard of anyone getting paid for this unless it was a mother bribing her child with ten cents.

With a new but younger headmaster at the helm, school opened with a rejuvenated sense of vigor and vitality; but soon Cy became engulfed in complications which increased the difficulty of breaking into a new job. Most of our young, physically fit masters were being inducted into the service. Since this was the case all over the country, there was a great shortage of teachers; so makeshifts were necessary in almost all departments.

To make matters worse, something unpredictable happened in that Germany decided to bomb England in earnest. So the British started dispersing women and children to all parts of the world, including the United States; and we were asked to accommodate at least fifty of these children at our school. In spite of the fact that our facilities were already bursting at the seams, Cy felt that, from an educational standpoint, this was too good an opportunity to miss so he decided to accept them. In about a month's time they arrived en masse, and there was great scurrying around for a while; but with the citizens of Milton responding nobly to the emergency, all of them were scattered about town in private homes. Of course, this meant much adjusting and bigger classes and more work for teachers; but in the end, it proved one of the finest things that could have happened to our students as well as to the British. Our children found out that basically there wasn't much difference between them and us. Also, they liked the congeniality of our teachers.

Our school found out that, comparing grades, their children were one year ahead of ours in knowledge. They, on the other hand, found out that our curriculum was much too easy, that we weren't all cowboys and Al Capones and that aside from football, which they considered brutal, we were much alike. In any case, I never heard of any unpleasant incidents involving national pride; so good relations were maintained throughout the war. At its end, they, of course, left for home. This emergency foreign exchange student program proved to be such a universal success that it has grown to monumental proportions everywhere.

For the first years, I was able to memorize the names of all the close to 700 students in the three divisions of the school and was able to greet them by name. But later, what with meeting many graduates, it became somewhat confusing; so I made no attempt to memorize the names of those students with whom I had no direct contact.

Through my study hall classes I got to know many boys whose antecedents were famous men such as Tom Paine; Paul Revere; two sons of Adlai Stevenson; Tom Cleveland, grandson of President Cleveland; Bob and Ted Kennedy; and others. Bob Kennedy and I became close friends. In study hall or, for that matter, most of the time his face carried a worried look. For that reason I would quietly approach his desk to chat with him. Usually I found out that it wasn't so much that he was worried but rather that life was a serious business with him. He was a person of strong character and even then showed signs of leadership, the boys usually trusting his fairness and good judgment to adjudicate disputes. He loved to play touch football, and I can still see him running the ball with such determination as if the world depended on his scoring. Frivolity didn't appeal to him. Ted, on the other hand, showed fewer outstanding characteristics that I could see. He was just one of the boys—happy-go-lucky.

After the war, the school settled back into its more normal pace and, with the return of inducted masters, many of whom nursed gangrenous feet and other tropical maladies, the teaching loads were reduced to a prewar level of about twelve students to a class.

By this time our orchestra had increased to around thirty players, with a corresponding improvement in quality. If there hadn't been a long-standing tradition of giving athletics (especially football) precedence over music, we could have done twice as well.

A separate orchestra was now functioning in the lower school, and the number of my private pupils increased to around fifteen—all that I cared to accept. The high quality of our four yearly concerts became talked about all over New England.

In addition to this, there were many Saturday evenings when Eunice and I invited a group of my pupils, both girls and boys, to supper, after which we would play chamber music until around 11:00 p.m.

There was a constant plethora of clocks needing repair amongst the faculty. Eunice was usually surprised if I didn't enter the house without at least one under my arm at the end of the day. Repairing these was a source of relaxation to me. In spite of the fact that I had been repairing clocks ever since I was fifteen years old, two years before I retired, the idea of taking a course in watch and clock repairing at the No. Bennet Street Industrial School—considered one of the best in Boston—occurred to me. This involved going into the city two nights a week from 7:00 to 10:00 p.m. for two years.

There were ten of us in the class, but the instructor soon saw that, since the others were all beginners, I was so far ahead of them he took me separately for private instruction. Here I learned that what I had learned all by myself was basically correct; but, as usual, there are tricks to all trades which taught me to accomplish the same objectives quicker and better in some cases. More important was the opportunity to learn how to make individual parts, which is a must when working on antique clocks for which the parts are no longer obtainable. With this training I am qualified to get a job in any jewelry store if need be. In poker they call it having an ace in the hole.

Aside from the Joneses, we had many other social contacts. This should now give a good picture of the busy but happy life we thoroughly enjoyed.

All through the war, life for the Joneses was very hectic; and while Cy seemed to thrive on it, Freddie's health, toward the end, began to fail. So they purchased a house right on the shore of Cotuit Bay on Cape Cod, to which they would retire on many weekends, often inviting us to go along. As a matter of fact, we had a standing invitation to go down and live in the place even if they couldn't go. This we took advantage of on many a weekend or holiday as opportunities presented themselves.

Alas, in another few years Freddie's health deteriorated to such an extent that their doctor advised them to leave the rigors of the

New England climate and spend their winters in some place that was warmer. This meant the retirement of Cy as headmaster, the news of which was received by all concerned as a shock. He was well liked by everyone, aside from the fact that he did an outstanding job as headmaster, contributing sound leadership and many innovative ideas.

They purchased a lovely home facing the Catalina Mountains near Tucson, Arizona, where they spent several winters, returning to Vermont summers where we were constant companions. All this time the doctors seemed unable to help Freddie, resulting in a situation wherein nurses were needed in three shifts around the clock. As they left us in Vermont that fall of 1948, we feared we would never see Freddie alive again. But no, when the Christmas holidays came, a letter from Cy arrived urging us to come to Tucson for our vacation. This we did, but it was a sad one, watching her in such a weakened condition. As we left, it was evident that the end was not far off.

Our hearts were heavy and eyes filled with tears as we departed for home, only to strike one of the worst blizzards within memory, with railroad tracks buried in eighteen inches of snow and telephone poles down across Kansas, Missouri, and Illinois. We arrived in Chicago sixteen hours late.

A month later on February 2, 1949, a telegram from Cy broke the news that the end had come. Although this would leave a great void in our lives, and though we were brokenhearted, after seeing her suffer for so long, we could only feel that it was a blessing. Poor Cy scarcely had survived this one shock when about a month later his mother passed away.

Next summer Cy spent most of the summer in Vermont, and we spent much of our time playing golf and bridge. But we could already sense the fact that, being essentially a saltwater man, his real love was the house on Cape Cod, which he already had started remodeling and to which in about a year he added a huge garden and large music room measuring about twenty-five feet by seventy feet. He loved gardening; so gradually he spent less and less time away from Cotuit. Winters we would drive down to see him at every opportunity, and so we continued being close friends.

Thus the years rolled by until I reached the compulsory retirement age of sixty-five in 1953. I could have stayed on as a private violin teacher; but osteoarthritis was taking hold in many of my joints, and I was beginning to notice it in my playing. On top of that, I was slowly beginning to acquire a lack of energy which some ten years later was discovered to be a lack of B-12 vitamin—hence, that constant tired feeling. One always hates to abandon a situation that has been a supremely happy one; yet common sense advised me to go while still wanted and not linger on, as I have seen happen so often, until one becomes a pain in the neck.

The following article, with my photo, appeared in the *Milton Academy Bulletin* at my retirement in 1953. It was written by Howard Abell, head of the Music Department.

On March 15, 1953, Shish and I played the Cesar Franck Sonata for Violin and Piano at a library concert. That evening, I recalled more vividly than ever our first reading together of that music in 1940, when Mr. and Mrs. Jones invited a few of us to meet Jaro and Eunice Siskovsky, who were to join our faculty the following September. For now, in June, they are retiring to Shelburne, Vermont, or, when their winter plans materialize, to Florida. Retirement from this community leaves many gaps to be filled.

Who will be so ready to mend our clocks? Who will really organize and spark the Orchestra? Above all, who can possibly bring to the teaching of the violin and the coaching of chamber music the wealth of unmatched background, both Sevcik and Auer and 17 years of professional experience as a member of the New York String Quartet?

Who but Eunice Siskovsky can so cheerfully and willingly organize the arrangements for chapel flowers or be so ready in the 101 often unseen jobs which the wives of the faculty do?

Scores of graduates will remember Jaro Siskovsky's patience and his perception as a teacher and coach. Many more will gratefully remember fine music well played in the library, concerts that could not have been given without him.

Those of us on the faculty who have worked closely with him will treasure and profit from what he has given us, the clear and simple fundamentals of playing together without eccentricity, with a deep respect for what the composer has written and an unfailing awareness that even the best performances may always be bettered.

So when the Shishes really leave they cannot take with them the important things—a vivid memory of the generosity of themselves, their sensitivity to what one may do in so many small but important ways for the community to which one may belong. Because they are made as they are, wherever they find themselves, they will never really retire, which is as it should be.

We wish them well and hope they will remember us as warmly as we shall remember them.

In addition, I received an illuminated testimonial signed by thirty-four members of the faculty, which reads as follows:

JAROSLAV SISKOVSKY—MASTER OF TIME—He has been the keeper of our clocks, a devoted coach for those who would play in time together, one who always found time to do for others—MASTER OF MUSIC—He has shown a generation of boys and girls how to make music, and through his own playing has given us an awareness of what well-played music can mean.

I can think of no single quotation in my whole life which gives me more satisfaction and heartthrob than the excerpt from the foregoing—"one who always found time to do for others." Thank you, my colleagues. It really came naturally. You were such nice people.

One of the most painful moments was when leaving our house, which we loved so much and sold. Immediately after graduation we put all our belongings into storage and left for Vermont. Cy came up shortly thereafter but only stayed long enough to make arrangements to sell his house, at the same time asking us if we wouldn't move into it in order to show it to prospective buyers.

When the house was sold in mid-November, we drove to Florida, where we had planned to make our future home. Having previously seen mid-Florida and its east coast, we were sure of one thing, and that was that Miami would be the last place we would choose to live. So we decided to take a good look at the west coast. Both of us having been water rats in our youth, the Gulf of Mexico acted as a great big magnet, especially to Eunice, who was partial to salt water. So we leisurely inspected every larger coastal town, starting with Venice, in the south, to Tarpon Springs, in the north.

There was something about Clearwater, which we had just passed through, which we liked. So we decided to return and give it a second look. The more we saw, the better we liked it. So within a few days a final decision was made to plant our roots there. From a motel in the center of the city we drove out in all directions for over two weeks looking to buy the house that would shelter us in modest comfort for the rest of our days. Much thought was given to such matters as minimum amount of upkeep, externally, on house and lot as well as minimal house-keeping.

Finally we found just what we were looking for in a brand-new house with five rooms and one and a half baths in a brand-new section, centrally located. It was something the two of us could take care of well into old age. Negotiations to buy were started on the spot. So after buying two single beds, two chairs, and a few cooking utensils, we moved in on December 15, 1953, and lived happily in the unfurnished house for over two weeks until all our furnishings arrived by van from the north.

It is a very rare house in Florida that has either an attic or a cellar; so we had to adjust our thinking to this fact. Fortunately, our supply of furnishings was more than adequate; so we spent the whole winter arranging and rearranging things until we became satisfied that that was what we liked best. And now we could dispose of the surplus which was cluttering up our garage to a secondhand man.

Spring had come, and our plans were to keep going to our camp in the summertime for as long as we enjoyed it. In the meantime, our very dear friend, Jeanne Gilfillan, had been urging us to visit her in Montevideo, Uruguay.

Now that we had established a home base in Clearwater, we decided to eliminate one winter, which we both hated, from our lives and go spend it with Jeanne below the equator, which would be their summer there. So, after making arrangements with our kindly neighbors, who offered to look after our house while we were gone, we drove to our cottage in Shelburne and as usual spent a delightful summer there, leaving in plenty of time to board a Norwegian-American ship, on October 2, 1954, departing from New York for Buenos Aires.

21

SOUTH AMERICA

Our ship, the *Bow Brazil*, was a freighter carrying miscellaneous cargo, a crew of thirty-eight, and twelve passengers. This number of passengers was limited by international maritime law, which decreed that any time this number was exceeded it was obligatory to add a doctor to the ship's personnel. Everything aboard was spotlessly clean. The captain and crew, all Norwegians, couldn't have been nicer or more obliging. The meals, giving evidence of an expert chef, were without exception first-class throughout the whole trip. The rooms were akin to those found in luxury suites aboard transatlantic liners, both in size and furnishings. The latter consisted of two single beds, one on each side of the room, a divan and coffee table in between, a combination desk and dressing table, a padded chair, two good-sized closets with drawers and plenty of clothes hangers, wall-to-wall carpeting, curtains for two large square portholes, a complete private bathroom with shower providing three kinds of water—hot, cold, and salt.

A good-sized dining room contained three tables of a size to seat eight people each, the captain presiding over one, the chief engineer over another, and a third used for smorgasbord, which was available along with regular meals if so desired. Adjoining the dining room was a large lounge containing an ample library, card tables, etc. Above these rooms was a top deck with deck chairs which we used for sunbaths and promenading.

Although it was understood that we had free access to any part of the ship, on this trip there were so many Ford automobiles anchored so closely together from bow to stern on the lower deck that very few, except seamen, ventured through the maze. Actually there was plenty of room to promenade both inside and on the upper decks so that no one found fault with this, especially since everything else was right to the queen's taste.

Now add to this a group of passengers of mixed nationalities, mixed sexes, mixed pursuits, and mixed temperaments. Still, we all got along together so well that we were like one happy family, due principally to our dear captain, whom everyone respected and loved.

Thus, in mostly good weather, at fourteen knots, we arrived at Rio in thirteen days without incident, although in the Caribbean area the captain thought it prudent to make a detour of 300 miles to the east because of a hurricane brewing there.

It took five days to unload all those autos and other cargo from the holds; so we had all that time to sight-see in Rio and its environs.

At this point I might restate what I said prior to this—that the only thing that made me persevere in writing these memoirs was that I felt my life and experiences were rather unusual and therefore might be of interest to a host of readers and, what would hopefully be more gratifying, an inspiration to some lonely straggler struggling along the rocky path of life in this sometimes cruel yet most exciting world. Therefore, when we retired and moved to Florida, we planned to slow up a bit and try to live a life that was more peaceful, yet useful, especially to others, as well as interesting, and not part of the rat race. As this is being written seventeen years later, I am happy to be able to say that this has been achieved.

Thus, the most interesting events in our lives from this point on were two trips around the world in opposite directions of almost six months' duration each on Norwegian and Dutch cargo ships and the trip to South America of eight months, which I have just started to narrate, on a Norwegian cargo ship going south on the Atlantic. After a four-month stay in Montevideo, Uruguay, we returned north via the Grace Line. There was, lastly, a six-month trip to Europe and the Scandinavian countries, leaving Tampa on a Swedish-American cargo ship and returning on the big German liner, the *Bremen*.

From this point on, this narrative might easily become a

travelogue, but these are a dime a dozen, written by people more expert than I; so, since I do have to account for the past seventeen years and the narrative is already lengthy, prudence demands that I describe only those events and places which made the deepest impression on my memory.

As usual in our travels, before we landed at any place, we would study up on its history and places of interest so that when we reached our first stop, Rio de Janeiro, we knew that Brazil had been discovered by the Portuguese shortly after Columbus discovered America; that it had been settled principally by them; and, with some interruptions, that it maintained a monarchical form of government until 1889, when it was made a republic. This is the one and only country in South America that speaks Portuguese as their national language.

In the latter part of the nineteenth century there was a great influx of Italians, African Negroes, and, in lesser numbers, immigrants from all over Europe. Thus, as we walked the streets, we weren't a bit surprised to find the names over shop windows and the architecture of buildings reflecting their European heritage, all except a few beautiful, distinctive, but modern buildings designed by Niemeyer, the famous Brazilian architect who also designed the new Brazilian capital, Brasilia. His name is German; the president's name, Kubichek, is Czech—two examples that show that South America is just as cosmopolitan as the United States.

There were innumerable shops selling jewelry mounted with butterfly wings, semiprecious stones, and what have you, which was something right up Eunice's alley. Here we purchased enough Christmas presents to last for years.

The view of the enormous statue of Jesus Christ with outstretched arms, high on the mountain overlooking Rio, is a very moving one from the streets below; but the view (from the pedestal of this statue) of Rio, Guanabara Harbor, and Sugarloaf Mountain must be put close to the top of the list of the most beautiful sights we ever saw in all our travels. Certainly we class the harbor as the most beautiful in the world. The usually published list of the most beautiful harbors gives San Francisco, Hong Kong, Rio, and Sydney, not necessarily in order of preference. We have seen the first three, and I have examined every picture of Sydney very carefully for this reason of comparison. Still, Rio, in my book, is easily the champion. For that matter, I can't understand why Naples isn't included in every list. Certainly the sight of Vesuvius puffing away every few minutes and surveying all the beauty that lies about him is most impressive.

We took the suspended cable car to the top of Sugarloaf, rode high in the air in a cab seating about twenty people for about a half mile, got out on top to admire the marvelous view of Rio and returned with our hearts tickling our Adam's apples all the way. But we thought it was well worth it.

While the autos and other cargo were being unloaded, we spent each day ashore either roaming the Rio streets or taking trains or autos out to surrounding points of interest. One sad sight was an immense *favela* (shantytown) practically in the heart of the city. The small shacks made out of discarded crates and other junk were a poignant contrast to the affluent tall buildings not far away. The rides by train were like rides through banana jungles.

Another thing that impressed us deeply was the complete absence of a color line. One saw mixed couples everywhere.

A visit to the famous Copacabana beach was a disappointment. The shore was lined with six- to ten-story hotel and apartment buildings from which sewage drained in little trenches above ground over the beaches and into the water in which the people were bathing, leaving an unpleasant stench.

In departing at dusk one evening, the ship traveled south, giving us all a chance to observe what is called the "diamond necklace"—the lights on the boulevard paralleling the shore for many miles.

It took us only a few days to reach Sao Paulo's port, Santos, but a whole week to get a docking berth; so we lay out in the harbor waiting all that time. To us it didn't matter; in fact, we were glad, since it didn't cost any more. But a few of the passengers did want to get to Buenos Aires and do things. After docking and ascertaining from the captain that the ship would be unloading for at least four days, four of us took the bus to Sao Paulo, a distance of about six miles up a steep winding road which we reached in one and one-half hours. Here we checked into a hotel and stayed for two days.

Sao Paulo impressed me as a big bustling metropolis with tall skyscrapers, the spitting image of Chicago, the only difference being in the language spoken and some unique buildings showing the masterful touch of Niemeyer.

On the third day we drove further inland to Campinas, into the heart of the coffee country, where we toured plantations and spent the night at a hotel, incidentally, run by a German. The next day we drove back to our ship, which departed for Buenos Aires in a few days.

It took two days to reach the 120-mile-wide estuary of the La Plata River, which we entered sailing close to the hulk of the German battleship, the *Graf Spee*, which was scuttled by the Germans in World War II, leaving only the masts visible above water. This was of particular interest to Eunice and me because our destination was the Quinta (Villa) Emma in Montevideo, where the top officers of the *Graf Spee* were interned for the duration of the war and which the Gilfillans purchased soon after the armistice.

It took another eight hours up the La Plata River before we arrived in Buenos Aires. Checking into a hotel, we had to fill out about two hours' worth of red tape before they would allow us out into the streets. But it was worth it, for here we lingered for a whole week, three days longer than we had planned.

This was in the days when Argentina was governed by the so-called benevolent dictatorship of Juan Perón and his Evita. How much good they accomplished is still questionable, but they did put Argentina on the map for the time being because of their ability to headline news all over the world more frequently than any other president of Argentina ever had.

No one thing remains memorable except the conglomerate picture of a very large, beautiful, progressive, cosmopolitan, European city (its architecture reminded me of Vienna). Spanish is the official language, as it is in all the other South American countries except Brazil and the three Guianas. There you could get a very delicious steak for fifty cents in the best of restaurants. We never tried to get used to the custom of having dinner at 10:00 p.m.; instead, we would order a sandwich or ham and eggs at what was supposed to be tea time, between 6:00 and 7:00 p.m.

Leaving Buenos Aires, we were subjected to a lot more red

tape; but we made it to a ferry boat which took us across the La Plata River to the town of Colonia in two and one-half hours. Now we were in Uruguay, reputed to have the most democratic government in South America, copying that of Switzerland. Here we caught a bus, which, on narrow roads through truck farming country, landed us in the center of Montevideo, where we transferred to a taxi, which took us to the Gilfillan quinta.

As we rang the bell at the gate entrance, I stood there ruing the fact that my dear friend Gil would not be here to greet us, for he had died several years prior to this.

After a wait of two or three minutes, a maid appeared with two big dogs, one a German sheperd and the other an even bigger mongrel, both of whom were barking their heads off and looking vicious. The maid, after identifying us, quieted the dogs, opened the gate, and led us down a lane through a fairyland of flowers for about 200 feet to the quinta, where Jeanne Gilfillan welcomed us with open arms.

It was springtime here. So the first thing we did after being settled in a very cozy room attached to the garage (containing twin beds with adjoining bathroom) was to be escorted on a trip through the premises by Jeanne. The whole domain was about the size of a football field, in the center of which stood an eight-room villa, all of which was surrounded by a masonry wall a foot thick and fourteen feet high. The portion from the gate to the residence was planted with scattered trees plus shrubs and flowers in great profusion, most of which, because of the season, were in full bloom, making the scene and aroma something that words cannot describe. The rest of the property in the rear of the house was devoted to truck gardening, with paths of grape arbors. At the extreme rear there were many cages in which chickens, ducks, geese, rabbits, and a small bird the size of a crow, called a teruteru, were kept.

When we got to this bird, Jeanne explained that many people kept one of these because of their habit of squawking loudly whenever a stranger appeared on the premises. Then she went on to explain that thievery and corruption were so prevalent that people used all possible means to protect themselves, and that was why she had two big dogs, the teruteru, and the high wall. To be sure, the wall was already built when they bought the place. As an example to show how crooked conditions were in Montevideo, she told about renting one of her apartments, which she owned for investment purposes, to the chief of police, where he had lived for two years without paying any rent. Then, after two years of court proceedings, he finally was evicted without his having to pay a cent for either rent or proceedings.

That evening just before dinner we met all the other members of the household—Henri, her brother, about forty years old, who was employed as clerk in an investment house; his wife, Ernestine, about the same age, he of French-Swiss and she of Italian-Swiss descent; along with their son, Paul Pierre, about seven years old. The help (living in the villa) was a Russian couple; she, purportedly an opera singer, did all the maid's work, while he, purportedly a Volga boat captain, did work as a handyman. They, having arrived in the country so recently, were not too conversant in Spanish. While Jeanne spoke six languages, Russian was not one of them; so ofttimes my knowledge of the language came to the rescue. I often enjoyed speaking to them because both were quite literate and obviously doing work below what they were capable of and what they were used to; besides, for me it was a refresher course in Russian. Then there was Eugene, a Swiss-German, about age forty, who was the gardener, on whom I often practiced my German. Ernestine did all the cooking. Jeanne had no difficulty ruling over this motley crew because she was the sweetest, gentlest, kindest and most thoughtful person I ever met, and everybody loved her.

Since we all had different things to do during the day, it was agreed to have pick-up breakfasts and lunches and then dine together in the evening. This arrangement suited us to a T because then we could sleep as late as we cared to. The employees, of course, ate separately.

After about a week, Eunice decided she would like to make a list of the number and types of flora on the place. So we spent several days and, I, with pencil and paper in hand, marked down the names of the different plants she spotted. We ended up with a total count of thirty-five different flowers, forty different shrubs, and forty-five trees of which there were some duplications, mostly in oranges. The climate is semitropical, similar to that of central Florida.

Now that I have set the stage for this story, I find myself

without a plot. Let's face it; there is nothing newsworthy in a blissfully happy yet uneventful life. That being the case, it behooves me to relate the rest of our five-month stay as succinctly as possible, yet give the reader a vague idea of how we occupied our time.

First of all, we looked for every opportunity to be useful and within an establishment of that size there were plenty of them. I helped the gardener and the handyman whenever possible. Jeanne called up all her friends and said, "If you have any clocks that need repairing, bring them over. I have a visitor who will do the job." An influx of clocks prompted me to set up a little workshop in the garage.

I taught the boy how to play the recorder; and by Christmas time he and Eunice at the piano were playing Christmas carols together, which Jeanne, his parents, and we enjoyed immensely. I also taught him to fly kites, which we ourselves made.

Eunice helped out in the kitchen and garden; and, of course, we read a great deal. The only thing I really missed was the daily newspaper, but Jeanne kept us informed of major happenings; and as we went to town at least once a week, where I purchased the South American English edition of *Time*, we kept abreast of major news.

We went to movies whenever a picture to our liking appeared, and that was often. Most of them were done in English, with captions in Spanish.

On weekends, more often than not, Henri would drive us out into the country on sight-seeing excursions or for a swim in the estuary of the La Plata River, whose water was pretty muddy at Montevideo. But the public didn't seem to mind it and neither did we. Everybody seemed to come out invigorated and clean.

Once we took a three-day camping trip over rolling hilly ranch country to a Brazilian border town named Chuey. Everything was still underdeveloped and primitive, yet colorful. At one point we were stalled a couple of hours while a herd of about 1,000 sheep, being transferred from one pasture to another, blocked the road. We passed innumerable flocks of ostriches running wild and many gauchos (cowboys) dressed up in their outfits, riding on such superb-looking horses that it made me believe they were chosen with more care than their wives.

We were fortunate to witness the inauguration parade of their new president. The Latins, as is well known, love bright colors. This propensity was well proven in the design of their military uniforms. Outstanding in this respect was the cavalry, which, mounted on the finest collection of horses I have ever seen, still remains in my memory as an inspiring sight. The British sent a battleship with a contingent of sailors who participated in the parade. The United States sent a big bomber, which kept flying back and forth over the line of march, making so much noise that people were shaking fists at it. A projected early visit by President Eisenhower inspired a deluge of writings on walls such as "Eisenhower, go home." In conclusion, let me add that never in the five-months' stay were we unhappy or bored.

Our plan was to go home via the famous Chilean lake region and up the west coast of South America. There were two ways to do this, one being to take the train from Buenos Aires, which travels south for some distance and then turns west across the pampas of Patagonia to the city of Bariloche. This was a forty-hour trip. The second choice was to fly from Buenos Aires to the same place. Everybody advised us to fly, because the train trip was too dusty. We chose number one because we came "to see," even if it involved a little discomfort—a decision which we never regretted.

Thus, one fine evening, the whole family escorted us to the night boat to Argentina, where we parted with tears in our eyes. And, after a night's journey up the La Plata River, we landed in Buenos Aires early the next morning. That afternoon we boarded the train, with comfortable accommodations in the sleeper. We traveled along the Atlantic coast for part of the next day, where the cities and towns were more progressive; but when we turned west, the train was a local. And that's where the fun began.

Every time we stopped at a station there was so much commotion and excitement that even though we were lying in our berths, both of us couldn't resist peeking out of our curtained windows at the antics of an excited crowd (apparently mostly illiterate) at every stop; therefore, we slept but little.

The scenery was nonexistent, for all night long we traveled over a flat, completely treeless plain. This, then, was the famous pampas that we had been warned about as being unbearably dusty. On this trip, at least, it wasn't so at all.

240

The second morning we started to climb at a slow, laboring pace; so we knew that we had reached the eastern edges of the Andes Mountains. At the 2,400-foot level we arrived at a perfect gem of a town, Bariloche, looking like a beautiful Christmas card after a light snowfall in the night. Practically every house in town was built of wood, stuccoed in white, with the wide overhanging eaves which are so common in Switzerland, Bavaria, and the Tyrol. Indeed, if there were some way of transferring the whole setup (houses and mountains) into the middle of Switzerland, I don't believe anyone could tell the difference. Everything was neat and tidy, showing evidence of expert and careful planning.

We checked in at a hotel with an awe-inspiring view over Lake Nahuel Huapí and the distant high Andes. After lunch and a nap we tramped around the town for several hours confirming the fact that this was almost exclusively a Swiss colony.

The next two days were spent on whole day excursions in a tourist bureau bus into the outlying mountains in all directions. Most memorable of these trips was the visit to the glacier, El Tronador.

The next morning we boarded a boat which took us to the western end of Lake Nahuel Huapí, where we got into a bus which delivered us to another boat in a succeeding lake. So in this way we hedgehopped three lakes with one overnight stop along the way, finally arriving at Puerto Varas, not far from the Pacific, in Chile. The town has no redeeming features except the magnificent view of stately snowcapped Mount Osorno (across Lake Llanquihue) which is the spitting image of Fujiyama in Japan. The views of the lakes were breathtaking, reminding me of the Norwegian fjords, that is, when we could see them in between a succession of showers. A Chilean on one of the boats, who obviously was not a member of the chamber of commerce, told us that here it rained 300 days in the year and the other 65 were apt to be foggy.

Having been advised to visit the very picturesque village of Puerto Montt, we engaged a taxi to drive us there the following day. In the meantime, we had met a delightful young Chilean couple from Santiago on their honeymoon; so we invited them to come along. It was about a six-hour trip, both ways, which we all enjoyed immensely—especially the old fashioned way things were done in the quaint old fishing town and harbor of Puerto Montt. Of particular interest was the way the people brought their boats in on the high tide and when beached on the low tide, they drove their wagons with teams (horses or oxen) right up close to the hulls, where unloading proceeded without difficulty. The four of us enjoyed each others' company so much we planned to have dinner together in Santiago in a few days.

We left by train to travel 800 miles on what is reputed to be the longest straight valley (1,000 miles long) in the world. After a twenty-four-hour trip through farming, cattle-raising, and grape-growing country, with high mountains on both sides, we arrived in Santiago about 10:00 a.m. and checked in at the Crillon Hotel. Immediately after lunch we went to the Grace Line office, which resulted in our securing passage on one of their ships departing in three days for Lima, where we would stop over for a week and then embark on another ship for New York. Two days were consumed seeing the sights of the city on foot and by taxi.

The general impression that remains is that of a great big bustling city of close to two million inhabitants, where the architecture shows European influence and most houses are built of lumber akin to redwood, which is weatherproof and bugproof and therefore is left unpainted. The population is a polyglot mixture, with Indians conspicuously in evidence. The one unique thing about the location is that it seldom rains there.

On our last night we invited our Chilean newlyweds (whom we had taken with us to Puerto Montt) to dinner, setting the time at 9:30. As is the custom down there, they arrived at 10:00. Anyway, it was a good dinner, with which we consumed two large bottles of Chilean wine, which is acknowledged to be the finest in all of South America. When we parted shortly after midnight, it was done in a jolly good mood.

Next midnight we were supposed to depart on a ship leaving San Antonio, a small town just south of Valparaiso. Why not sight-see in the latter city and its famous beach, Vina del Mar? Since Santiago is inland some 100 miles, we got up early and made a deal with a taxi driver to take us to our ship. Chile at that time was in the throes of a galloping inflation; so the price was ridiculously low—something like $3.00.

It took four hours to reach Valparaiso. So after lunch and a tour of the city, we finally boarded our ship, where, after a good dinner, we were so tired that staying up until midnight to witness our departure did not intrigue us in the slightest. So we hit the hay (as they say in the army) very early.

After sleeping as late as possible without missing breakfast, on going outside, we noticed that the air temperature was much colder. Then we knew that we were in the Humboldt Current, which flows north from the South Pole, a condition of which all ships going north take advantage. Another thing was the gentle pitching motion, like that of a porpoise, when the bow and the stern were alternately going up and down.

After five days we arrived in Callao, a city made famous because it was from here that the Norwegian, Thor Heyerdahl, sailed on a balsa raft to the South Pacific. As Callao and Lima were almost contiguous, it took only about ten minutes by taxi to reach the Hotel Bolivar, where we checked in.

Since it was only about 10:00 a.m., we went strolling about the center of town to see what there was to see. Here again was a big bustling city of about two million people; but, somehow or other, we got the feeling that it was more sophisticated than the other South American cities we had been in. Here for the first time did we get away from the heterogeneous European influence. Also, here for the first time did Spanish influence prevail, often with artistic effects, such as in the planning of the city. People in the streets were mostly white or tan, but there were a great number of Indians in their picturesque hats, lugging various sizes of bundles on their backs, who obviously had come to the city from outlying districts to do some shopping.

The main purpose of our stopping here for a week, however, was to visit the ruins of the Inca stronghold of Machu Picchu, high up in the Andes. The closest big town was Cusco, which could be reached by plane in two hours; otherwise, by a roundabout train and bus trip, it would take three days. Neither of us had ever flown; so this would be our first flight—and what a flight it was! Every inch of the way was over 20,000-foot mountains with nary a landing field in between. The decision was not difficult to make, because it was either go by plane or don't go at all in the week's time we had in between ships.

Thus, with faltering steps, and great apprehension, we boarded the plane for Cusco one morning. After about five minutes, in which we had reached the required altitude, all passengers were handed flexible tubes, which we held in our mouths and from which we breathed oxygen. This pumped a little more bravery into me, because I could look down at those snow-covered mountain peaks without being so scared. We landed in Cusco, which itself had an elevation of 12,000 feet, located at the bottom of a cup-shaped hollow surrounded by mountains 6,000 to 8,000 feet higher.

After checking in at a modern hotel, we decided to take a short walk about the ancient town. This turned out to be much shorter than intended, because soon our hearts began to pound, we were short of breath, our legs began to wobble, our knees began to buckle, and we began to feel very weak; so we retraced our steps back to the hotel, took to the beds, and slept until dinner time. After dinner we ventured out again, with better results, although still feeling a bit feeble.

Next morning, having become acclimated to the rarefied atmosphere, we tramped the streets all day, mingling with the Indians, fascinated by their folk art, of which there was an abundance wherever one looked.

The next day we hired a taxi to visit the picturesque but poverty-stricken Indian villages in the surrounding area. Their markets alone were sideshows well worth the price of the trip. Along the way we passed many an Indian woman tending a herd of llamas, all the while spinning wool, in fields that apparently were public property, because there wasn't a fence in sight. We also passed innumerable Indians, loping with heavy loads on their backs, evidently too poor to buy a burro. This also was a common sight on the busy auto-jammed streets of Lima.

On the third day we arose at 5:00 a.m. to catch a rail car leaving for Machu Picchu at 7:00, which proved to be one of the outstanding sights of all our travels. We passed picturesque but dilapidated Indian villages where people lived in adobe houses with thatched roofs, as we rode along in a deep ravine alongside the wildly rushing Urubamba River, full of rapids and cataracts.

When we reached the rail station of Machu Picchu, after about a three-hour ride, we were transferred via a footbridge over the river to a bus which drove us to the top of the 2,500-foot mountain on which the ruins were located. Seen from our starting point at the bottom, one noted that the road looped up in innumerable hairpin turns hacked out of a side of the mountain, which looked almost perpendicular all the way to the top. On seeing this, my remark to Eunice was, "Never mind the motor; I am interested at this point in what kind of brakes this bus has." We counted fifteen hairpin turns on our way up. No matter how you look at it, it's a hair-raising trip and an amazing engineering feat. Fortunately, the motor worked properly; so we didn't need brakes. But as we stepped from the bus at the top, I could have used oxygen, because the view was so awe-inspiring it almost knocked the wind out of me. I never saw such a dramatically heroic, awesome sight in my life. It seemed to be a perfect setting for Valhalla. Words just can't describe it; so I'll stop right here.

We had lunch at a small inn, the only abode there, where I found a photo on the mantlepiece which was of special interest to us. It was of United States Senator Hiram Bingham, who spent practically a lifetime searching for Machu Picchu. His grandson was a favorite pupil of mine at Milton Academy.

After some three hours surveying the ruins with a guide, three things still amaze me. How could they cut such immense granite blocks so perfectly with crude tools that when fitted together, the joint is so tight a knife blade will not enter them? I was amazed at the amount of work they put into building such narrow terraces on such steep slopes at such high elevations and the enormous amount of climbing it took to plant, care for, and harvest the crops planted therein. It seems to me miraculous.

Everybody looked forward to the descent on the bus with apprehension. After three hours' exploration we were quite tired and well cognizant of the fact that one little misjudgment by the driver, or a failure of the brakes, would surely plummet us into the gorge and river below; but we made it and got back to our hotel very hungry and in time for dinner at seven.

The next day we flew back to Lima without any qualms; and the day following we boarded a Grace Line ship bound for New York, making a few intermediate stops, such as Guayaquil, Ecuador, and Buenaventura, Colombia, where we went ashore while the ship was loading bananas, coffee, and cocoa beans.

Our first trip through the Panama Canal proved to be of great interest. I was to discover that a large part of it was Lake Gatun and that because of the crook in the umbilical cord that joins the two continents we would actually be traveling east to west, going from the Pacific to the Atlantic.

We arrived in New York on May 16, 1954, and soon thereafter proceeded to our camp at Shelburne, where, as usual, we spent the summer and left early in October for our home in Florida. There we found everything in good condition, just as we had left it eighteen months previously, barring the landscaping, which was in a shambles. It appeared that we had chosen a good winter to be away, for it was central Florida's coldest winter on record, with the thermometer dropping to sixteen degrees. All our flowers, shrubs, and citrus trees had to be cleaned out and replaced, which took about six months to accomplish.

22

AROUND THE WORLD WESTWARD

It wasn't long before we began to have visions of another trip, this time around the world. But it would have to be on a Norwegian cargo ship. It took about six months of perusing travel folders and correspondence with a New York travel agency before we found just what we wanted. And then, after signing up and making a deposit, we had to wait a whole year before our reservations could be honored.

Finally, we boarded the M.S. *Queensville* of Klaveness Line in New York on November 11, 1957, at 4:00 p.m., just about two years after our return from Uruguay. To our delight, we found the ship and our stateroom even more sumptuous than that of the *Bow Brazil*, on which we had traveled to South America. She was practically new; and this being only her second voyage around the world, everything everywhere was spotlessly clean.

We were served a delicious supper at 6:00 p.m., which three-fourths of the twelve passengers proceeded to lose as soon as we reached the Atlantic about two hours later, since it was very rough. There was no fraternization among passengers that evening. I was surprised at how much the ship rolled and began wondering what it would be like in a real storm, but my apprehension was dispelled on reaching Newport News the next day, where we spent two days loading innumerable tons of coal into our holds. It was then that I realized that we had been traveling only partially loaded and that we would be riding much more smoothly from now on, and so it proved to be.

I might mention here that the first officer, who has charge of loading, is informed in advance of the kind and amount of cargo to be loaded and discharged at each port according to which he can estimate the time of departure, which is posted in a conspicuous place for all to see. Passengers are free to come and go at all times; so from now on, it may be assumed that Eunice and I debarked at every port to our hearts' content, usually coming back in time for dinner, to sleep and then start out again the next morning after breakfast.

As we entered Hampton Roads, we passed close by the aircraft carrier, the *Forrestal*, whose immense size made our ship look very small in comparison.

Our next stop was Charleston, South Carolina, and then Cristobal in the Canal Zone, where we had to wait several hours to take our turn being admitted into the Panama Canal. By this time all the passengers had become so well acquainted with one another that we were like one happy family, due in great part to the fact that at meals we sat at one table headed at one end by kindly Captain Berntzen and at the other end by his wife. This was the first and only time I had seen the wife of a captain accompany him on a trip, although it is common practice on Norwegian ships to have wives of lesser officers and crew serving as dining room waitresses, room service maids, etc. The Norwegians found out that this system creates a higher standard of morality among the crew. There were fourteen of us seated at one table for lunch and supper. Breakfasts were served ad libitum from 7:00 to 9:00. Early risers, like Eunice, could get a hot cup of coffee by simply walking into the galley and helping themselves.

Among the passengers were two pseudo comedians, one a widow, the other a widower, both about age seventy and close friends for many years, who kept taunting each other in such a humorous manner that it kept the rest of us in stitches throughout the whole journey.

Though we had passed through the canal, which takes the better part of a day, only two years previously in the opposite direction, we still were just as eager to watch the maneuvering at the locks as before; so we climbed to the highest vantage point on deck, which was atop the wheelhouse. Here we stayed until we reached Balboa, at the other end, allowing only time out for lunch.

Particularly noticeable to us was the enormous amount of grading that had been done in Culebra Cut. The last time the sides were almost perpendicular. Now they sloped up from the water's edge. It looked as though work on this troublesome spot, which had been caving in for so many years, was finally coming to a close.

It felt good to get to San Francisco (our next port) to replenish our diesel oil for the engines and other supplies necessary for the long trip across the Pacific to Manila, our next stop. Almost everybody who comes to Frisco loves it. True, it is the most beautiful port on the North American continent, but there is something else about it that gives one a feeling (here I'll have to dig into my German to come closest to what I mean) of *Gemütlichkeit* that people find hard to describe. Here it was, too, that the New York String Quartet gave many enthusiastically received concerts; so we visited many friends while in port.

Crossing over, we couldn't see why the Pacific was named so, because at times it was anything but peaceful. As we approached the latitude north of the Hawaiian Islands, had we continued on our regular course, we would have headed directly into a hurricane brewing in that area. So the captain, having been forewarned, changed course to one some 200 miles north, where we only got the edges of the wind and sea. By this time fully loaded, our ship was riding the waves comfortably; and we passengers, now with steady sea legs and stomachs, were enjoying every minute of our trip.

The most vivid recollections I have of Manila are of the great number of peons, sitting on their haunches in bunches, especially around the docks, for hours at a time, doing nothing but gabbling and the abundance of gaudily painted jitney buses (converted U.S. Army jeeps), which they called jeepneys, busily plying the streets, loaded with chattering passengers.

A sobering two hours were spent at the enormous, neatly kept graveyard for thousands of United States soldiers killed in the Second World War. We were surprised to see so many gravestones marked with the inscription "Known only to God."

From one of the natives we learned something that as far as we know had never been reported in the United States. When we were retaking Manila from the Japanese in World War II, our air force bombed the center of the city so devastatingly that there was nothing left of that part of town except one of the many churches to which the people had flocked thinking that the Lord would protect them there. The other churches were levelled, and, as a result, the loss of life was in the thousands.

It took us exactly twenty-one days to cross the Pacific, at nineteen knots, from Frisco to Hong Kong, including the three-day stopover in Manila. Now we had a chance to compare two of the most beautiful ports in the world. I wouldn't argue either way. In my estimation it is a toss-up.

Theoretically, this is the port where all around-the-world passengers on this line change ships, but we learned from our captain that our next ship wouldn't be leaving for ten days and that, if we chose, we could stay aboard until we arrived at the first port in Japan without extra cost. This was too good an unexpected opportunity to miss; so we and another couple decided to stay with the ship while all the others debarked. It was a sad parting, since we had been together for thirty-seven days; but we had no time to linger, for with this new arrangement, we had to busy ourselves getting a visa to enter Japan. This, along with a few other matters, took the better part of two days, which was about the length of time it took to unload the cargo for this port.

Arriving at Hirohata, (a suburb of Kobe) at dusk one evening, the scene that met our eyes (excluding the frying of victims on red-hot coals) could easily be used to depict hell on a busy day. There seemed to be at least a hundred chimneys pouring out the thickest, dirtiest, blackest smoke I ever saw, and I spent my youth living in between the stacks of the Otis Steel Company and the Standard Oil Company works (within ten blocks of each other) in Cleveland. To make matters worse, aside from being dusted with soot and coal dust the minute we stepped ashore, we couldn't help feeling ashamed, because here we were bringing more of the stuff that was the cause of all of this pollution, namely, the enormous amount of West Virginia soft coal that we had loaded at Newport News. To this day it seems inconceivable that the Japanese could not find a supply of the nasty stuff closer to home; but, of course, there must have been a reason. We had to walk several hundred yards amid coal cars to reach the office of the steel company, where we had to wait a couple of hours for a customs officer to clear us and for a taxicab to take us to Kobe. It was after working hours; so the office was empty except for an affable young boy about eighteen, with whom we had much fun while he tried to teach us Japanese.

We only stopped a day in Kobe, most of which was spent with a representative from the Japanese Tourist Bureau, with whom we made arrangements to be provided with a guide who would travel with us for a week and handle all the business affairs of the trip, which included points of the greatest interest.

We did visit one beautiful shrine that day, where it became apparent how practical the Japanese are even in praying. They work it on the cash-and-carry system. They would step before an image of Buddha, alongside of which was a rope hanging from above. Underneath was a large bowl. They stepped up to the image; pulled the rope, which rang a bell; then dropped a coin into the bowl; clapped their hands twice; crossed their arms across their breasts; and prayed to their hearts' content.

The next morning our guide, Shiro Endo, took us in tow; and we made the short trip to Kyoto by train. Kyoto was the ancient capital of Japan. So there was much to see in the way of palaces, shrines, etc.

It wasn't long before we became aware that we had struck a trump in our guide. He couldn't have been more efficient nor more accommodating.

Here was my first real contact with Oriental art, and I was thrilled with the beauty of it. But I swore not to make a travelogue of this, so must limit myself. I was fascinated with the artistry and deftness displayed by the craftsmen in shops working on the justly famous cloisonne ware, laquer and silk weaving. We stood for at least an hour on a riverbank watching workmen washing bolts of silk and then spreading them out on the bank to dry.

It was Christmas Eve, 1957; so the four of us had our guide arrange a geisha party. In a private room in one of the big geisha houses, we sat on the floor on pads with back and arm rests around a low, round table while a cook, kneeling beside us, prepared a sukiyaki meal and two beautiful geisha girls enter-tained us with song, dance, and music on the samisen—a guitarlike instrument—all the while keeping our tiny cups filled with warm sake wine. To those raising their eyebrows at this sort of disport, let me disabuse their minds by saying that geishas are not prostitutes, but cultured, educated girls of good reputation who go through a rigorous course to learn the many facets of the entertainment profession.

We left Kyoto on the 100-mile-per-hour express that runs between Osaka and Tokyo. The crowds reminded me of the New York subway during rush hour, the only difference being that the cars and stations were much cleaner and the people more polite. We couldn't help noticing, as we traveled along, how neatly kept the small farms looked and how every inch of space was taken advantage of, even the banks of the railroad tracks.

We hoped to see Fujiyama as we passed it, but misty weather prevented that.

We got off the train at a small station before reaching Tokyo from which we were driven to what is supposed to be one of the most opulent watering places in the world. Since none of us were troubled with rheumatism or other ailments, we didn't take advantage of the great variety of baths at our disposal; but we did take full advantage of the day spent there roaming the fantastically beautiful garden surrounding the place. The Japanese are famous for their horticultural expertise, and this one, along with many others we saw later on, confirmed this fact. It is the Fujiyama Hotel in Miyanoshita in Hakone National Park.

Then on we went to Nara, where we visited a magnificent five-story pagoda decorated in brilliant red and gold. Here, too, we saw in the center of a huge auditorium what was purported to be the largest Buddha in the world—fifty-three feet high.

Hundreds of small tame deer were roaming the streets all around us; so I went up to one and started to pet it. A teen-age boy came up on the run and, shaking his head, stopped me. Our guide then explained that it was permissible to feed them but not to pet them, because they represented the spirits of ancestors.

We were especially fortunate in Kamakura, because here lived a Japanese woman who attended Vassar and was in the class of 1916 with Eunice and the other girl in our group. She was contacted; but as she lived some distance out of town, it was arranged that we meet at the foot of the Kamakura Buddha, the most famous of them all, the replica of which, in all sizes, graces homes all over the world.

She was a most charming person and, fortunately for us, an intimate friend of the wife of the priest in charge of the Buddha, whose house was close by. Here we were invited to tea and to see how a middle class Japanese family lived. Fortunately, none of us had holes in our socks; and we followed the custom of taking shoes off at the entrance to the house. This custom was possibly a hand-me-down from olden times, when most people wore wooden shoes.

Indeed, at this time many of the women wore thonged sandals with wooden soles. They wore specially constructed socks which had an interstice between the big toe and the other toes into which the thong fit. It would seem that this custom is more sanitary than the western one, where we carry much dirt on our shoes from the street into the houses.

One more reason for this custom is that the Japanese like to cover their floors with reed mats, which are not nearly as wear-resistant as our carpets. When bedtime comes, they merely drag the required number of mattresses from an adjoining closet, lay them on the floor, and there they have as therapeutic a bed as anyone could wish. The next day the process is reversed; and all the paraphernalia—sheets, pillows, and mattresses—are returned to the closet, leaving the room free for other purposes. I don't believe there ever was a woman born who didn't swear every time she had to clean out that mound of dust that accumulates under beds.

Our hostess was such a charming person and we were so interested in learning how the Japanese lived that two hours passed all too quickly and we had to bid her a fond farewell.

On our way by car to Tokyo, as we neared Yokohama, the traffic consisted of a greater variety of vehicles—hand-drawn carts, horse-drawn wagons, bicycles, motorcycles, and autos of every description—weaving in and out. It seemed as though we would never get to the Imperial Hotel, the building which helped make the American architect Frank Lloyd Wright famous, because it was one of the few buildings which withstood the big Tokyo earthquake.

The city underwent extensive bombardment by American flyers during the war; but most of the damaged buildings had already been replaced by modern high-rise buildings. So it looked like Chicago, Sao Paulo, or Buenos Aires, with but little evidence of the battering it went through. Its famous shopping street, the Ginza, could stand up to New York's Fifth Avenue and make just as good an impression.

Not only was western architecture being imitated, but so was our popular music and mode of dress, as well as gum chewing and tough talk. There still were a few women wearing colorful native kimonos and sandals; but it didn't take much imagination to foresee the demise of these in the very near future, because— let's face it—western dress was more practical, even though the other was much more picturesque.

If things keep changing the way they are and Hilton hotels keep proliferating, one will be able to go from the hotel in Siwash to the hotel bar in Chicago and sit there drinking for several days, all the while imagining he is in Tokyo. It won't make much difference as to the sights one sees. These will be standardized in the name of efficiency.

After two days of sight-seeing, we were put aboard the midnight plane for Hong Kong by our loyal and obliging guide, who, at the last minute, presented each couple with an album containing snapshots of us which he had taken on our trip. We had been wondering why he took snapshots of us.

The next morning we made an instrument landing at Hong Kong in a pea-soup fog. The first thing we did after registering at the Miramar Hotel in Kowloon was to take the ferry to Victoria Island (actually Hong Kong proper), a ride of only a few minutes, and up the cog funicular which takes you to the top of the peak, from which we had a glorious panoramic view of the harbor and surrounding country into China. We lingered there for several hours, entranced with the beauty of it all; but there was an added attraction—watching several hundred Chinese men and women painting one of the big liners in the harbor below. They swarmed all over it like bees on a honeycomb. We were told they can do the job in a couple of days.

That evening we had a delicious supper at a famous seafood restaurant on Aberdeen Bay where hundreds of sampans are moored together like sardines in a can. Families live on them from cradle to grave.

The next day we toured the city, sight-seeing with a tourist guide, visiting innumerable temples, museums, etc., the most unusual of which was a park containing many cement figures representing gods and fabled figures in folklore and built by a rich man by the name of Haw Par, who made a fortune manufacturing and selling a concoction called Tiger Balm, which claimed to cure every ailment tormenting mankind and some that hadn't been thought of as yet.

At the end of a full day, our Chinese travel agent surprised us with an invitation to come to his home and celebrate New Year's Eve with him and his family. After a nap, we arrived at his apartment (furnished about as well as any in an upper middle class family in the United States) to be greeted by his wife, his sister, and two small children, all of whom spoke English.

While his wife was out in the kitchen preparing dinner, he and his sister regaled us with their harrowing escape from China.

It was about 10:30 before we sat down to dinner of fourteen courses, the likes of which I had never experienced. My father taught me a guideline to follow when eating which I found sound and followed with but a few exceptions all my life: "If you get up from the table feeling full, you have eaten too much." By the end of the fifth course, I felt as though another mouthful would be my Waterloo. So from then on, thinking that it might be an insult to our hard-working hostess if I stopped eating, I nibbled at the remaining nine courses and concentrated on the delicious various kinds of wines being served with each course. The only thing I remember about leaving is that it was in the New Year and that there was no feeling of pain. That came the next day, about noon, when both of us awoke with splitting headaches.

Since we had just received word to be aboard our departing Norwegian ship, the *Glenville*, by 6:00 p.m., this was no time for complaining. So we each downed two cups of black coffee and set about doing the necessary chores of packing and transferring to the ship that would carry us back to New York. With all this hustle and bustle we forgot about our headaches, had a good dinner aboard, and sailed out of beautiful Hong Kong harbor at 7:00 the next morning.

As we arose from a very sound sleep, we looked out the windows and saw that the decks were stacked high with crates of cabbages, which had been loaded while we slept. Each day, as we progressed to Singapore, which lies only a few degrees north of the equator, the odor of these cabbages increased in potency. By the end of the fourth day, as we entered Singapore's harbor, it wasn't necessary for us to give warning to the harbor police of our arrival—they could smell us coming! We all took it in stride as an adventure but at the same time breathed a sigh of good riddance.

In the two days we were there, we visited the sights of interest. But there was nothing unusual except a duplicate of the Tiger Balm park we had visited in Hong Kong; quite a large British military headquarters; and a diversified population consisting of Chinese, Malays, East Indians, etc., who got along fairly well under British rule, although the Chinese, being more numerous, more energetic, and more industrious, and therefore more wealthy, seemed to be somewhat disliked by the others.

Arab Street in the Indian quarter is a long thoroughfare consisting of nothing but colorful dress goods shops selling saris, batiks, and the like, which we both found intriguing. We enjoyed ourselves going from one shop to another bargaining for materials which we liked and which were relatively inexpensive.

By this time we had gotten pretty well acquainted with the other passengers on our new ship, who all seemed quite congenial; but there was one couple, a Dr. and Mrs. Lewis, who appealed to us more than the rest. This proved to be a blessing at Bangkok, our next stop, where their knowledge of the most colorful, fantastic, Arabian Nights fablelike city of my whole life, was of immense help.

Dr. and Mrs. Lewis were returning from a year's sabbatical in the States after having spent some ten years in the Orient. As a missionary doctor in one of the Bangkok hospitals, he knew the city and surroundings well. They devoted much time and effort to guiding us about the five days we were there; so we undoubtedly saw more than we otherwise would have seen.

Our next stop was in Viet Nam, where we spent just one day rickshawing around Saigon, which had just been liberated from the French. Law and order were somewhat awry, but there was no denying the fact that the French left behind their artistic touch in such matters as ladies' apparel, architecture, etc. Eunice and I agreed that we had never seen women as pretty and nattily dressed as they were here. With their slender, short builds (not over five feet), they looked like fairies.

There was sufficient evidence all around us to warrant the statement that the city had seen better days under French rule, since they had invested a large share of their financial gains for the benefit of the country. This statement applies even more to the British, who, by the evidence, showed even more consideration for the goose that lays the golden eggs. *Not* so with the Dutch.

On our first tour of Djakarta, our next stop, it was perfectly plain that the Dutch had bled the goose to the point where it was barely breathing. The whole city was a conglomeration of poverty-stricken shacks intermingling here and there with mansions. The highlight in this city was a stop at a home industry plant, operating under three dilapidated sheds, printing batiks. In amongst the various paraphernalia were a father and mother and several children working on bare ground, while chickens, ducks, kids, and dogs were roaming the place at will. In spite of all this bedlam, they did manage to produce beautiful batiks.

We arrived just at the time Sukarno was expelling the Dutch from Indonesia; so there were armed soldiers swarming all over the city. For a time it looked as though they wouldn't let us land. At the dock we were berthed between Holland-America liners which had been sent there by the Dutch government to bring home those of its citizens whose businesses had been confiscated by the Indonesian government. Many of them had been there for years; and, judging from their demeanor, this was one time when people weren't happy to be going home.

Now back again to Singapore, the shipping center of this section of the world. Here it is where most cargo ships make it a rule to change passengers to another ship, because no matter how friendly and agreeable they are at the start, they fight among themselves and scrap about the way the ship is run. We, having changed at Hong Kong, were not obliged to do this.

Since we were anchored out in the harbor, stopping there for at least a week, and since the clambering into and out of the launch that took us ashore was a hazardous undertaking (especially in rough weather), we decided to go to the Cathay Hotel for an indefinite number of days. Of course, we were free to come back to the ship at any time; but we spent five most enjoyable days roaming the streets of Singapore and its environs from morn till night.

We were very fortunate when one of these days happened to fall on the annual event of the Hindu immolation festival of Thaipusam. I can't imagine anyone witnessing the proceedings ever forgetting them. The routine started out with the penitent, surrounded by a coterie of relatives and friends, at his local outlying temple, where the priest prepared him for the ordeal with a bath in coconut milk, after which innumerable steel and silver needles about twenty inches long were driven through his skin, mostly up around the shoulders. In the newspapers the next morning, we read that one man endured 220 of these. Then a kavadis, a wooden frame weighing twenty-five pounds, adorned with flowers and resembling a big collar, was planted on the man's shoulders, after which the coterie would start out up the main streets, headed for the principal temple in the heart of the city, where other priests would perform proper rites and then relieve the penitent of his needles and his sins.

We watched these processions wending their way, the penitents' faces contorted in pain, seemingly in a trance, legs and body in a circular motion ala a dervish dance, while the coterie chanted and urged them on. The closer they got to their destination, depending on their stamina, the violence with which they danced, and the distance they had come, the more faltering there was, in which case their escorts would come to their assistance, either dragging or even carrying them the rest of the way. We saw many brought into the temple completely unconscious, but at no time did we see any traces of blood nor any female penitents. The temple was heavy with burning incense and jammed with Hindus in prayer. We stood watching other rituals, such as the shaving of babies' hair and the anointing of the head with some kind of salve.

Two days later we sailed up the Strait of Malacca to Port Swettenham, Malaya, where we spent a day ashore visiting several rubber plantations while latex (liquid rubber) was pumped aboard our ship. Then, crossing the strait, we put in at

Belawan, Sumatra, where another day's loading took place; but, owing to the serious revolutionary conditions existing there at the time, the local authorities refused to allow us passengers to land. Looking down onto docks from our vantage point at the railing of our ship and seeing the number of odd characters roaming about carrying guns on their shoulders and impersonating soldiers, absolutely no persuasion was necessary to keep any of us from trying to go ashore.

Crossing the strait again, our next stop was Penang, Malaya, which, with its beautiful surroundings, in the light of hindsight, I like to call the garden of Eden. Entering the harbor, the ship plowed through several miles of jellyfish floating atop the water.

On a sight-seeing trip around the city, we found the houses, lawns, and streets all neatly kept, showing signs of care and affluence, probably due to tin mines close by. One Buddhist temple was unusual in that it had a great variety of snakes hanging on altars and roaming all around. The women in our party weren't amused; so we made a hasty retreat.

As we made a trip around the island, up hill and down dale, through lush tropical sylvan and jungle areas, passing here and there lonely, neatly kept huts of rubber plantation caretakers and scattered villages, I had that idyllic feeling that here was a place where people live and die in contentment and happiness.

This same feeling pervaded me while traveling through the island of Ceylon, our next stop. Both islands were administered by the British, and it didn't have to be a very experienced eye to notice that they left a few more crumbs for the local population than most other nations did in their colonial exploitation.

There was a stevedore strike on at Colombo, the main port; so we put in at a small town named Galle on the south coast. Being advised that there would be at least three days of loading here, a party of us took the train to Colombo, which is the capital. A tour around the city turned up nothing unique, but on the train trip to Kandy we passed many small, colorful villages. We found the unusual on the outskirts of the city, where hundreds of semitame monkeys would come in from the surrounding forests to beg for food from the tourists and local inhabitants.

Most exciting of all was a visit to a nearby lumber camp, where we watched elephants dragging immense logs and loading them onto railroad cars. It was uncanny the way the elephant would pick up the log with his trunk so that it would balance evenly when lifted. We were told that these pachyderms would work diligently for about four hours, after which they would go on strike. The mahout would then lead them to the river, where they lay down, completely immersed in the water, while their masters scrubbed them down from top to bottom with a brush. This they seemed to thoroughly enjoy, for they lay there placidly not moving until told to turn over.

After an overnight stay at a good hotel, four of us decided that we would prefer to go back via another route, through the interior of the island and the tea plantations. A man with a large car was soon engaged to drive us to our ship, which took us from 9:00 a.m. until 4:00 p.m.

Again the villages along the way were so picturesque that at one point where we stopped to have lunch we got to talking with one of the local inhabitants, who was so friendly that we told him we were Americans and that we had never seen the inside of one of their houses and asked if he would mind showing us his. He was flattered; so we saw how simply an average Ceylonese family lived. Of course, we rewarded him well; but it was worth it, for the picture of the inside of that cabin still lingers in my mind. In this thatched mud hut with practically no furniture, their pride and joy was a Singer sewing machine, which really worked, as was demonstrated by the man of the house.

The journey through tea groves was idyllic almost all the way except for an occasional large tree from which hundreds of flying foxes (a large type of bat) were hanging upside down, which, as we approached would fly into the air in a cloud, squawking their heads off. We arrived back at the ship very weary; so it was early to bed that night, dreaming about the bullock carts we kept passing all day.

At dinner that night the captain announced that he had just received orders to make two additional stops that were unscheduled. This was greeted with joy because it gave most of us a chance to get acquainted with Africa. The first of these was Djibouti, French Somaliland, just below the narrow neck of the Red Sea, where it empties into the Gulf of Aden. A tour of the city revealed no features of the French artistic touch which had struck the eye in Saigon. A visit to the market was picturesque but nauseating. More interesting were the sights outside the city, where we were fortunate enough to encounter a herd of about a hundred camels being driven in to the docks for shipment to some other port. Picturesque, too, were the many herds of sheep and goats grazing on the sparse, scrubby growth that managed to grow in the desert.

Discharging our taxi in the center of the city, we decided to take a walk amongst the huts in the residential part. We hadn't gone but a few blocks when a big burly Arab with a big club in his hand approached us with advice not to go any further; otherwise, the probability was that we would be robbed, if not murdered. We lost no time getting out of there, thanking him profusely.

After luncheon at a French restaurant we took a taxi back to our dock just in time to witness the loading of the camels which we had passed in the morning onto a Yugoslavian ship moored close to ours. This was more fun than a circus. The boom would lower a canvas sling just the width of the belly between the camel's fore and hind legs. Then, bringing the two sides of the canvas up over the back, there was a loop through which the hook of the hoist was inserted; and up into the air went the beast, with both legs wildly flailing, only to be deposited a few moments later on the top deck and freed. Most of us usually associated a camel with a placid temperament; but when the animals on the dock saw what was happening to those being hoisted, they became restless. A great many were so enraged that the drivers had great difficulty getting them aboard ship. But by sundown they had them loaded, with only one casualty—a broken leg, and this happened after the camel was already aboard ship. We watched the proceedings all afternoon, fascinated by the clever way in which those drivers handled the animals.

The next day our ship moved up only a short distance into the Red Sea to Assab, Eritrea, administered by Ethiopia. The population, like Djibouti, consisted mostly of Arabs and Negroes, the only difference being that in Djibouti there were a good number of French who apparently were the elite, whereas in Assab, these elite were Italians.

This city appears to be the only seaport in all of Ethiopia; and the fact that the docks were only big enough to accommodate four larger ships gives one an idea of how feeble the export and import business of that country was at that time. In any case, Assab was much smaller than Djibouti and even more drab and poverty-stricken.

Walking about town, we couldn't locate any business district; but we did find a place to buy some mangy postcards. Since New York City would be our next stop, we returned to our ship and spent the afternoon writing them to everyone we knew. Before doing so, however, we took one last stroll into the surrounding country where we encountered several camel caravans bringing in bags of coffee for our ship from the hinterland.

Don't ask me why the Red Sea is red, but it really is. We anchored close to the southern end of the Suez Canal, waiting for our turn to enter. This came the next day at noon, when we were sixth in a convoy of thirty-six ships. The canal is ninety-four miles long and 350 feet wide. Ships must travel at an exact eight-knot speed and one-half mile apart. There are only two places where convoys traveling south pass those traveling north, namely, at Bitter Lake and a bypass north of it.

Just before we started, two rowboats were hoisted aboard, one at the bow and one at the stern, each with a two-man crew who, in case of a blinding sand storm, pea-soup fog, or breakdowns, are lowered into the canal with mooring ropes with which they secure the ships to rings in the concrete embankment 100 feet apart along the shoreline. Each rowboat also carried a miniature souvenir shop with which they apparently increase their income, selling Egyptian novelties to passengers and crew. Besides, it's a form of amusement, haggling over prices. If you are a novice at the game and pay the first price asked, they chuckle with glee, all the while thinking what Barnum thought, "There's a sucker born every minute."

We didn't reach the terminus until shortly after midnight, which made it a twelve-hour trip. The weather turned very cold, which to us seemed all the more so, having just come from two months of meandering in the vicinity of the equator. Eunice and I bundled ourselves up well and sat on a bench just over the bridge, where we had a clear view in all directions. She deserted me about 9:00 p.m., feeling cold; but I stuck it out until we

262

reached the beautiful Suez Canal port authority building, all ablaze with electric lights, in Port Said.

Aside from a few scattered towns in the northern part, the eastern shore of the canal was a barren desert, except for an occasional lonely hut. I kept wondering why anyone in his right mind would want to live there.

When we awoke the next morning, we were far out into the Mediterranean Sea, which wasn't what it was cracked up to be, namely, blue. It was brown, stormy, and cold; and the weather continued that way all the way into New York, which, according to our captain, was par for the course for the month of March.

As we approached the Rock of Gibraltar from the east, we noticed that the whole slope was paved with concrete, creating a reservoir for the water supply for the city of Gibraltar. The southern side, looking toward Africa, slopes gradually into the Strait of Gibraltar, through which all ships must pass, leaving or entering the Mediterranean.

As we approached New York, I begged the captain to give me a manifest of the cargo we were bringing into the United States, which may be of interest to those with inquisitive instincts. The list included tapioca, flour, rubber, tea, sisal fiber, wolfram ore, duck feathers, coffee, goatskins, beeswax, mother-of-pearl shells (for buttons), pepper, resin, refined tin, nutmeg, gum, dammar, and latex. These products came from Bangkok, Java, Sumatra, Malaya, Ceylon, Ethiopia, French Somaliland, and, by trans-shipment, from Australia.

We landed in New York on March 18, 1958, having spent four months and eight days traveling around the world. Even though the weather was stormy all the way from Port Said, the last few days were so bad that the captain had to reduce speed, which delayed our arrival a whole day. Still, we both regretted the fact that the trip was over. In another week we were back home in Florida after an absence of over five months.

23

EUROPEAN TRIP [1961]

After about two happy but uneventful years, we decided to make another European trip, principally to show Eunice Norway and Sweden, of which I had spoken in most glowing terms, and also to assuage a deep-felt longing to revisit the haunts of my student days.

It didn't take long to make arrangements to leave Tampa on a Swedish-American Line cargo ship on August 7, 1961. Passenger quarters weren't quite as luxurious as on Norwegian ships, but our large room with private bath was neat and clean, as was the whole ship. So, with comfortable beds and excellent meals, we were completely satisfied.

There were three other couples on the passenger list. We got along splendidly, except for one old gentleman, an ex-army officer, who enjoyed being grumpy and was therefore avoided— no doubt to his complete satisfaction. We very quickly struck up a close friendship with a delightful young Swedish couple who were returning to Sweden after two years of medical study in the United States. We were inseparable for the whole journey; indeed, the friendship has lasted to this day; each year we exchange Christmas cards.

Thus, with good weather, good accommodations, good companions, and a genial captain, the trip to Gothenberg, Sweden, with stops at Le Havre, Antwerp, Rotterdam, and Bremen, lasting twenty-three days, seemed to have come to an end all too quickly. We, of course, went ashore at all the above cities, and it was pitiful to see the ruins still in evidence from World War II. Rotterdam in particular looked like a completely new city, having suffered 80 percent destruction by Hitler's emissaries.

Debarking at Gothenberg, we barely made connection with the little ship making the famed trip up the Gotha Canal to Stockholm. We chugged along at eight knots, through sixty-five locks and numerous lakes for 347 miles, for three days and nights, through some of the most delightfully lush farming country imaginable. Our ship, taking it easy, cows grazing in the meadows, hills in the distance, numerous picturesque villages looking neat and well kept—all combined to create such a peaceful picture of well-being that it felt good to be alive. This rosy state of things must be somewhat qualified when I describe the sleeping arrangements as two bunks fastened to the wall. Although long enough, they were only eighteen inches wide. A broad band of netting had to be stretched along the outside to keep one from falling out of bed! However, the food was good and the room spotlessly clean; so we accepted this inconvenience in good spirits.

Arriving in Stockholm, having been forewarned that hotel rooms were in short supply, we took a taxi to the railroad station, where for fifty cents a tourist service found us a very nice room in a private home within an hour. While waiting for them to locate this room, we couldn't help but reminisce about the numerous groups of graceful aristocratic wild swans we had passed all during the latter part of our journey.

Arriving at the apartment, in a fashionable neighborhood, we were welcomed at the door by a kindly elderly gentleman who, replying to my query in poor Swedish as to whether he spoke any of five languages which we could speak, apologetically said, "No, only Swedish." So, with my Swedish plus some arm motions, we got settled in a very nice comfortable room.

The next morning we called up our young Swedish couple, the Magnussens. They invited us to come visit them at their home in the suburbs. From that time on, except for nights, we were with them constantly for three days, either at their home or rousting about the city being shown the points of interest, the most unusual of which was Skansen, a reproduction of an ancient village on the order of our Williamsburg.

The next stop was Christiania, now named Oslo, where we again were put up in a very nice room in a private home to which we were directed by the Railway Information Service. It was to this city that Professor Auer migrated from Petrograd every summer that I was with him. These were three of the happiest summers of my whole life, even though they were at the beginning of World War I.

I loved Norway and the Norwegians, and the memories that returned to mind as we explored old haunts were most endearing ones. Added to this, two of my dearest friends, Helge and Aase Koenig, lived here. While Helge had made several trips to the United States since 1917 during which we saw each other, Aase, who was the famed Edvard Grieg's niece, I hadn't seen in forty-five years; so it was with great anticipation that I looked forward to seeing her. When we met we both threw our arms around each other and hugged for a full minute. At this time she was chief receptionist for the Norwegian Tourist Bureau, so she was a very busy girl but did take every free opportunity to be with us. Her husband, Helge, was with us almost constantly while we visited friends and places which were dear to our hearts.

High spots during the week were a dinner at their home, attended by their four daughters, with husbands whom I had heard much about but had never met. Eunice had heard me speak often of these dear friends; so it was a big get-acquainted party.

Then there was the unique maritime museum built at Bygdo (a suburb) in recent years, which housed several ancient Viking ships; the vessel, the *Fram*, which Nansen used on his polar explorations; the original raft, *Kon Tiki*, on which Thor Heyerdahl and party sailed and drifted from Callao, Peru, to the South Seas; as well as some stone monuments he brought back from Easter Island.

To get to Bergen, our next stop, we traveled over a railroad which is still considered quite an engineering feat because it has to cross a range of mountains almost 4,000 feet in altitude. Much of the way, at the higher elevations, the tracks are covered with snow sheds. Fortunately, the trains are run by electric power. There is no inconvenience, but you continually keep ruing the fact that you are missing so much beautiful scenery.

I had been to Bergen once before and regretted the fact that at that time, for some unremembered reason, I had not visited Grieg's home, Troldhaugen, beautifully situated on a lake in the mountains about an hour's trip by taxi outside the city. The rustic two-storied home was open to tourists, but to me it was particularly endearing because he was the aforementioned Aase's uncle, because there were several pictures of my good friend, Percy Grainger, hanging on the wall, and, of course, because Grieg was one of the all-time giants of music whose compositions I enjoyed playing and hearing. A little cabin on the shore of the lake was used by him as a retreat, where he did most of his composing. And some twenty feet up a high perpendicular cliff, in a vault blasted out of solid granite, the remains of Mr. and Mrs. Grieg lie peacefully interred. As we slowly wandered about the estate we had a feeling of great reverence and serenity.

Points of interest unique to Bergen were the ancient Hanseatic houses, especially their interiors, and the monument in a central park to the great violinist, Ole Bull.

We were fortunate enough to be in the city at the same time as King Olaf of Norway, who was there to dedicate a government museum. Quite noticeable was the fact that he moved freely in the crowds without bodyguards. I wonder how many kings, or presidents, for that matter, could claim that distinction?

One of the principal reasons for coming to Bergen was to show Eunice the fantastic beauty of the fjords, which she had heard me eulogize for years. Having already been there in my student days, I more or less knew the ropes. So, since we had no set schedule to cramp our style, we planned to make the whole trip fancy-free, by using small packet steamers which stopped and delivered mail and supplies at practically every town along the way.

Since it was the end of the tourist season, there was no fear that hotels would be filled up. Thus, by getting off the ship at places that appealed to us and staying as long as we cared to, we hedgehopped up the Sogne and Naero fjords to Gudvangen, where we took several bus trips through Stalheim and Voss to Ulvik on the Hardanger Fjord, a drive of over five hours over mountains with breathless scenery as well as breathless corkscrew turns.

From Ulvik we took another packet steamer down the Hardanger Fjord, which returned us to Bergen after a most exciting ten-day voyage through Valhalla country. Here we engaged passage on another cargo ship which would take us to Bremen in three days with a stopover in Stavanger.

To our surprise and gratification, we soon discovered that the only other passengers making the trip were a delightful Norwegian couple who were the owners of the ship. They confided that they were on their annual anniversary splurge to Hamburg, where they surfeited themselves by attending the opera every night for a week.

The four of us were having a pleasant chat until we reached the north sea and rough water, when the lady excused herself, saying, "I am a very poor sailor who gets seasick very easily; if this weather keeps up, I will be obliged to stay in bed the whole trip." And so it was. She didn't put in an appearance until we reached Bremerhaven and took the train for Rotterdam, where we were fortunate enough to get accommodations on the good ship *Basilea*, leaving the next day for a week's journey up the Rhine to Basle.

Embarking at 9:00 the next morning, we found the *Basilea* to be an almost new ship designed to carry about fifty passengers, Swiss managed, which is synonymous with saying well managed, with good food, and clean. We were fortunate in having ideal weather for the whole trip. We spent much time seated in comfortable reclining chairs on the top deck with views in all directions.

The ship's schedule was planned so that we traveled by day and tied up to a wharf in some city overnight, allowing the passengers to debark at will to explore the different places, which Eunice and I always did. Thus, we made stops at Emmerich, Cologne, Rüdesheim, Speyer, and Strasbourg. The Rhine is a very busy river, full of scow tows and tugs until it reaches the juncture with the Moselle, where much of the traffic branches off.

The first two days out of Rotterdam are through the Ruhr district, Germany's biggest industrial complex, full of factories with high chimneys pouring out dirty black smoke. The most beautiful part is between Cologne and Mainz, where you travel between hilly slopes covered with vineyards interspersed with ancient castles.

On landing at Basle at 9:00 a.m., we hurried to the tourist office to make arrangements for a trip down the Danube from Passau to Vienna, only to learn that this service had been discontinued for the winter a week previously. So with a few days stopover in Zurich, we proceeded by train all the way through

Alpine scenery, which, as everyone knows, is magnificent.

It was heart-warming to be back in Vienna again after an absence of twenty-five years. Even though the city had been severely bombed during World War II, it looked much the same as my memory recalled it. Even the famous opera house, which was reduced to rubble by bombing, was rebuilt almost exactly as it had been.

A pension on the Graben two blocks from Stefan's Cathedral, in the heart of the city, had been recommended to us; so we were happy to get a comfortable room there, especially since our plans were to go on a musical spree. Vienna had been home for such musical greats as Beethoven, Brahms, Mozart, and many others. It was a rare night when there weren't at least ten major musical events taking place. So from our centrally located pension, we were able to walk in fifteen minutes to the opera, concert halls, museums, and palaces, the latter of which, now that the government was operating under a socialist regime, were being used as concert halls. The opera house was sold out for every performance; so tickets couldn't be purchased at the box office. But two of my cousins, through some influential contacts, were able to get us into three performances.

With visits and excursions with five cousins living there, walks in the Vienna woods, climbs up surrounding mountains, operas, concerts, and an occasional good movie, we spent three busy, ingratiating, and rewarding weeks, the detailed account of which might be interesting in a diary, but not here, where I promised to report only on the unusual. As an example of my condensing, it took Eunice forty-four pages to tell about our peregrinations in and around Vienna in her diary.

Leaving Vienna, we were apprehensive as to what would happen at the border of Czechoslovakia, since it was behind the iron curtain. Actually, the officials couldn't have been friendlier. They didn't even inspect our baggage. One slight mistake was made by the Austrian Tourist Bureau, which, when I inquired about exchanging dollars for Czech money, informed me that we would find an exchange office at the border, which was not the case. This was remedied several hours later when we stopped to change trains and I was able to perform the task at a bank near the station.

Arriving in Písek in a heavy rain at 9:00 p.m., we went to the

269

best hotel in town, only to find that the owner, whom I had known well, had been accidentally killed during the Russian occupation, that the hotel was now being run by the government, and that, because of a delegation of about twenty Cubans stopping there for a few days, not a single room was vacant. The clerk called all the other hotels, only to learn that they were full, too.

By the time this all took place it was 10:00 p.m., raining hard outside; and, after a long day's railroad trip, both of us were very tired and having visions of spending the night sitting up in some corner of the lobby when in walked a gentleman who, after giving me one querulous look, shouted, "Siskovsky, what are you doing here?" I didn't remember ever having known him, but he remembered me from my student days. As though this wasn't enough of a surprise, it soon developed that he was the manager of the hotel, and, on hearing of our predicament, took measures the result of which was that soon we were ensconced in the choice suite in the hotel reserved for dignitaries. What a godsend! And didn't we appreciate it! It was the only suite in the hotel with a private bath. To be sure, it was always a surprise when warm water flowed from the hot water spigot. Usually it was as cold as the other spigot; but, otherwise, we were very comfortably situated there, especially since we were continually on the go visiting friends and relatives so that we seldom used our privileged quarters except for sleeping purposes during the week we were there.

I had brought along two albums of photos which depicted the life in the city and the Sevcik colony in those bygone student days. These I presented to the local museum, and they were very happy to get them. As it happened, Sevcik left a stack of memorabilia to the museum with no annotations, so the museum officials took advantage of my presence to help them identify the various objects, photos, and papers. With the help of my good friend Professor Velenovsky, we were able to identify almost half the material. Though it consumed the better part of two days, it was a most interesting and gratifying task.

Much of our time was spent with my good friend Franta Kolar and his sister. On one of our excursions into the surrounding country on a local bus filled with peasants carrying baskets of various kinds of produce, chickens, geese, rabbits, and whatever, we had a circus listening to the passengers josh one another. The bus was in a continuous uproar. At one point a chimney sweep, black with soot from hair to foot, boarded the bus and stood on the outside doorstep. One of the passengers called out to him, "Aw, come on in and join the crowd; we won't hurt you." Quick as a flash, he answered, "Not on your life. Do you think I want to get my new 'soot' dirtied up?"

We were continually mixing with the peasants, whose standard of living had been improved immensely since our last visit. They were more literate, much healthier, better fed, better clothed, their mouths showing proper dental care. On the other hand, we heard of a few instances where businessmen were mistreated for not cooperating with the government. In the worst case we heard of, a man who ran a successful coffeeshop and bakery, whose business was confiscated, was given a job delivering newspapers because he wouldn't cooperate. "What happens to those who do cooperate?" I asked. "They continue on as usual," was the answer, "only they must abide by certain rules which many of them dislike."

As far as we were concerned, we were allowed to roam about freely, with nobody, as far as we could see, spying on us. We had, however, agreed to one thing before entering the country. There was a system whereby each tourist had to buy a certain number of certificates according to length of stay and class (first, second, or third) of accommodation. These certificates were then used in place of money. The catch was that there was an estimate made of how much a good spender should spend in a week. Here is how it worked with us.

We asked and got a visa from the Czech consulate in Vienna for a week's stay along with which we bought first-class certificates good for that length of time. At the end of our first week's stay, even though we were living in a privileged suite, but due to the fact that we were eating away from the hotel much of the time, we had a surplus of certificates left over. So I went to the proper authorities to get an extension of our visa. "Yes, we will be glad to give it to you, but you must buy another batch of certificates, depending on how long you wish to extend your visa."

"But why should I be buying more certificates when all these are left over?"

"Sorry," he said, "those are the rules and I have to abide by them."

"Sorry," I said, "we would like to have stayed at least another week, but in this case we will leave at the expiration of our visa."

Except for a trip to the Hungarian border, where my Viennese cousins took us, crossing the border into Germany on our way from Písek to Nuremberg was the first time we had come in close contact with the iron curtain. Here they had quite a detachment of soldiers, wire fencing galore, with observation towers strung along at strategic locations, and a compound in which were the fiercest German shepherd dogs I ever saw.

The only two things a polite female customs officer was interested in were our passport and how much Czech money we were taking out of the country. I pulled a handful of change out of my pocket and told her this was all we had and would she please let us keep it as a souvenir. She did. Others who had too much were obliged to step off the train into a nearby general store and spend it on merchandise which could be taken out; otherwise, it was confiscated.

Arriving in Nuremberg, we were surprised to see what a devastating attack from the Allies the city had suffered. Most of the old historic buildings were destroyed and replaced by modern ones in a style which harmonized well with the ancient ones that survived or were repairable. Most of all we missed Hans Sach's house and the Bratwurst Glocklein. Yet there remained enough that interested us; so we stayed here three days before moving on to Dinkelsbuhl.

Now I'm stuck. Words fail me. It is so much like something out of Grimm's fairy tales that you have to pinch yourself to be sure that you are not dreaming. I'll take the easy way out and swipe a paragraph from Eunice's diary, which has served me well in refreshing my memory.

This ancient feudal city is a beautiful gem surrounded by a high wall and moat, all of which were spared from bombing by the Allies; therefore, they are well preserved and well taken care of. It was founded in about the year 900 and gradually grew into a town of some prominence around the

Renaissance period, after which, from the looks of everything, time stopped and there you have it just as it was.

We stopped at a delightful old inn, the Weisses Ross (White Stallion), where the only concession to modern improvements seemed to be modern beds and a running water toilet and bathtub in neighboring rooms down the hall. The flooring consisted of one-foot-wide planks which squeaked under every footstep. A bureau, a washstand, and two wooden chairs were the furnishings.

I can imagine if these lines ever reach the eyes of some affluent skeptic, he will be raising an eyebrow, thinking, what a hell of a way to live if you can afford something better. Let me remind that skeptical reader that with the quartet we always stopped at the best hotels in the country. On our travels around the world, Eunice and I did stop at the best hotels in the country much of the time. And in retrospect, I have asked Eunice many times this question: "Have you any endearing memories about those hotels similar to those we have of the Dinkelsbuhl and other inns?" Her answer is always a resounding "No!" Once I asked, "Can you think of at least one that remains endearingly in your mind?" She couldn't think of one, and neither could I.

To describe Dinkelsbuhl properly would require a book. Many such books have been written in many languages by authors more proficient than I. One, in English, we carried with us as we roamed the streets for a week, reading about the fascinating history of almost every house in the walled town with its population of only about 7,000. As we left the city by train, we had a feeling akin to waking up from a dream. The only other time we ever had a similar feeling was on a visit to Rothenburg several years previously, but it was much less primitive.

Our next stop was Munich. The purpose of this stop was to visit a dear old friend of mine for a few days, at a time when all Germans were celebrating the annual Oktoberfest, a time of much gaiety, singing, dancing, and beer drinking. The Bavarians, being of a much more easygoing temperament (more like the Austrians), took to this sort of thing wholeheartedly, and hilarity pervaded the air wherever we went.

The result of this was that, with sight-seeing in the daytime and merriment at night, our plans to stay only a few days were put aside, and we stayed for a whole week. Fortunately, we had no date set for our departure from Europe; so it was a nice feeling to be free as the birds in regard to time.

After much unsuccessful effort to secure passage home via a cargo ship, we reluctantly purchased tickets to make the crossing on the super-liner, the *Bremen*, leaving Bremerhaven the following week.

Along the way, we stopped at Heidelberg to visit a German pupil of mine at Milton who, with his mother and sister, had been living there as refugees for the duration of the war. He was now attending the University of Heidelberg, and it took some time to locate him; but we finally spent a delightful evening reminiscing.

We both hated the trip back on the *Bremen*. While the food was good and the rooms comfortable, it all was so impersonal and crowded with people that we looked forward to the day of landing in New York. Little did we know what a disgusting performance it would be.

It was well known that the customs officers in New York were champions of the world when it came to rudeness, but this time they outdid themselves. When leaving the ship at 9:00 a.m., we were given instructions to stand in the sections of the pier shed marked with the first letter of our last names. Half drunken officers kept passing us by all morning without paying any heed. There we stood or sat on boxes without any lunch until about 2:00 p.m., when along came a customs officer, smelling like a Bowery bar room, announcing that the porters were on strike, and if we would go to where our luggage was stacked on the pier and carry it to our places, they would proceed with the inspection. Of course, there was a big rush to do just that; and the inspection got started, but with only a handful of men. So that we didn't get out of there until 5:00 p.m.

All this time Janet Robarge, a niece of ours, and her parents who had come in from Ridgewood, New Jersey, to meet us, stood at the outside gate with three children, ages five, three and one. We all were certainly glad to get out of there. It was 7:00 p.m. before we got to Ridgewood, half-starved. But after a few drinks and a good dinner, the world looked much brighter.

Here we lingered a few days and several more days with

another niece, Frances Moretti, on Long Island. Then we took the train back to Clearwater, arriving home after an absence of about four months, close to December 1, 1961.

We soon got back into the stride of our busy yet unnewsworthy life, but it wasn't long before we developed that itch for another trip around the world—this time in the opposite direction. True, we had already seen much; yet there still remained much more that we hadn't seen.

Contacting our travel agency in New York and telling them what we wanted, we were soon receiving brochures on cargo ships around the world. We had made up our minds to travel on a Norwegian ship. But after a year's search, it developed that those ships made stops at too many of the ports we had been to; so we finally settled on a Dutch line. The cruise and itinerary chosen were so popular that we had to sign up for it over a year in advance. Of course, that year seemed unusually long; but it was a nice feeling to have something so delightful to look forward to.

24

AROUND THE WORLD
EASTWARD

Time has a way of catching up with you. The date of our departure from New York finally arrived right at the beginning of a stevedore strike; so we didn't sail until six weeks later, on March 27, 1965. The ship was spotlessly clean, as was our large cabin with two full-sized beds, a desk, a bureau, two chairs, a table, and an adjoining bath and one large window. The floor was parquet, which wasn't quite as pleasant to walk on in bare feet as the wall-to-wall carpeting we had become accustomed to on Norwegian ships; otherwise, it was just as comfortable and as nicely furnished as a good hotel room. The meals were first-class, although, for our taste, a bit fatty.

By and large, the Dutch are more reserved than Norwegians. Therefore, the relationship between passengers and crew was not as genial; but let me hasten to add that they couldn't have been more accommodating. The passengers were three elderly married couples; two middle-aged schoolteachers from Louisiana, and an eighty-five-year-old woman in her dotage, but full of pep, who was continually losing her glasses, pocketbook, etc. She was such a busybody that she was perpetually in trouble. So all the passengers were inclined to be sorry for her and offered to be of assistance, which she more often than not declined, with the remark that she was perfectly able to take care of herself.

When we got to Tripoli, it developed that her son-in-law was the United States ambassador to Libya. He boarded our ship and stealthily informed us that the family had long ago given up offering advice to her because it only irritated her; so they let her bumble her own way through life and hoped for the best.

From then on, we passengers stopped trying to be helpful and gave assistance only when requested.

The weather was cold, rainy, and windy, resulting in our having to spend most of the ten days it took us to reach Gibraltar indoors. From then on we were blessed with warm, bright, sunny weather for almost the whole trip.

Tripoli was our first contact with the Arab world, and most picturesque it proved to be. Here is where the camel was still a popular means of conveyance. Wanting to see the city in a leisurely fashion, we hired a driver with a rickety carriage and an even more rickety horse to drive us around for the whole day. This proved to be a most successful experiment, for we felt we were absorbed in the atmosphere and life of the city.

By noon we were fairly hungry; so we asked the driver to take us to a typically Arabian restaurant. Arriving there, we found the place crowded with about a hundred diners, all men, seated at tables, while some five or six late arrivals stood in the center of the room around a series of basins washing their faces and hands before being seated.

Just about then Eunice decided she had to go to the ladies' room; so after much scurrying around, I learned such a thing was nonexistent. But there was a men's room in the corner of the kitchen. On examination, I found it to be nothing but a cubbyhole with a small round bowl sunken level with the floor, all of which was filthy and had an overpowering stench. Oh well, this was an emergency—any old port in a storm—so it was here that Eunice found relief while I stood like a watchdog at the door.

Eunice being the only woman on the premises, all eyes were upon us when we reentered the dining room from the kitchen. They were wondering what we were up to. Then, in our ignorance, we proceeded to break all the rules of Moslem law by seating ourselves at a table without washing our faces and hands. I invited our driver to have lunch with us, but he apologetically declined, saying he had some business to transact with a friend at another table. Although he allowed me to pay for his meal, according to his way of thinking, and I didn't blame him, who wants to sit and eat with a couple of pigs? In spite of the fact that we wanted to get out of the place as quickly as possible, we found our meal of couscous very tasty. It was brown cereal topped with goat's meat and gravy.

The rest of the afternoon was spent exploring the city in our ramshackle rig, the most exciting part of which was a visit to the public livestock market, at which hundreds of sheep, goats, and camels were bought, sold, and bartered. Altogether, there must have been some 500 animals howling, braying, or making whatever noises their mammas taught them to make. Now add to that the bargaining yells of the herders making their sales, and you have a cacophony that defies description. Anyway, we spent about an hour there watching what to us seemed like fun.

Returning to our ship at 4:00 p.m., we struck up a conversation with the local guard who was there to see that nothing was smuggled off the ship. We hadn't been talking long before Eunice said, "Let's go." When we got to our room, she said, "Imagine the nerve of that S.O.B.; he pinched my fanny twice with you standing there." These are some of the vicissitudes of travel. Still, we wouldn't have missed our visit in Tripoli for anything.

We found Latakia, Syria, our next stop, a hodgepodge city with no especial architecture nor charm except for numerous Roman arches, pillars, and ruins intermingled with newer buildings all over the city. Still, it is famous all over the world because a very fine grade of tobacco is grown in its environs. It is also the only large seaport in Syria, and the ancient Phoenician ruins of the city of Ugarit are close by.

It was a big change and surprise when our ship moved on to the city of Beirut, Lebanon. Aside from a few ancient ghettos, one could transpose it to any modern city in Europe and very few would know the difference. Even the speech in the streets is multilingual. Gone are the veils that covered women's faces. Gone are the man- and horse-drawn carts, only to be replaced by automobile traffic jams. All visible evidence seemed to say, "This is a well-managed prosperous Western city which doesn't seem to belong here." Though we took a comprehensive tour, we saw nothing striking enough to impress itself on our memories.

The next day we and another couple from the ship hired a taxi for an all-day visit to Damascus. It was about a three-hour trip through mountainous desert country all the way. Periodically, we would see small colonies of nomadic Arabs pasturing their herds of sheep and goats while they lived in large camel's hide tents which they moved from place to place as the fodder gave out. From the auto the desert appeared completely barren; so at one point we got out to take a look. Still we couldn't see anything that seemed edible; yet there were those animals finding something to assuage their hunger.

As we approached the center of Damascus, I had the same eerie feeling when as a child I read *Tales of Arabian Nights*. It is popularly known as the oldest inhabited city in the world. From what we saw, it certainly gave that impression, especially since we had just come from Beirut, which was almost completely up to date. Latakia had a half-ancient look. There you have three large cities within a short distance of each other, yet so unlike that thinking about it creates a paradoxical problem not easy to solve.

Here we were in Damascus, imagining that this was what life must have been like in about the fifteenth century. We mingled with the crowds which jammed the streets, full of pedestrians and carts of all descriptions, all straining to perform some errand of importance to themselves. An occasional auto would try to weave its way through that mass of humanity with progress so slow and hazardous that one wondered why the attempt was made; besides, it seemed sacrilegious, so out of context was it.

We noticed that there had been made slight condescensions to progress. The muezzins no longer had to climb to the top of the minarets to call the people to prayer. No doubt loudspeakers installed up there were more efficient, but they certainly were not as picturesque. A great proportion of the women still wore veils, which left only their eyes exposed, and long black dresses.

In the heart of the city, we entered what was supposed to be the largest of 250 mosques in operation. On entering, we were obliged to put on felt slippers over our shoes, while the local residents simply doffed their shoes and, carrying them in their hands, entered barefooted or in stockinged feet. The interior was beautiful beyond description; and after about an hour's milling about amongst the madding throng, the serene quiet within was like a refreshing balm on frazzled nerves.

Since it was against the law for our Lebanese taxi driver to operate in the city, we had hired a local one to show us the chief points of interest. Of a city as ancient as this, so much has been written over past generations that my attempt to abstain from writing a travelogue is easy to adhere to by closing the account of our visit right here, fascinating as it was. But I just can't resist mentioning the innumerable side streets we drove through, lined on both sides with cubbyholes about six feet wide and six feet long (let's call them shops) in which artisans were hammering out the most beautiful copper, brass, and silverware imaginable. These streets were so narrow that as our taxi passed through at a crawling pace, the pedestrians would back up against both side walls and let us pass.

We were told that these streets have remained unchanged for centuries. Since each generation passed on this art of metal decoration to its progeny, it seems reasonable to assume that each cubbyhole was passed along in the same way. Imagine how proud each generation must be of the number of years their family has worked in that cubbyhole.

Our plans were to stop at the famous ancient ruins of Baalbek, but it was already too late to get back for supper. Also, it was raining, and our get up and go was gone. So we skipped that part of our plans, had supper in Beirut, and immediately went back to the ship and bed. This was one of our more memorable days. As we returned to Beirut, we went by an immense Palestinian refugee camp composed of shacks made of the most dilapidated junk material imaginable. It was a heartbreaking sight.

The next day we learned that in our absence the two school-teachers among the passengers had decided to fly down for a few days to Jerusalem for the Easter holidays and would rejoin the ship at Alexandria. Arriving there, one of our married couples had reached their destination; so our passenger list dwindled down to two married couples, two schoolteachers, and the unpredictable old lady. By this time, however, she had become more predictable and created more amusement than nuisance.

Alexandria was the capital of Egypt in ancient times; but with the expansion of trade, it grew into its largest seaport, thereby presenting an old town and a relatively new one. We did the usual tour of points of interest, of which, of course, in the old town, there were many, but none significant enough to warrant mention here. Possibly King Farouk's ornately grandiose palace might qualify. Done in Western style architecture, we might call it a modified Versailles. We spent one whole morning going through just one wing of it.

With Cairo only 120 miles away and plenty of time on our hands, we decided it was a must to go there; so we hired a car with chauffeur by the hour. The road along one bank of the Nile through rich farm lands was an interesting spectacle of local life, teeming with pedestrians, donkey carts, laden camels, assorted animals, and autos. Add to this the adobe villages and the men, women, and children working in the fields along the roadside, and you have a kaleidoscopic panorama which captivated our interest all the way into Cairo.

This city is huge—four million—crowded with cars, bustling, modern, with handsome department stores and shops. After visiting many points of interest, we arrived at the citadel (an old fort), from which there was a glorious view in all directions, including the pyramids, which were situated right on the outskirts. This came as a great surprise to me because I had visualized them further out in the desert. This was an incentive to go there posthaste.

On arrival, I got another big surprise when I found the Sphinx much smaller than it appeared in pictures. No doubt this was due to the fact that it usually was portrayed standing alone with people peering up at it from its base; whereas, in comparison with the huge size of the pyramids, in close proximity, it looked dwarfed.

There were several hundred tourists milling about amongst these famous objects of adoration, while others were being led about on the backs of camels having their pictures taken with the pyramids in the background. By this time it was close to 4:00 p.m., and we hurried over to the Cairo Museum before it closed in another hour.

The first things that struck our gaze were the three exquisitely beautiful mummy form coffins in which King Tutankhamen's body was placed in 1343 B.C. The goose pimples were running up and down my backbone, and still do every time I think of what to my mind are the most beautiful objects ever made by the hands and mind of man. An hour passed all too quickly as I passed from one to another of the relics discovered in the young king's tomb, marveling at the skill and ingenuity of the artisans of that day, using crude tools. The bell was sounding for us to clear out of the building, awakening me from a trance.

On the return to Alexandria and our ship, we chose another road further south from the Mediterranean, which, although somewhat longer, was completely in the Sahara desert, well paved and almost devoid of traffic, although at many points we did have to maneuver through sand drifts. This was the road the British built from Cairo to the west in their operations against Rommel in World War II. Although we traveled most of the way in darkness, the moon was bright. So we could see much discarded war material still lying along the roadside. Only an occasional auto was met along the way, but nomadic Arab tents were quite frequent. The absolute stillness of the desert was a novelty which we thoroughly enjoyed, but not the quick drop in the temperature soon after the sun went down. Consequently, we arrived back at our ship half-frozen shortly after 9:00 p.m., happy and thankful for another exciting banner day in our lives. A hot bath and a cup of coffee, which was available at all hours, in the kitchen, and we hit the hay without further ado.

Within a couple days our two schoolteachers returned from Jerusalem with a collection of religious bibelots, one of which they presented to each one of us.

It wasn't long thereafter that we made the short run to Port Said, where we did a lot of maneuvering getting into the order of precedence in the lineup of ships to be convoyed through the Suez Canal. Finally there were about thirty of us proceeding in this order: battleships, tankers, passenger liners, cargo ships carrying mail, and, finally, anyone else. The last time we made the trip from south to north in the darkness. This time it was vice-versa on a sunny day in good weather. Again, the startling contrast between the two sides of the canal seemed unbelievable—the east side, barren desert; and the west, lush green farming country almost all the way, thanks to irrigation from the Nile.

We then proceeded down the Red Sea, which was not red but blue while we were in it, though we have heard that during severe sandstorms, which are frequent, it really looks red. Now the weather was at last getting hot, and the cooling system was put into operation. It took us ten days from Alexandria to traverse the Suez Canal, Red Sea, Gulf of Aden and Arabian Sea to reach Bombay, with only one short stop of four hours at Djibouti, French Somaliland.

At Bombay the immense harbor was so crowded with ships and dock space so occupied that we had to anchor several miles out from shore. This meant that all loading and unloading had to be done to and from lighters (scows); and passengers wishing to go ashore were transferred there in launches, which was quite a hazardous operation in choppy seas. Both of us being good swimmers, we had no fear of the water; but in the five or six times we chanced the trip in our nine-day stay there, we had a few close calls when it came to getting on and off the landing stairs on the ship and the wet landing stairs on a concrete seawall while the launch was constantly rocking.

Bombay is a city crowded with teeming masses of ragged Indians seemingly just drifting around, with many sound asleep under dirty blankets on the sidewalks and under arcades, mercifully unaware of the heat of the sun and the crowds of pedestrians and traffic passing by.

As was our custom, of course, depending on the ship's length of stay in a port, we chose the most comprehensive tour of the city we could find. The next day we would study up on those subjects which intrigued us most and then go back and enjoy them at liberty, without having to be herded about in a crowd and having to listen to a guide's spiel.

So the first time out we went to the Taj Mahal Hotel to hire a guide for a half day's sight-seeing trip. We were lucky to get a charming, young, native college girl, who was so articulate, knowledgeable and efficient that we took her out to lunch and engaged her for the full day. She was the best guide we ever had.

On subsequent trips to the city, we visited those places of preference which we had boned up on more thoroughly, then went to some restaurant that local people patronized for lunch and ordered strictly Indian dishes—such as curried prawns with chapatties (whole wheat pancakes made of flour and water and similar to Mexican tortillas) and candied ginger for dessert, along with ginger beer. Afternoons we would sit on the balcony of the Taj Mahal, famous as one of the finest hotels in the world, looking down on the street below, where entertainers such as musicians, snake charmers, and performing monkeys were doing their specialties for the tourists.

Something we had never seen anywhere was an outside laundry, which we watched from a bridge overlooking the site. Imagine looking down on a city block composed of about a hundred symmetrically aligned concrete basins about six feet by six feet by about three feet deep, level with the ground and filled with dirty clothes. Beside each basin stood a man who would take out a bunch equal to about five men's shirts, then lay it on the cement paving to straighten it out, pick up one end of the mass in both hands, lift it above his head, and then repeatedly slap it down with all his might over a rounded cement block, with occasional dips in the water, at the same time turning the bundle end for end until it was supposed to be clean. We questioned our nice guide about the longevity of the laundry under this process. She assured us that her clothes lasted longer when she sent them to this laundry than they did when she sent them to a mechanical one.

During the nine days Eunice fell in love with so many saris that we brought home a dozen of them along with other mementos from which we derive never-ending pleasure.

Leaving Bombay, we rounded the island of Ceylon, at which we threw kisses because we loved it as a place where nature took particular pains to make it beautiful.

Docking at Madras, on the Bay of Bengal, it struck us that the city gave the appearance of being more poverty-stricken than Bombay, even though many universities and a Maharaja's palace were located here. It was at this place that we received some bad news from headquarters of our ship, the Holland-American Line. Our itinerary booked our next stop as a 12-day layover in Calcutta, at which time Eunice and I had planned to leave the ship and go off on our own to the following places: Katmandu, Delhi, Agra (Taj Mahal), Benares, and Jaipur. Due to the prolonged strike of stevedores in the United States, ship schedules all over the world were disrupted; so at this time, every effort was being made to bring them back into order again, resulting in instructions to our captain to unload our cargo for Calcutta onto another ship and proceed to Penang, Malaya, without delay.

This, of course, was a big blow to all of us passengers, because it meant we would be done out of seeing those world-famous spots mentioned above. Of course, we put up an awful protest, but deep in our hearts we knew that the captain had to follow orders, that the strike created a shambles of shipping schedules, and that we had signed an agreement with the company that we would not hold them responsible for any changes beyond their control that they would have to make in their schedules, provided the length of the tour remained the same.

We were a disgruntled lot of seven passengers as we proceeded to Penang, another island which we had visited on our first trip around the world and on which we had thought nature had lavished extra care to make it beautiful. There we did what we enjoyed most the first time, and that was to take a taxi around the hilly, lushly fertile tropical paradise. This time we were fortunate in having a driver who had a friend who was in charge of one of the many rubber plantations; so along the way, we stopped to pay him and his family a visit.

Their hut was a one-room affair about fifteen feet square with a thatched roof mounted on stilts about ten feet off the ground and a crude ladder leading to the front entrance. The furnishings were so sparse that I only remember seeing a table, three chairs, three rolled up mattresses, a small kitchen stove, and a few rows of shelves with kitchenware and, their prize possession, a small radio. They were a couple and small child and seemed like gentle people and were flattered and delighted to see us.

That night we ascertained that our ship would be in port at least two days loading palm oil and raw rubber. On learning this, we decided to take the train the next day to Kuala Lumpur, capitol of Malaysia, and get a general idea of what the interior of the country looked like. From there it was only about thirty miles to Port Swettenham—its port on the Malacca Strait—where we would rejoin our ship in a few days.

We found our trip a most interesting and delightful one, especially since we met up with a United States colonel and his wife (he an advisor to the Thai army in Bangkok) who were on their way for a vacation in the Cameron Highlands. They had much of interest to tell us and vice-versa. The ever-changing scenery consisted of miles of rice paddies, huge fields of pineapples and sugarcane, rubber trees, banana trees, and coconut palms galore. As everywhere, where they had only one or two trains a day, half the villages would be out to meet us, which created an unorganized circus at every station. Suffice it to say that when we arrived at our destination in the evening, we were immensely pleased to have thought of this diversion.

The next day we did an all-day comprehensive tour of the city and environs, of which nothing outstanding remains in memory except an overall picture of a relatively modern city with many handsome new buildings interspersed with many ramshackle ones, a nice new residential section, and enormous sections of slums, which guides invariably avoid unless you demand to be taken there.

The following day we rejoined our ship at Port Swettenham. Incidentally, Kuala Lumpur translates as "Muddy River." From here it was only a short run down the Malacca Strait into Singapore, which is considered the halfway mark for most round-the-world trips. Here we struck upon some good luck. With sailing schedules so badly scrambled, the company had no ship to which they could immediately assign us; so they transferred us and our baggage to the Goodwood Hotel, one of the newest and finest, for an indefinite stay at their expense, which in the end turned out to be exactly eight days. Though we had already done Singapore quite thoroughly on our visit six years previously, we were delighted at the turn of events.

The first thing that struck us as we roamed about was the big building boom that had taken place during the interim. High-rise modern buildings, completed or in the process of construction, were in evidence wherever one looked. This evidence was applied in reverse regarding rickshaws, which were prominently absent and had been replaced by pedicabs, three-wheeled bicycles to which a wicker basket seat had been attached to carry another person.

Most of the sampans were now propelled by outboard motors, which seemed a sacrilege, as did the same crime committed on gondolas in Venice. Not only was the charm and grace of the oarsmen coupled with the silent majesty of the picturesque ship gliding noiselessly through silent waters gone, but the noisy din created was enough to shatter nerves of steel until one became accustomed—or should I say hardened—to it.

Another big innovation was in the change of government from British rule to a semi-independence, with Britain acting only in an advisory capacity in military and foreign affairs. Though the population is almost a million—75 percent Chinese, 15 percent Malay, 8 percent Indian, and 2 percent British—it will be a long time before the British flavor is completely gone from an area almost completely Oriental.

At the time we were there communism had gained quite a foothold in nearby Indonesia. There was hardly a morning that newspapers didn't give an account of some raiding party from there trying to infiltrate Singapore and its vicinity, but the local people were such loyal citizens that the raiders were soon caught and incarcerated.

There was no dearth of interesting places to visit during our eight-day stay, so we tramped the city all day, often winding up, weary afoot, at the famous Raffles Hotel for one of their equally famous gin slings.

One narrow street in the slum district was unusual in that within two blocks, nicknamed death alley, there were two death houses (three-or four-story-high apartment buildings) jammed with aged persons so decrepit that they had (excuse the expression) one foot in the grave. They had become too much of a burden for their families to keep at home so were sent here to live with others, each of whom presented a picture of miserable dotage, the likes of which would sicken Goliath. So there they existed until merciful Buddha came to snuff their lights out. Now here is what might be called efficiency in Oriental manner. In those same two blocks there are innumerable undertakers' establishments which have artisans hollowing out logs with hatchets and fashioning them into plain and ornate coffins. This operation takes place in the street in front of each establishment.

Now imagine the street crowded with pedestrians, pedicabs and carts of all categories, then you look upward and see three rows of laundry strung on lines hanging from windows on all floors all the way down the street and you will get a picture that will never be forgotten of a jungle of humanity striving to make a living. One remarkable feature that impressed me greatly was that, in spite of the bedlam, it all looked so clean. Aside from the wood chips made by the coffin artisans, which were swept up frequently, the cobblestone pavement was barren of trash; and the pedestrians (particularly the women) looked as though they had just been processed through laundry machines, body and all.

A favorite spot of ours for lingering was along the river docks to which junks were tied, unloading their cargos of raw rubber, copra, rice, tapioca, etc., from Borneo and other islands. The steady procession of coolies from the junks to the shore carrying heavy bales on their backs gave the impression of ants busily performing some task important to them. Ashore, the sidewalks were crowded with girls, sorting out and baling the crude rubber in preparation for shipment to all parts of the world.

Thus, eight days passed all too quickly. Then we received notice that the ship taking us to Hong Kong would leave the next day. For once there were no complaints from any of the passengers, who by now had dwindled to five, namely, the married couple, the old lady with bats in her belfry, and us, the two schoolteachers having flown to Japan on a bat of their own. Who could ask for anything more from our shipping company? They had put us up for eight days in the most modern hotel, in their best rooms, free to order anything we wished on their regular menu, the only proviso being that we pay for our tips and beverages. Eunice and I got used to drinking a certain delicious Australian white wine with dinner that we mourned having to part with.

The next day, aboard ship, gathered about the captain, the five of us were informed that his ship was of a more ancient vintage than the one we had left and therefore had upper and lower bunks instead of twin beds in the staterooms, which also lacked private showers and toilets but did have running water sinks. Though the rooms were smaller, we obviously would have to use the public toilets and bathtubs. Otherwise, the accomodations were exactly the same.

Furthermore, there was no alternative to making the three-day trip to Hong Kong on this ship, but there we would be given an option to change to another ship or remain aboard for the trip home. Since we didn't have to make up our minds until we got there, we decided to wait and see how we liked the ship we were on and what the others would do.

When we arrived there, it couldn't have turned out more to

our liking. On the trip we found the captain and officers most amiable people, the cooking exceptionally good; and, as far as we could see, all other facilities for passengers were equal to or better than our other ship. On top of this, when we found out that our quixotic old lady had made up her mind to debark and lay over, we didn't hesitate a moment to tell the captain we would stay with him. The other couple were undecided, so went to a hotel to make up their minds. This left us the only two passengers aboard.

Entering the beautiful harbor of Hong Kong, we were dumbfounded at the enormous changes that had taken place since our last visit six years previously. The building boom had been even bigger than that at Singapore. Buildings that had extended only to the foothills on Victoria Island now reached all the way to their tops. The Kowloon section across the harbor had been transfigured from an area of low buildings into one of high-rise apartments and office buildings. To be sure, we did recognize some old landmarks such as Haw Par's villa and the adjoining Tiger Balm garden, with its conglomeration of statues of humans and monsters taken from Chinese mythological and Buddhist history. Then, too, almost next to it there still was the immense ramshackle shantytown which the British apparently weren't able to do much about. Yes, big changes had taken place. Even the sampans and junks had been motorized.

As we proceeded, we kept passing anchored ships and then free-floating buoys, finally anchoring in an isolated spot far from the rest. We wondered why but thought nothing of it until the next day, when we noticed that the cargo being loaded onto our ship was fireworks. At last we knew why we were ostracized. By then we had become quite friendly with the captain and crew and had gained full confidence in them. After all, their lives were at stake as well as ours. To show how careful they were, every four hours at the change of the watch a thermometer on a string was lowered into every hold through tubes from the main deck, thereby taking the temperature therein.

We were in port three days, and we spent every one of them ashore, returning to the ship in the evening. On our first trip in we noticed that there were still a few rickshaws operating; so we each took one for a long ride, after which we had our pictures taken and then mailed 200 to our friends as Christmas cards. Evenings after dinner we would relax on the upper deck, watching the lights come on all over the Hong Kong hills, the junks go by, and the loading of our ship just below us.

One evening as we sat there talking with the first officer, a beautiful young lady appeared on the lower deck and proceeded directly to the crews' quarters on the stern of the ship. I asked the first officer who she was. His reply was, "She is a lady of leisure come to administer to the sexual desires of our men. Our company finds it safer and more profitable to allow selected ladies certified by our own doctor to come aboard rather than having our men go to town promiscuously."

Time for departure came all too soon. Then the captain told us that unless someone turned up at the last minute we would be the only passengers on the ship. We were so happy about this development that to suit us the ship couldn't leave port fast enough. And so it was that we left Hong Kong the only two passengers, Eunice the only woman on a large cargo ship with a crew of thirty-six men on the long journey across the Pacific with Cristobal, Canal Zone, our next stop. This meant that all the facilities for twelve passengers were at our private disposal and that we had the use of two rooms; so neither of us had to sleep in an upper bunk. But what we liked best of all was the fact that by the end of the journey we got to be very good friends with the captain and his crew. Practically the whole crew spoke English; so we had pleasant chats with many of them.

As soon as we got onto the high seas, I asked our steward to pass the word around that anybody with a clock or watch in need of repair should bring it to me and I would be glad to make the repair free of charge. This is a procedure which I followed on all our voyages. The result was that, working spasmodically whenever the spirit moved me, it was about three weeks before the last watch was repaired.

We had our meals with the captain, first officer, and chief engineer; and we had many a talk fest in the lounge or captain's office with them at cocktail hour as well as after meals. Much of the time was spent up on the bridge, where an officer and a seaman were on four-hour shifts, watching for derelicts and other ships, while the automatic pilot set for a certain course held the ship there.

Trying to keep the ship clean and free of rust was a never-ending problem which faced these men eight hours a day, six days a week. This work was always interesting to watch, especially when they were doing high climbing.

We got the news daily over the radio; and there were plenty of good books to read in the library along with a stack of *Reader's Digests* which we had brought, including *Time* magazines, which were purchased at all ports in the world in order to keep up with current events. There were movies on deck four nights a week for everybody. Eunice, of course, worked at her diary; and as I peruse it to refresh my memory, I marvel at the fact that not a single day passed but what she found something interesting to report.

What I am trying to convey is that during all our trips never did we find time hanging heavy on our hands.

An interesting coincidence happened on June 21, the longest day of the year, when we arrived at the international date line where all ships set their calendars back twenty-four hours or, if you will, let their calendars stand still twenty-four hours in order to compensate for the half or full hours that they had been setting their watches ahead. In short, it amounted to our having the longest day of the year last forty-eight hours.

It just so happened our beloved cook's birthday fell on that date. Everybody loved this cook. There was never any time that one of the crew could not walk into the kitchen and find some delicious snack waiting for him. He was so proficient and artistic at his job that once speaking about him to the captain, I ventured the opinion that he was so good that he would have no trouble getting a job as chef in some fine restaurant. The captain laughed and replied, "Oh, he keeps getting tempting offers periodically; but, no, the guy has the sea in his blood and just won't leave it." And so it was that the assistant cook took over, told the chief to go sit on his fanny; and we all celebrated the birthday that lasted forty-eight hours with plenty to eat and drink.

We had ideal weather the whole twenty-five days it took us to cross the Pacific, which this time lived up to its name, although the captain steered clear of two hurricanes which lay in our path.

We found our third passage through the Panama Canal as exciting as the first. On learning our ship was making a two-day stopover at Cristobal, we decided to go right back to Panama

City via the narrow gauge railway, which revealed that much of the canal was lake and swampland which extended into the interior as an impenetrable jungle.

We rattled, swayed and bumped on the one-hour-and-twenty-minute run all in the Canal Zone, making frequent stops at army posts for military personnel. There were supposed to be monkeys and parrots visible along the way, but we didn't see any. Otherwise, there were innumerable wild mangoes loaded with fruit, as well as durian, coconut palms, banana trees and other trees that Eunice could identify from our car window.

On our tour of Panama City, one noteworthy thing that struck us was the mixture of French and Spanish influence. This was due to the fact that so many Frenchmen chose to stay after their venture to build the canal failed.

We returned to Cristobal that evening in time for supper, feeling that the trip was well worthwhile.

As we approached the estuary of the Mississippi a few days later, we were disgusted to see how the beautiful Gulf of Mexico had been desecrated by oil derricks. Not only that, but as we proceeded up the 120 miles of river to New Orleans, its banks were lined with oil tanks almost all the way. Seeing such a sight makes one wonder if it should come under the heading of progress or degeneration.

Our ship spent three days in New Orleans unloading large quantities of fireworks and artificial flowers, giving us a chance to roam the streets at will.

One more stop was made at Mobile, Alabama; and then, proceeding south in the Gulf of Mexico, as we reached the latitude of Clearwater, we threw it a kiss from the captain's bridge, where we had spent so many pleasant hours.

Often, in bathing at Clearwater, I had wondered what the distance was straight across to Corpus Christi, Texas. So the captain measured it off for us, and it came to 940 miles.

Off the coast of North Carolina we had a most exciting experience. About 11:00 p.m. one night I was awakened by an unusual amount of activity taking place on the deck above. Dressing hurriedly, I went up to see what all the commotion was about and saw that the sky was bright as day, all lighted up by flares being dropped by several airplanes while we and about twenty-five ships were slowly circling about with all searchlights on.

I awakened Eunice and we went up to the bridge, where the captain informed us that an S.O.S. had been received; a fishing trawler had exploded. We contributed four sharp eyes to the searching party but failed to spot anything; so went to bed at 3:00 a.m.

At breakfast our captain said that they kept on the hunt until 5:00 a.m. when a message from our Coast Guard, with profuse thanks, advised him to proceed, as the wreckage had been located. Later on, a more detailed report from a radio station in Norfolk, Virginia, informed us that a fishing trawler dredged up a World War II mine in its nets, which, when being hauled aboard, exploded, leaving it a total wreck, with four badly burned men rescued, one body picked up, and nine still missing. To us it was a heart-warming display by seamen of responsibility for one another the world over, regardless of nationality, creed, or color.

We docked in New York on a Sunday morning; and I phoned our niece, Janet Robarge, who drove over from Ridgewood, New Jersey, with her whole family (her husband and three small children) to get us. They had a whirl being shown all over the ship by the captain.

One nice thing about coming into port on a cargo ship is that the customs officer boards the ship, and you thereby avoid the bedlam you get into in the shed when debarking from a passenger liner. Our customs officer couldn't have been nicer.

Parting was such sorrow when it came time to bid good-bye to our captain, officers, crew, and the ship which had been our private yacht for fifty-four days.

Three days were spent with our family at Ridgewood; then a week with the Swains (Eunice's sister's family) at their camp on the Green River, near Greenfield, Massachusetts; and another two weeks with our very dear friend Cyril Jones at his beautiful home on Cotuit Bay on Cape Cod.

25

BACK HOME IN FLORIDA

A flight to Tampa (our first by jet) got us home on July 15, 1965, after an absence of five and one-half months. Of course, the garden was somewhat weedy, but the house seemed just as though we had left it overnight. Soon we were in the swing of things.

It took Eunice and me about a month to get our 75-by-110-foot yard back in shape again. In this we complement each other. I like to do the big things and she likes to piddle with the little stuff. Just to give you an idea, we have four orange, one grapefruit, one lime, one kumquat, one persimmon, three coconut palms, and a large clump of banana trees on the place. A two-foot-wide border surrounding the house and one four feet wide marking the rear property line planted in bushes and flowers supply us with a multicolored succession of blooms the year around.

Believe it or not, here in Florida, where almost everything grows so profusely, grass is just about our biggest headache. A strain impervious to some kind of blight hasn't been developed as yet; so spraying with an insecticide is a must several times a year. Of course, this entails quite a bit of work, all of which we have so far been able to handle by ourselves. In fact, I can't ever remember doing work that didn't give me pleasure and satisfaction, providing it did some good and gave the joy of achievement.

I have always been envious of the painter, who can work at his art in the quietude of his studio or a sylvan glen, alter his work at will, work only when inspired, and end up with something permanent, which he and future generations can admire. Compare that with the efforts of a concert artist and see how evanescent his performance is. He appears before the public in a highly nervous state at a certain time on a certain date in a straitjacket (for that is what his full-dress clothes are) with a high, stiff collar, stiff-bosom shirt front, and a coat with two long tails attached. He starts playing the most delicate passages with trembling fingers. Now he must wait until the end of the first selection, which, if it is a sonata or concerto, can be forty or more minutes, before he can be inspired by the applause of the audience.

This latter is the only advantage he has over a painter. I doubt if any painter has ever felt such an overwhelming emotional and spiritual uplift. Yet how fleeting it is!

After the concert there is that wet strait jacket and underclothes, a souvenir program, and possibly a few press clippings, which if you stay in town until the next day you may accumulate and paste into a scrapbook. In my own experience, we usually left the city on the midnight train; and therefore I only have about one-third of the concerts accounted for. But this is no great loss, because the number of knowledgeable music critics outside the largest cities was so negligible at that time that we paid scant attention to them.

Now to get back to how my time was occupied in Clearwater. After finishing our gardening chores, I resumed repairing clocks for one of the clockshops in town. I enjoyed it so thoroughly that for about a year I was working at it almost constantly.

Along with this and my reputation as an all-around handyman, my neighbors kept calling on me to repair their washing machines, toasters, blenders, vacuum cleaners, door locks, cameras, etc.; in short, I can't think of a thing on the inside or outside of a house that I can't repair except TV and radio sets. Repairmen, whether they were carpenters, painters, electricians, cabinetmakers, plumbers, or cementworkers, would have starved to death if they had depended on the Siskovskys for a living.

Even with the busy life I led concertizing and then teaching, I always managed to find time to paint the three houses (two of them two-story affairs) we lived in as well as our summer cottage. I replaced the plumbing in two seven-room, two-story houses; built a complete garage, including the cement floor; built a lean-to garage; and dug a fourteen-foot well.

These are but a small number of the things I was capable of doing, all without a lesson; but they give a good idea of my versatility. I am often asked, "How is it possible for you to do all those things without ever having learned how?" My only answer is that I have a good analytical head; take pleasure in watching those who know how; and, possibly more importantly, am inherently a dare-doer for whom everything in life is a challenge.

So, for the discerning reader, it will be easy to conclude that my problem as I write this at age eighty-two is not what I shall do today, but what I shall do first. From my point of view, as I look about in this haven for the elderly, it appears that the deadly malady of boredom is the most potent form of suffering invented by the greatest inventor of them all. Why? Because it lasts so long and is so hard to pinpoint. Pathetic is the person who comes to the conclusion that the world has passed him by and can find no niche of usefulness in it. So it is with this feeling of usefulness that I have lived all my life, doing extracurricular things for people and never charging them for it. Time and again, I was told that I was an idiot—"Look at all the money you are losing"—to which my reply was "Of course. But if I charged you, it would be a business deal; and I would not have the satisfaction of doing a favor for a friend."

In the evening we like to listen to TV programs (especially those on the educational network) and our favorite records. We do exchange dinner dates with our good friends. Otherwise, we always seem to be doing something which seems interesting but not noteworthy. Exceptions to the latter were three events.

The first took place when Erick Friedman, the famous violinist and pupil of Heifetz, gave a concert in Clearwater and came to our house after the performance, where he fell so much in love with my Guarneri violin that he played it till 2:00 a.m.

Three years later another fine violinist, James Buswell, a pupil of my buddy, Paul Stassevitch, of Petrograd and Oslo days, also gave a concert here, after which he also came to our house and played on my violin for several hours.

The greatest thrill of all, though, was when Erick Friedman recently came to town for a return engagement, played on my violin all afternoon at our home, and then played half his program on it that night at his concert, at the beginning of which

Professor Auer (seated) and five of his pupils. *Left to right:* Max Rosen,
Jascha Heifetz, Jaroslav Siskovsky, Toscha Seidel, and Margaret Berson.
Heifetz and Siskovsky stayed up all night printing and developing this
photo, summer of 1916 in Christiania (Oslo).

he made the following announcement: "I have the very great privilege of playing on a violin that is not mine tonight. You have a famous violinist in your midst—Jaroslav Siskovsky—and he has a very wonderful violin. It is a 1733 Guarneri, considered the sister violin to my teacher's, Jascha Heifetz. Heifetz and Siskovsky were fellow students of the great Leopold Auer in Russia. I've never done this before in my life—played on a strange violin at a concert. Thus, it not only is an honor for me, but I hope it will mean something to Mr. Siskovsky to hear this wonderful instrument again."

Thank you, Erick. It was an honor to have you play it so beautifully, and it did mean much to me. The tears kept filling my eyes all evening. We returned to our house after the concert along with a few guests, where Erick beguiled us with his adventures on concert tours.

I have reached the end of my narrative. Now the problem is how to write an ending without a premature obituary. Mine has been a most varied, active, and sometimes sensational life, rich in sweet memories. But I am not one who dwells long on sweet memories; hence, I live mostly in the future, which can be changed and improved. Each day is another challenge. I am grateful to be alive, especially when I consider the number of close calls I have had driving autos the last forty years, the three perilous (because of German mines and submarines) crossings of the Atlantic in ships during World War I, and finally because I am the sole survivor of the original New York String Quartet.

Clearwater, Florida
June 1971

ADDENDA

Here are the questions about old violins I have most often been asked.

Q. Why are old violins more valuable than new ones?

A. The law of supply and demand is at work here. With the passage of time, more and more of the fine old violins are withdrawn from the market either because of deterioration and destruction or placement into museums and private collections. As no new violins are made equaling the old, the supply becomes smaller and the price higher. Today the violins of Stradivarius and Guarnerius reign supreme as the most prized possessions of violinists. Fifty years ago a few other makes, such as the Amati and the Stainer, were esteemed almost as highly as the aforementioned two. At that time the concert artist was called upon to play in halls seating at most a thousand people. Today he is playing in halls of immense size; and the only violins with enough carrying power to fill these large spaces are those of Stradivari and a Guarneri. Others, though possessing a sweet enough tone, sound anemic and therefore have lost favor and declined in value.

Q. Were Stradivari and Guarneri famous as violin makers in their time?

A. Stradivari was, but Guarneri was not. Stradivari was

almost as famous in his day as he is today. Orders for violins, violas, and celli poured in to him from all over Europe, especially from the nobility and the churches, which fostered music. They paid well for the product, and therefore he was able to devote much painstaking care to each instrument. The reputation of Guarneri was not outstanding; indeed, aside from his violins and a few official records, very little is known about his life. His customers were the average fiddlers who couldn't afford to pay much, all of which shows up in the workmanship. Some of his violins show care being taken, while others show the man in a hurry. In spite of this, however, his work is distinguished by an artistry, imagination, and boldness that are a never-ending source of delight to the connoisseur. What is more important to the violinist is the fact that with but few exceptions, they all sound good, and that is why fully 70 percent of the top violinists today prefer them to Strads, Heifetz being one of them.

Q. Did the violins of Stradivari and Guarneri sound good the day they were finished?

A. The world's foremost experts, Hill and Sons of London, estimate that it takes from thirty to forty years for these violins to mature. That is, it took that long for the wood to age properly, the varnish, glue, and wood to blend; and, of course, they had to be "played in."

Q. What makes the tone of old violins superior to new ones?

A. With the death of Guarneri in 1746 the skill in violin making gradually declined until today it is a lost art. The answer to the above question has been puzzling amateur and professional violin makers all over the world for the past hundred years. So fanatically did some search for the lost secret that they became insane. For one thing, with all our scientific advances, the glorious varnish has become a lost secret and cannot be duplicated today. Chemists have tried in vain to analyze it. Some experts therefore claim that the hidden secret lies in the varnish.

The great majority, however, are of the opinion that this is not the only missing link. Certain it is that these masterpieces have been taken apart time and again, all measurements taken down to the minutest detail, the wood studied. And with everything duplicated as closely as is humanly possible, still the new violins are inferior in quality to the old. What is even more disconcerting, as has been proven in past generations, is that the aging process does not improve them enough to put them on a par with the old. Three basic qualifications are demanded of the violins by the artists of today: tone quality, ease of response, and carrying power. The best old violins possess a rich, mellow tone which, oddly enough, does not sound exceptionally big in a room, yet carries to the farthest corners in fairly large auditoriums. They respond instantly to the slightest touch of the bow. The new ones, on the other hand, respond sluggishly and are apt to have a harsh, brittle tone which sounds big in a room and feeble in a hall.

One of the vicissitudes in being a professional violinist is that people constantly keep bringing you violins which have been lying in their attics for years and on which uncle Joe took lessons when he was a boy. These have a Stradivari or Guarneri label in them and look very old. These are all fakes and can be spotted immediately by the average violinist who has taken the trouble to view and examine a good number of violins. Every once in a long while, an old violin is discovered in Europe which has lain in some out-of-the-way place for untold years and therefore was unknown. There is no record of this ever having happened in America. The general public assumption is that if you play the violin well you ought to know all the fine points in its makeup. Actually, the great majority know only the rudiments. This is a highly specialized field in the violin making and repairing business in which Rembert Wurlitzer and Company in New York excel in America. Under the masterful tutelag of Mr. Sacconi, this firm has established an enviable reputation in this field. The last time I was there, they had sixteen repairers working in their shop. Hill and Sons in London also have a fine reputation. Otherwise, in this country there are quite a few repairers scattered around (many are disciples of Mr. Sacconi) who could be trusted to do a good job on a fine violin, but by and large, the majority are good artisans who do well enough on ordinary violins.

The list of artists with whom we gave joint concerts reads like a "Who's Who of Celebrities in International Musical Life." With the majority—especially singers—we gave only one concert; with others, many more—and as many as twenty with Percy Grainger.

Harpists	*Pianists*
Carlos Salzedo	Ossip Gabrilovitsch
Salvatore de Stefano	Harold Bauer
Marcel Grandjany	Joseph Lhevine
	Rosina Lhevine
Vocalists	Wilhelm Backhaus
	Wanda Landowska
Louise Homer	Elly Ney
Sophie Braslau	Mischa Levitzki
Mme. Johanna Gadski	Ethel Leginska
Clara Clemens	Catherine Bacon
Lawrence Tibbett	Olga Samaroff
Richard Crooks	Rudolph Ganz
Tito Schipa	Jose Echaniz
John Charles Thomas	Percy Grainger
Reinald Werrenrath	Charles Courboin (organist)
Frazer Gange	
Frederick Jaegel	

Over the lifespan of the quartet, joint concerts with the above artists were an exception rather than the rule and consequently were only a very small part of our complete itinerary. But it was a stimulating experience to make friends with such famous names on an equal footing; so we always looked forward with joyful participation to those dates. Then, too, it was a relief from our regular routine and programs. With singers, the usual program consisted of five numbers we doing the first, third and fifth, while the singer did the second and fourth. Rarely did we ever do a number together. With pianists it was quite the opposite. We followed the same order as above except for number five. We combined forces for a grand finale which was one of the four quintets by Schumann, Dvorak, Franck or Brahms. No two pianists played alike; so we had fun.

CHRONOLOGY

August	8, 1888	—Born in Cleveland, Ohio.
September	1893	—Entered public school in Cleveland and started violin lessons.
June	1902	— Quit high school at the end of the sophomore year.
June	1903	— Left home to room and board with another family.
February	8, 1904	— Left Cleveland for the Southwest.
March	1904	— Until August 1904—Hachita, New Mexico.
August	1904	— Until June 1911—El Paso, Texas.
June	1911	— Until October 1911—Cleveland.
October	28, 1911	— Sailed on S.S. *Vaderland*, Red Star Line, from New York enroute to Prague.
November	1911	— Until June 1912—Prague, Czechoslovakia.
June	1912	— Until January 1915—Písek, Czechoslovakia (summers), Vienna (winters).
January	20, 1915	— Sailed from Rotterdam on S.S. *New Amsterdam*, Holland-America Line.
February	1915	— Until June 1915—Cleveland.
June	10, 1915	— Sailed from New York on S.S. *Oscar II*, Scandinavia-America Line.
June	15, 1915	— Until July 1917—Oslo (summers), Leningrad (winters).
March	12, 1917	— Russian Revolution.
July	20, 1917	— Sailed from Oslo on Norwegian-American Line, S.S. *Bergensfjord*.
August	3, 1917	— Until October 1917—Cleveland.

October   14, 1917 — Until July 21, 1919—U.S. Army at Fort
Slocum, New York.

July   1919 — Until October 1937—lived in New Rochelle, New York

October   1919 — Joined the New York String Quartet.

November 4, 1921 — Married Eunice Ball in New York City
and lived in New Rochelle, New York.

October   26, 1922 — New York String Quartet debut at Aeolian
Hall.

May   1936 — New York String Quartet disbanded.

October   1936 — sailed from New York on the S.S. *Exermont* for an eight-month stay in Europe.

June   7, 1937 — Returned to New York and Shelburne,
Vermont on S.S. *Veendam,* Holland-
America Line.

October   1937 — Until June 1940—taught violin at the University of San Antonio, San Antonio,
Texas.

September 1940 — Until June 1953—taught violin at Milton
Academy, Milton, Massachusetts.

November 1953 — Moved to Clearwater, Florida.

October   2, 1954 — Left New York on the M.S. *Bow Brazil,*
Klaveness Lines (Norwegian), for a South
American tour, mostly in Montevideo,
Uruguay, returning through the Panama
Canal via Grace Line—May 1955.

November 10, 1957 — Sailed from New York on a Norwegian
cargo ship, the *Queensville,* on our first
round-the-world tour.

March   18, 1958 — Arrived back in New York, changing to
another Norwegian ship, the *Bronxville,*
of the same line, in Hong Kong.

August   7, 1961 — Sailed from Tampa, Florida, on the
Swedish-American Line cargo ship, the
Trolleholm, for a Scandinavian European
tour.

November 21, 1961 — Returned to New York on the passenger
liner, the *Bremen.*

March	27, 1965 — Sailed from New York on the Holland-America line cargo ship, the *Musi Lloyd*, for our second round-the-world trip, this time eastbound.
July	25, 1965 — Returned to New York after changing to another Holland-American Line cargo ship, the *Wonorato*, in Singapore. We spent thirty-seven glorious summers of three to four months duration from 1921 to 1957, inclusive, on Lake Champlain in Vermont. The first three were at Oak Ledge near Burlington and the rest at Shelburne Farms near Shelburne.
July	1971 — Still living in Clearwater, Florida.

Dear reader: You have now reached the end of the Odyssey, and I have now reached the end of hoofing. It was an exciting and fascinating life, and I hope you enjoyed reading about it.

Sincerely,
Jaroslav Siskovsky